The Creative Process in Music
from Mozart to Kurtág

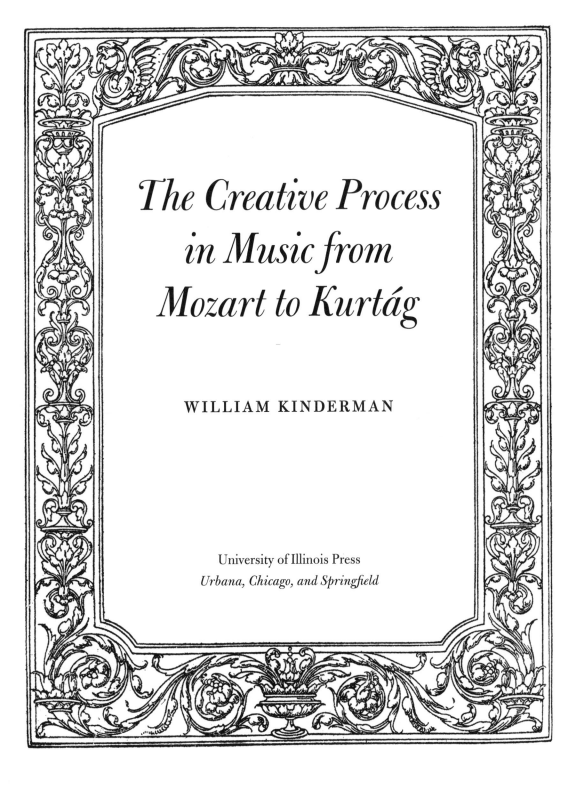

The Creative Process
in Music from
Mozart to Kurtág

WILLIAM KINDERMAN

University of Illinois Press
Urbana, Chicago, and Springfield

Library of Congress Cataloging-in-Publication Data
Kinderman, William.
The creative process in music from Mozart to Kurtág /
William Kinderman.
p. cm.
Includes bibliographical references and index.
ISBN 978-0-252-03716-0 (cloth : alk. paper)
1. Music—History and criticism.
2. Creation (Literary, artistic, etc.).
I. Title.
ML193 .K56   2012
781.1'7   2012024400

For Katherine

Contents

Illustrations

EXAMPLES

FIGURES

PLATES
Following page 156

Introduction

Works of art have been compared to icebergs: what is visible is but a small part of the whole. An artwork might seem to exist in splendid isolation, but that impression is misleading. Cultural products inevitably arise from a context, a submerged landscape that is often not easily accessible. It is an undertaking of research to bring such things to light, and studies of the creative process find their cutting edge by probing beyond the surface, opening new perspectives on the apparently familiar.

In the case of Beethoven, whose music has served as a locus classicus for studies of musical genesis, part of this missing context is preserved in voluminous sketchbooks. Johannes Brahms, another composer who labored long and hard on his compositions, himself collected sources bearing on the creative process, including some of Beethoven's manuscripts. Just weeks before his death, Brahms examined one of his predecessor's later sketchbooks.[1] Yet he curbed the access of later investigators to his own creative method by destroying not only sketches but also many of his early unpublished works. Artists do not always welcome others into their workshop.

In the present study I open the door to that workshop, investigating not just the final outcome but the *process* of creative endeavor in music. The most rigorous basis for the study of artistic creativity comes not from anecdotal or autobiographical reports (although they have their role) but from original handwritten sketches and drafts and preliminary studies, as well as from revised manuscripts and similar primary sources. Especially since the eighteenth century, the issue of originality of style has encouraged intense preliminary efforts preceding and leading toward the production of finished artistic works.

Study of the creative process has an interdisciplinary context. The term "genetic criticism," or *critique génétique*, relates not to the field of genetics but to the genesis of cultural works, as regarded in a broad and inclusive manner.[2] This approach stands in contrast to a formalist focus on the text itself and the related disinclination to probe issues of creative process lest these involve entanglement with the so-called intentional fallacy. Although the turn away from such formalist thinking in literary studies occurred several decades ago, its lingering influence was felt much longer in music scholarship. More recently, growing recognition of the value of contextual studies and of the problematic nature of the notion of a single definitive text has exerted a welcome impact. Particularly promising are approaches that integrate source studies with interpretative analysis, probing the aesthetic meaning of artworks in a rich contextual field.

The approach of genetic criticism offers a valuable antidote to the fragmentation of music scholarship into subdisciplines cultivating discrete methodologies. The integrated field as understood by Guido Adler and others in earlier times has split into a colorful array of discrete subdisciplines, with weakened connections between what have become largely autonomous areas of activity.[3] Since the tendency toward fragmentation has gained ground in recent decades, it is useful to describe the background in order to clarify the enhanced relevance of creative process studies, which have the potential to help counteract this trend. In a much-discussed article from 1978, for instance, Douglas Johnson sought to confine the relevance of Beethoven's sketches strictly to the biographical sphere; in so doing, he overestimated the capacity of musical analysis, guided by a belief that the structure of a given work can be read as though it were transparent in the published score.[4] Johnson's model of musical analysis was the system of Heinrich Schenker, who was concerned to construct "a theory of musical coherence that will not open pieces to the infinite intertextuality of the *déjà entendu*," as Kevin Korsyn puts it.[5] If the musical text is understood as a closed system of relations—exuding an aura of infallibility—then *avantes-textes* such as sketches and other preliminary compositional documents seem excluded from the aesthetic field of the work itself. Yet underlying this position is an attitude of dogmatic ideology. As soon as we embrace an open view of the work—acknowledging its continuity with historical sources and the intertextuality of the *déjà entendu*—the potential enrichment of such contextual studies becomes apparent.

By the 1980s Joseph Kerman had advocated a model for musicology involving a shift "from the various branches and methodologies of music history towards actual music," but this model was not embraced by the "new musicology," whose proponents were concerned to distance themselves from a work-based canonic repertory of "pure music."[6] Despite its use of a rhetoric of liberation, the new musicology did more to divide rather than integrate music scholarship. Lawrence Kramer set out in 1995 to recast "musicology as the rigorous and contestable study, theory, and practice of musical subjectivities. This would be a musicology in which the results of archival and analytical work, formerly prized in their own right, would become significant only in relation to subjective values—which is not to say the values of an atomized private inwardness, but those of a historically situated type of human agency," whereas Susan McClary proclaimed in 2000 that "music never seems so trivial as in its 'purely musical' readings. If there was at one time a rationale for adopting such an intellectual position, that time has long since past. And if the belief in the nineteenth-century notion of aesthetic autonomy continues to be an issue when we study cultural history, it can no longer be privileged as somehow true."[7]

A belittlement of archival and analytical work and of the "purely musical" as "trivial" betrays a lack of sympathy for research and naïveté about the nature of musical meaning. The target of attack is largely a straw man; and the related demand that cultural contextualization be given priority over individual aesthetic response should be resisted. In a 2004 response to this ideological agenda, Robert Hatten wrote:

> In the face of postmodernism, I maintain that the "aesthetic" is no illusion. Within a realm of scholarly discourse that is increasingly aware of contingency and relativity, I maintain that we still have access to *relatively objective* (by which I mean *intersubjectively defensible*) historical meanings—both at the general level of style (which can be *reconstructed* to a degree that the evidence will allow) and at the more detailed level of a work (which must be interpreted not only from stylistic knowledge but also through hermeneutic inquiry). The latter requires a mixture of deep empathy for the potential expressive significance of a musical work, and careful argumentation that can justify unusual structures as the plausible outcomes of work-centered expressive motivations.[8]

Scholarship relies fundamentally on a distinction between knowledge and opinion, *scientia* and *doxa*, whereby precision is preferable to polemical exaggeration. McClary's claim that the "kinds of processes" and "conditions for the production and reception of artworks" are "intensely ideological formations" is overstated, assuming in advance what needs to be tested empirically as a hypothesis.[9] In this regard, it is problematic to emphasize the "work-concept" as key to the historical emergence of a "musical museum" of canonic compositions. Lydia Goehr has argued for the primacy of the work-concept beginning around 1800, depicting Beethoven as representative of a deep separation between improvisation and composition proper, a development bound up with the creation of a dominant canon of musical works.[10] This view underestimates the role of spontaneous invention for Beethoven. To oppose extemporization to composition proper misrepresents his creative process by ignoring the crucial interdependence of freedom and determination in the concrete stylistic context in which Beethoven worked.[11] Furthermore, in early nineteenth-century aesthetics, as in E. T. A. Hoffmann, discussions of the autonomy of music did not imply abstraction.[12] Only decades later, in the polemical writings of Richard Wagner, did this connotation arise, whereby "absolute" music is characterized as "detached" music and hence as merely abstract.[13]

The ramifications of the work-concept beginning in the later nineteenth century are double-edged. An increased concern with originality of style and the allure of the cult of genius motivated some artists to cover their tracks and suppress their sources; yet more than ever before, musical creativity expressed itself through self-conscious allusion to earlier models.[14] When Anna Ettlinger was reminded by the accompaniment of a Brahms song of the inverted form of Beethoven's "Appassionata" Sonata, Brahms is said to have responded: "You have discovered my tricks! I have always done it that way. I always took things from Beethoven and turned them upside down."[15]

The notion of artistic autonomy, whereby a musical masterpiece was regarded as having a highly determined canonical character toward which responsible performers and listeners might appropriately display an attitude of distanced reverence in the spirit of *Werktreue*, or "faithfulness to the work," proved to be a very mixed blessing. The approach of genetic criticism frequently undermines this assumption, productively deconstructing the impression of artistic autonomy. Such study can reveal unsuspected links between musical projects, bring to light the aesthetic qualities of unfinished or fragmentary efforts, and disclose the fluid, blurred boundaries between biography and art, genesis and structure, historical and analytical concerns.

To what extent, then, should the "conditions for the production and reception of artworks" be regarded as "intensely ideological formations," as McClary insists? Let us assess this issue by examining late nineteenth-century works by two influential composers from the European musical tradition: Brahms and Wagner. We shall first consider the "conditions for the production" of Brahms's pieces by taking note of his engagement with Beethoven's music and sketchbooks. In Wagner's case, we shall focus on issues of reception, particularly how his final drama, *Parsifal*, was promoted at Bayreuth after his death.

❧

Although Brahms destroyed many of his own working papers, his fascination with the creativity of his predecessors was reflected in his impressive personal collection of music manuscripts and other sources as well as his own editorial work on Schubert, Schumann, and other composers. He was aided in his research into earlier music by his friend Gustav Nottebohm, the pioneering scholar of Beethoven's sketchbooks. Brahms studied such manuscript sources not merely out of antiquarian curiosity or a desire to enhance his knowledge of biographical details of the lives of earlier masters. His interest was clearly linked to his own ongoing compositional activity. Whereas our examination of the German reception of Wagner's *Parsifal* will demonstrate the hazards of a narrow branding of a cultural product for ideological purposes, Brahms's own preoccupation with Beethoven's manuscripts points in another direction, to the inner drama of creative work as a quest for originality to be achieved through a *Rückblick nach vorn*, a backward glance paradoxically pointing the way forward.

If we understand ideology as a closed body of doctrine harnessed to a political plan, it is unclear how Brahms's cultural focus can be properly regarded as ideological.[16] On the other hand, the character of Brahms's engagement with Beethoven's manuscripts affirms the aesthetic relevance of these sources, contradicting the view that would confine the import of sketches to biography. Through Nottebohm, Brahms obtained an entire sketchbook for Beethoven's "Hammerklavier" Sonata, op. 106;[17] his collection also included the corrected copy (*Arbeitskopie*) of Beethoven's *Missa solemnis* as well as the autograph score of Mozart's G Minor Symphony, K. 550. Brahms helped Nottebohm to publish his musicological studies while joining his friend in exploring the world of musical creativity that is superbly documented in Beethoven's voluminous sketchbooks.

It is no accident that Brahms exploited in some of his own pieces the artistic possibilities of specific compositional strategies documented in such sources. Beethoven's "Hammerklavier" and *Missa solemnis* and Mozart's G Minor Symphony all prominently emphasize descending third-chains, a device Nottebohm described as *Terzen-Ketten* or *Terzen-Zirkel* and identified in various other works by Beethoven.[18] Nottebohm compiled entire sheets of such examples and shared his transcriptions and analyses with Brahms, as Marie Rule has demonstrated in her recent study of sources held at the Gesellschaft der Musikfreunde in Vienna.[19] The sketchbook that passed into Brahms's possession includes entries showing Beethoven at work on the extensive chain of falling thirds interrupted by contrasting episodes that is employed in the introduction to the fugal finale of the "Hammerklavier" Sonata.

Our appreciation of Brahms's achievement is enhanced when the evolutionary context of such ideas is set into relief. As so often, an awareness of the genetic context reveals new biographical perspectives but also proves suggestive for musical analysis. It has long been recognized that Brahms's Fourth Symphony, op. 90, from 1884 employs elaborate chains of thirds that give rise in turn to harmonic and tonal juxtapositions; the first four notes (B–G–E–C) of the opening movement already imply a pairing of E minor and C major triads, a relationship that is connected to the beginning of the second movement in the key of C major as well as to the use of this tonality as tonic in the third movement. Brahms's exploitation of third-chains in his final symphony is comparable to Beethoven's in the "Hammerklavier," a work that lurks in the formative background of Brahms's op. 90. The biographical context is revealing here, for it appears that on one of its many levels of meaning the Fourth Symphony represented Brahms's private homage to his friend Nottebohm, who died in 1882.[20]

The artistic possibilities of *Terzen-Ketten* continued to preoccupy Brahms into his last years. His seven Fantasies for Piano, op. 116, from 1892, embody an extension of these compositional ideas, especially the three swift framing capriccios in minor keys (nos. 1, 3, 7), which lend a sense of coherence to the whole cycle. Whereas the opening motto theme of the first capriccio features a rising sixth followed by falling thirds, the secondary theme contains chains of falling minor thirds in the bass forming diminished-seventh chords. In the coda, the opening theme achieves a decisive cadence as the structural intervallic chain is rendered as a canonic series of rising sixths, the inversion of the descending thirds. The outer sections of the third capriccio unfold a subject based on descent by thirds through the minor triad and beyond, reinforced by dense counterpoint; the final capriccio employs a version of the idea based on diminished-seventh chords between the hands in contrary motion. Even more remarkably, in the intermezzo marked Adagio (no. 4), Brahms employs a motive that expresses the progression of the descending third as a harmonic shift from E major to C♯ minor triads, an idea he later reinterprets in several different ways. It is revealing to observe how the compositional technique of third-chains integrates this cycle of highly contrasting pieces.[21]

For Brahms, the falling third-chain represented not just a technical procedure but an expressive resource often bound up with darker emotions. The Fourth Symphony evoked for him the astringent, bitter quality of "unripe cherries." Describing one of his subsequent piano pieces, the exquisite opening Intermezzo in B Minor, op. 119, no. 1, the composer confessed to Clara Schumann that "the little piece is exceptionally melancholy and to say 'to be played very slowly' isn't saying enough. Every measure and every note must sound ritard[ando], as though one wished to suck melancholy out of each and every one, with a wantonness and contentment derived from the aforementioned dissonances!"[22] In this intermezzo, Brahms "bleeds" the chords based on stacked third-chains by sustaining their notes; the penultimate sonority sounds all seven pitches of the scale simultaneously, creating a poignant dissonance that emerges as an embodiment of the basic structural idea. This melancholic expressive quality, which the aging Brahms attributed to *Terzen-Ketten* in this intermezzo, is reflected as well in some of his later songs, notably "Feldeinsamkeit," op. 86, no. 2, and the third of the Four Serious Songs of op. 121, "O Tod" (O Death). Walter Frisch regards the falling third-chain and its ensuing inversion as rising sixths in "O Tod" as "one of Brahms's most profound thematic transformations" conveying "two viewpoints on death," one "harsh" and the other "blissful."[23] We can perceive in "O Tod" an affinity to another Beethovenian model: the fugue on "Et vitam venturi saeculi Amen" that crowns the Credo of the *Missa solemnis*. The corrected copy of the Mass containing

Beethoven's numerous handwritten revisions belonged to Brahms, who must have been keenly aware how his predecessor built up the fugue subject from a chain of falling thirds yet reshaped this configuration into a rising progression containing ascending sixths as the music reaches the fugal climax on a high sustained E♭ chord. This sonority is identical to the framing chords from the beginning and end of the movement and similar as well to the musical setting of the final line of the Schiller text in the choral finale of the Ninth Symphony: "Über Sternen muß er wohnen" (Above the stars must he dwell). In the "Et vitam venturi" fugue, as in Brahms's setting, the substitution of rising sixths for descending thirds contributes to the quality of spiritual aspiration conveyed through the music.

No sharp separation can be made here between historical, biographical, and analytical concerns or between musical techniques and their expressive qualities. The connections between these various works by Brahms and Beethoven are intimate and far-reaching, involving self-referential and intertextual threads that might have made a systematic theorist like Schenker cringe. In the case of Brahms and the device of *Terzen-Ketten*, the connection to Nottebohm and to Beethoven's sketches is sufficient to suggest how this internal aesthetic context contributed to Brahms's creative enterprise.

In turning now to the context of reception history of Wagner's *Parsifal* in Germany during the half century after the composer's death, we confront a completely different array of issues and problems. Here the role of ideology understood as a closed body of doctrine becomes urgently important. In some ways, *Parsifal* represents an extreme example of the autonomous work-concept in that its author not only devoted unusual attention to the drama and music but also specifically designed the piece for the special conditions of the Festspielhaus in Bayreuth, reserving staged performances for this single unique theater. The notion of *Urtext* (original text) applies here not only to the relation of verbal text and music but also to the staging, and after Wagner's death in 1883 his widow, Cosima Wagner, sought to preserve the memory of the original production for decades.[24] For a generation thereafter, until 1913, the Wagner family and cultlike Bayreuth circle exploited their privileged possession of this work, assuming the role of guardians of the Grail, whereby the religious aura of *Parsifal* made it suitable for the hypnotic depiction of collective identity.

The negative impact of this reception of *Parsifal* at Bayreuth became fully evident by 1911, when Leopold von Schröder published his book *Die Vollendung des arischen Mysteriums in Bayreuth* (The fulfillment of the Aryan mystery in Bayreuth), according to which the Bayreuth Festspielhaus itself represented a miraculous Grail temple, the culmination of a process extended over five thousand years, whereby "through Wagner, Bayreuth became the ideal center of all Aryan peoples."[25] Schröder had been recruited for the Bayreuth circle by Houston Stewart Chamberlain, whose friendship with Cosima Wagner began in 1888. Before he married Wagner's daughter

Eva and moved to Bayreuth in 1908, Chamberlain had resided in Vienna, where he exerted potent influence on the Germanic racist groups from which the young Adolf Hitler assembled his ideology. Chamberlain's popular 1899 book *Die Grundlagen des neunzehnten Jahrhunderts* (Foundations of the nineteenth century) promoted a brand of racism according to which Jewish and Aryan principles were fundamentally incompatible. Having absorbed much from pan-Germanic, anti-Semitic sources that themselves owed a debt to Chamberlain, Hitler was bound to be well received by the Wagner family when he met them at Bayreuth in 1923; his enthusiasm for Richard Wagner's works was the icing on the cake.

Only in the German political context can we understand the framing argument of Alfred Lorenz's still overrated 1933 monograph on *Parsifal*.[26] Lorenz did not hesitate to identify Wagner's redeeming Grail king, Parsifal, with Hitler. Granting Wagner the power of political prophecy, Lorenz announces in his preface that "Wagner conveyed his prophetic thoughts about leadership of the Führer and regeneration in his work and bequeathed thereby an e x a l t e d m i s s i o n."[27] Following the cue of Chamberlain, who had proclaimed Hitler as "god-sent bene-diction" to Germany a decade earlier, Lorenz placed his interpretation narrowly in the service of National Socialist ideology, treating the artwork as a vehicle for political propaganda.

The approach of genetic criticism enables a productive deconstruction of the evolution of *Parsifal* and the distortions of its German nationalist reception history. From source studies we learn, for instance, that its opening Communion theme was adapted by Wagner from an obscure cantata by his father-in-law, Franz Liszt, a work that was inspired in turn by the American poet Henry Wadsworth Longfellow.[28] On the other hand, as Katherine Syer has recently shown, prominent theatrical features of *Parsifal*, particularly in its second act—which lacks extensive models in the medieval sources—stem from Carlo Gozzi's *La donna serpente*, the eighteenth-century Venetian play that forty years earlier had served as the basis for Wagner's first complete opera, *Die Feen* (The fairies).[29] Study of the genesis of *Parsifal* shows that it is far from the embodiment of German racial purity as was claimed by members of the Bayreuth circle and National Socialist ideologues like Lorenz. The German nationalist appropriation of *Parsifal* involved misrepresen-tation driven in part by the hope of the Wagner family that Hitler, once in power, would reestablish their control of this work, the copyright of which had expired in 1913. But the most serious problem is lodged in Lorenz's conviction that the closing affirmative music of the work discloses a "new Parsifal religion," enabling the listener to experience through the music the following insight: "W e s h o u l d o v e r c o m e d e c a y a n d a s a r a c i a l l y h i g h-b r e d p e o p l e a d v a n c e t o v i c t o r y, Wagner wishes."[30] Lorenz's view was not shared by some other National Socialist ideologues. Responding to the passivism of the title figure and the central importance of the theme of compassion in Wagner's work, Alfred

Rosenberg stated that "*Parsifal* represents a church-influenced enfeeblement in favor of the value of renunciation."[31] Nevertheless, the view advanced by Lorenz is a chilling example of an overdetermined work-concept, an ideological reduction of an artwork to serve a murderous totalitarian regime. For those who accepted Lorenz's view of Wagner's "prophetic thoughts" and the "new Parsifal religion," *Werktreue* became inseparable from commitment to Hitler's "New Germany."[32]

Brahms once told Karl Reinthaler in reference to *Ein deutsches Requiem* that he would gladly have called the piece "Ein menschliches Requiem" (A human requiem); at the same time, he declined Reinthaler's request to make the work explicitly Christian in doctrinal terms.[33] Lorenz's interpretation of Wagner's *Parsifal* moves in the opposite direction. In his 1933 essay, "Die Religion des Parsifal," Lorenz first describes how "Parsifal as king brings together the entire ethos of humanity," using the word *Menschheit* as the collective noun for "humanity." However, at the end of his essay, it becomes abundantly clear that what is meant is not *Menschheit* after all but just the "German people," for Lorenz the only real "humanity" because of their being "racially well bred."[34] If we understand ideology as a body of doctrine tied to a political or cultural plan, Lorenz's interpretation clearly belongs in this category. Brahms, by contrast, sought to limit or avoid the narrowing effect of any such doctrine, affirming an unrestricted use of "humanity," the term that was hypocritically redefined by Lorenz in the service of the racial policies of National Socialism.

Artworks are by no means inevitably ideological but are sometimes used as vessels of political ideology or misappropriated when the context of their reception conflicts with the intrinsic content of the work. Claims that the meanings of artworks are socially constructed should be tested to assess how and to what extent this may be true. In the context of reception history, some socially constructed "meanings" may lack much connection to aesthetic experience, while others may in extreme cases be unmasked as lies and sham pretension. No work so powerfully critiques every regime that denies human freedom as does Beethoven's *Fidelio*, but this opera was also pressed into use during the ceremonial mass rallies of the National Socialists in the 1930s. In 1945 Thomas Mann wrote about the opera in Germany during the Third Reich: "How could it happen that Beethoven's *Fidelio* . . . was not forbidden in the Germany of the last twelve years? . . . For what utter stupidity was required to be able to listen to *Fidelio* in Himmler's Germany without covering one's face and rushing out of the hall."[35]

The "aesthetic" is indeed no illusion, often involving as it does a personal response of "private inwardness" or "deep empathy" that need not remain isolated from other concerns. As Friedrich Schiller claimed, artistic activity can represent an "effigy of [the] ideal" or goal for human striving, whereby the work, if it is to represent the highest human potential, must embody the principle of self-determination while avoiding ideological determination from without. This view is compatible with Susanne Langer's description of the successful artwork as presenting "an unconsummated symbol" through a "process of articulation."[36] The approach of genetic criticism prizes the results of both historical and aesthetic investigation—archival and analytical work—as vital components of the exploration of musical meaning.[37]

❧

The essays in this volume address music of six major composers from the eighteenth century to the present, from Wolfgang Amadeus Mozart to György Kurtág. The choice of composers traces the continuity of a central European tradition that has displayed remarkable vitality for over two centuries, as accumulated legacies assumed importance for later generations. Certain of these composers had personal contact with one another. Beethoven reportedly met Mozart at Vienna in 1787, and he received "Mozart's spirit from Haydn's hands" beginning in 1792.[38] During a period of personal trauma in the 1830s, Schumann was so haunted by Beethoven that their respective yearnings for a "distant beloved" merged into a composite expression. Gustav Mahler's intense preoccupation with Wagner's art assumed personal and artistic significance in 1901 as he labored on his Fifth Symphony. The yearning to which he gave expression in its Adagietto is linked in turn to works in other artistic genres, from Thomas Mann's novella *Death in Venice* to Luchino Visconti's 1971 film of the same title. Another kind of cultural continuity is reflected in the more recent works of György Kurtág, who—like his colleague György Ligeti—waited in vain at Budapest in 1945 for the return of Béla Bartók, who sadly died of leukemia that year. The music of Bartók nonetheless continued to inspire them. For Kurtág today, in the second decade of the twenty-first century, the music of Bach, Schumann, and Webern, among others, continues to play a crucial role.

Our investigation of Kurtág's creative process benefits from the input of firsthand witnesses, including András Wilheim, who helped shape the order of the forty songs for soprano and violin that make up the *Kafka Fragments*, Adrienne Csengery and András Keller, the performers who worked closely with the indefatigable composer in preparing performances and recordings, and Kurtág himself, together with his pianist wife, Martá Kurtág. Since the premiere of this work in 1987, Kurtág's *Kafka Fragments* have found growing international recognition. The number of concert performances and recordings has increased steadily. In addition to the classic recording by Csengery and Keller from 1990, another distinguished recording by Juliane Banse with Keller was issued in 2006 in honor of Kurtág's eightieth birthday.[39] Further attention was drawn to the *Kafka Fragments* by a staged version from 2005 directed by Peter Sellars, with soprano Dawn Upshaw and violinist Geoff Nuttall. A genetic study of this comparatively recent work can assess the surviving compositional documents in light of living memories while taking note of a dynamic reception history that is still taking shape.

The topics discussed in the following chapters illustrate the wide range of issues and problems that can be addressed through studies of the creative process. The misleading cliché of Mozart's effortless creativity, for example, invites further examination. Early or alternative versions of familiar works force us to assess the result of revisions while not assuming that the final text is always the best. The need for critical judgment is obvious when an obscure unfinished work is unearthed through manuscript study, as with Beethoven's fragmentary Piano Trio in F Minor from 1816. Other examples, as in the chapters devoted to Schumann, Bartók, and Kurtág, remind us of the diversity of sources, rejected passages and movements, or aborted projects that preceded or were absorbed into finished compositions.

A through-line of these essays pertains to the essential continuity between a work and its genesis. Genetic criticism might appear to undermine the work-concept, deconstructing the work through its own history. However, such an approach often opens perspectives that serve as a promising platform for critical interpretation, and analysis remains vitally important to the evaluation of sketches and drafts, whose significance can be elusive and enigmatic.

As already noted, the approach taken here is by no means confined to source studies per se. It is my conviction that the potential of such philological investigations can be realized only if this work is pursued in an enhanced interpretative field that goes beyond traditional philology in its quest for meaning. In his 2003 book *The Powers of Philology*, Hans Ulrich Gumbrecht argues for such an approach as an alternative to an often free-floating textual interpretation and to the more recent redefinition of humanistic scholarship as "cultural studies," which sometimes entails a loss of intellectual focus. Such revitalization of philological scholarship can achieve its potential only if it takes into account the hidden desire that has inspired philology since its Hellenistic beginnings: the desire to make the past present again by embodying it. Gumbrecht calls upon the humanities to recover the concept of individual aesthetic response or "lived experience," and he sees virtue in this proposal precisely on account of "the impossibility of making this notion compatible with the sphere of the collective and social," insisting that "lived experience, as that which precedes such [collective and social] interpretation, must remain individual."[40]

Can we detect traces of "lived experience" in our investigations of the genesis of Schumann's Fantasie in C or Kurtág's attempt to depict the impossibility of a "true path" as a deterministic goal in his "Hommage-message à Pierre Boulez"? While Gumbrecht does not privilege the "original *Erlebnis* [lived experience] of the great artists," he does credit Wilhelm Dilthey's notion of a "retranslation of objectivations of life into that spiritual liveliness from which they emerged," a formulation that comes close to describing some of the kinds of insights enabled through genetic studies. The goal is not simply to reconstruct the past but to utilize source studies as a focus and springboard to fresh insights in the present.

The search for such traces of "spiritual liveliness" reminds us of the importance of an aesthetic dimension in music analysis. In its original sense as *epistēmē aisthētikos*, aesthetics refers not only to art or beauty but to sensible awareness more generally; the opposing complement to this concept is the anesthetic, involving a loss or deadening of feeling. A musical work is not an abstract entity but an experience in sound and time. As with any creative act, the product cannot be fully envisaged in advance but represents an imaginative synthesis consisting of elements that are intimately known. The unity or integration of a musical work is best understood not as a tautological concept or even as an organic whole but rather as that totality of concrete elements and relationships that demand realization in sound. What is meant is a unity that is entirely compatible with tension, contrast, diversity, and the individuality of a work. Our apprehension of unity or integration is wholly dependent on our internal sound image, or *Klangvorstellung*, of the music. Without this key ingredient, analysis is empty and criticism blind. It follows that analysis, properly considered, must engage the immanent temporality of the work, not merely the visual notation of the score nor a structural matrix posited by a priori theoretical constructs.

Since a primary focus in these essays is aesthetic, some familiarity with the musical works is desirable; the chapter on Beethoven's fragmentary trio is supported by a sound recording of the music. The discussions of pieces aim toward an integrated approach that strives to avoid sacrificing artistic sensibility to systematic method. Analysis at its best is not an end in itself but a means to an end: it enables us to hear more in the music. In this sense, analysis resembles an inward performance.[41] It depends vitally on our imagination of the sound, and it needs to be verified by the reader: how does it feel?

At the same time, the biographical sphere remains vitally important; the study of original sources reminds us of the irreducibly personal aspects of creative endeavor. Within the contextual field of genetic criticism, there is no sharp separation between biography and musical analysis; issues of authorial motivation need not be shirked. Where the genesis and structure of a work intersect, each dependent on the other, is lodged the mysterious phenomenon of the creative process—the ultimate subject of investigation. In a sense, the point of this book is to show the nature of this interdependence. Since the early nineteenth century, the metaphor of the submerged iceberg has been used to describe the unconscious aspects of creativity as a vast wellspring that leaves its traces on our conscious realm.

How can we discern traces of authorial motivation or "spiritual liveliness" in a finished artwork? The topics chosen in this book display commonalities and differences while surveying a variety of genres and historical settings. Mozart's decision to join his Fantasia and Sonata in C Minor into a single opus in 1785 and his reworking of the piano entrance of one of his most imposing concertos in 1786 provide suggestive contexts for interpretation. The genesis of an unfinished project such as the first movement of Beethoven's Trio in F Minor is best grasped once we retrace how the composer, after preliminary work in his sketchbook, transferred and elaborated his ideas in a draft on loose papers resembling a rough score. The outcome is a performable musical excerpt that casts fresh light on Beethoven's creativity, especially when regarded in relation to the complex of compositional projects to which the trio belonged. Some of the trio's substance was absorbed into finished works, including the Sonatas op. 101 and op. 106, and the investigation illuminates these pieces as well.

The chapter on Schumann's op. 17 Fantasie explores the intertwined spheres of the biographical and musical, whereby the notion of an overcoming of distance through the artistic imagination assumes primacy. Thought provoking is Schumann's removal of his allusion to Beethoven from the end of the entire work, a late compositional decision revealed in a manuscript held in Budapest. This decision represents a retrenchment of his original idea, which mirrored the formal context of Beethoven's song cycle *An die ferne Geliebte* (To the distant beloved), in which the first song is recalled in the last, reaffirming the theme of unfulfilled yearning as an aspect of the overall design. Is the author always the best editor of his own work? In Schumann's case, as with some other composers, it is appropriate to weigh alternative versions on their own merits.

An interpenetration of biographical and aesthetic concerns is no less fascinating in relation to Mahler's Fifth Symphony, whose songlike fourth movement, the Adagietto, bears an intimate relationship to his own Rückert setting "Ich bin der Welt abhanden gekommen" (I have become lost to the world). While the duality of inner and outer realms of experience reflected in Mahler's pair of closing movements resonates in the Wagnerian works that influenced his composition, it is also reflected in aspects of Mahler's life, particularly through his love for Alma Schindler, who became his wife. Playing with the analogy of Hans Sachs and Evchen in Wagner's *Meistersinger*, Mahler struck a chord with Alma that helped cement their relationship, yet as years passed, his hesitation to marry her proved to have some basis after all. In this complex interplay between life and art, the narrative moment of *Durchbruch* (breakthrough) assumes importance, providing a suggestive psychological context for interpretation. The dynamic trajectory of this work also encourages us to test the recent idea of rotational cycles as an alternative analytical approach to more static concepts of form, while the evidence of the compositional process offers further clarification of the musical meaning. In Mahler's finale, a theme drawn from the Adagietto seems bound up with the subjective quest of the isolated self and becomes by stages increasingly integrated with the sound world of the last movement.

The more compact dimensions of Bartók's *Dance Suite* allow for more comprehensive analysis in which the impact of biographical and historical factors can be assessed. As an artistic assimilation of multicultural materials, Bartók's work strives toward a synthesis reflecting a political context that had collapsed by the time the piece was composed. It is in that sense a work of retrospective cast, but, like Beethoven's Ninth Symphony, its guiding theme of "brotherhood" avoids the perils of reductionism while preserving the notion of folk music as an authentic communal expression, aspects of which can be productively absorbed into art music. As he did with Mahler's Fifth Symphony, the influential modernist critic Theodor W. Adorno found fault with the *Dance Suite*, underestimating how Bartók achieves a synthesis by means of his succession of contrasting dances, with ritornello and finale. Although the work was composed for the anniversary of Budapest as a unified city, Bartók's aesthetic range in this work is broader, encompassing sources of inspiration from diverse regions while avoiding mere eclecticism, as his elimination of the planned Slovakian dance implies.

Our final example, the *Kafka Fragments* by Kurtág, is a work that defies simplistic notions of modernism and postmodernism. One recent critic described this "great and mysterious Hungarian composer" as "wreck[ing] all categories as [he] moves along" and as "a composer of neither/nor—neither ruthlessly new in his methods nor remotely traditional, neither atonal nor tonal."[42] In the *Kafka Fragments*, a deterministic path is thoroughly critiqued and paradoxically replaced by a process of searching; an inability to narrate is absorbed into the musical narrative itself. As the sources show, Kurtág conceived additional songs not included in the finished work. The boundaries of the cycle are fluid, with some pieces, like "Der begrenzte Kreis ist rein" (The closed circle is pure), connecting to other works by Kurtág and other composers, including Schumann, whose dualistic pair of characters Eusebius and Florestan appear in the "Scene on a Tram" at the end of part III. The phrase "der begrenzte Kreis ist rein," drawn from Kafka's 1913 diary, became a motto for Kurtág, who uses a version of the setting as well in his *Hommage à R. Sch*. In its association with the inner sanctuary of the self, his settings of this motto invite comparison with Mahler's Adagietto or Schumann's allusion to the "distant beloved," pointing thereby to the rich continuity of a musical tradition that remains urgently relevant in the present.

❧

The following archives and libraries kindly allowed access to sources in their collections: Biblioteka Jagiellońska, Cracow; International Stiftung Mozarteum, Salzburg/Archiv, and Bibliotheca Mozartiana; Ira Brilliant Center for Beethoven Studies, San José State University; Library of Mr. William Scheide, Princeton University; Musikabteilung, Staatsbibliothek zu Berlin preussischer Kulturbesitz; Willem Mengelberg Foundation, Nederlands Muziek Instituut, The Hague; Pierpont Morgan Library, New York City; National Széchényi Library, Budapest; Paul Sacher Stiftung, Basel. Many friends and colleagues offered helpful assistance or comments, including Bernhard Appel, Valentina Bertolani, David Campbell,

Hermann Danuser, Warren Darcy, Bradley Decker, Judit Frigyesi, Philip Gossett, Robert Hatten, Wolfgang Hesse, Joseph Kerman, Lewis Lockwood, Felix Meyer, Balázs Mikusi, Ulrich Mosch, Paul Needham, Friedemann Sallis, Michiko Theurer, J. Rigbie Turner, László Vikárius, Rainer Waubke, and András Wilheim. Michael Warner offered valuable assistance in preparing the final typescript for publication.

I am especially grateful to György Kurtág, who granted me an interview at Zurich in June 2010 and who offered invaluable response to my chapter on his music. More than a decade earlier, at the "Musiktage Mondsee" Festival held near Salzburg in 1998, I enjoyed the opportunity of hearing many works by Kurtág in memorable performances in the presence of the composer. One of these concerts included the *Kafka Fragments* performed by Adrienne Csengery and András Keller. Several years later, my interest in Bartók's *Dance Suite* was deepened by the chance to conduct parts of this work at the California Conducting Institute at Bakersfield led by John Farrer, Daniel Lewis, and Donald Thulean. Especially valuable to my project was the opportunity to present my work on Bartók's *Dance Suite* at the colloquium "Scholarly Research and Performance Practice in Bartók Studies" held at Szombathely, Hungary, in July 2011. It was in Szombathely that Kurtág conceived many of the *Kafka Fragments* twenty-six years earlier, in 1985. While in Hungary, I discussed the genesis of Kurtág's work with two of his important artistic collaborators, Csengery and Wilheim.

My research was supported by an Arnold O. Beckman Grant from the Research Board of the University of Illinois at Urbana-Champaign. A Research Prize from the Alexander von Humboldt Foundation enabled me to spend prolonged periods of research based at Munich in Germany during 2009–11, during which the final chapters of the book were written.

Material from this book has been delivered as lectures at various conferences and universities. The Mozart and Beethoven chapters were presented at meetings of the American Musicological Society in 2005 and 2003, respectively. The Schumann chapter has been presented as lecture recitals at Boston University, the University of Chicago, the Humboldt University in Berlin, and the Ludwig Maximilian University in Munich; material drawn from the Mahler chapter was given as a lecture at Cornell University. During 2011 I spoke about Bartók's *Dance Suite* at the aforementioned Bartók Colloquium at Szombathely and about Kurtág's *Kafka Fragments* at the annual meeting of the American Musicological Society in San Francisco.

Some parts of this study intersect with my earlier published work. Chapter 1 draws on material in chapter 6 of my book *Mozart's Piano Music* (Oxford University Press, 2006). Chapter 2 appeared in somewhat different form in the *Journal of Musicological Research*; chapter 4 was first published in the *Musical Quarterly*. All of these essays have been revised and updated. Chapters 3, 5, and 6 are printed here for the first time. All translations are my own unless otherwise noted.

Mozart's Second Thoughts

The popular image of Mozart's music as having sprung into existence fully formed as the miraculous product of genius, as is conveyed in Peter Shaffer's play *Amadeus* and in Milos Forman's film of the same title, is seriously misleading. While Mozart did not make nearly as many sketches and drafts for his works in progress as did Beethoven, he nevertheless invested much labor in the compositional process, and he was by no means always satisfied with his initial attempts to work out compositions. Mozart not only composed in his head but tried out ideas at the keyboard and made written sketches and drafts, some of which have survived.[1]

Some scholars have long recognized that the notion of Mozart's having composed his important works rapidly and without much effort is inaccurate. The debate reaches back to early published writings on Mozart. In the first monograph devoted to Mozart, the book *W. A. Mozarts Leben*, first published in 1798, Franz Niemetschek wrote concerning Mozart's creativity of the "incomprehensible ease with which he composed most of his works."[2] On the other hand, Georg Nikolaus Nissen, in his *Biographie W. A. Mozarts* of 1828, claimed that "one doesn't believe the gossip at all, according to which he [Mozart] tossed off his significant works swiftly and hurriedly. He carried the main ideas with him for a long time, wrote these down briefly, and worked out the principal matters fully in his head. Only then did he write out the whole, and even then, not as quickly as one has imagined: he carefully improved his work and was extremely strict with himself regarding those compositions that he himself valued."[3]

The surviving manuscript sources offer confirmation of Nissen's statement. Mozart often made revealing changes after having devised an initial version of a work. Some glimpses into Mozart's compositional process are provided by four concerto fragments written on a type of paper also found in the autograph score of his Piano Concerto in A Major, K. 488.[4] Of particular interest is a fragmentary draft that was presumably intended for the finale of K. 488, a manuscript that is cataloged as K. 488c (Anh. 64).[5] Instead of the duple meter of the finale in the finished work, this music is written in $\frac{6}{8}$ time; the opening rondo theme shifts between the piano and clarinets in four-measure phrases. Remarkably, this theme has a siciliano rhythm, clearly reminiscent of the slow movement as we know it. In the end, Mozart confined the siciliano idiom to the slow middle movement while devising thematic connections of a rather different kind between the two last movements of the concerto.

New insight into Mozart's revision process emerged as well from the rediscovery of the autograph manuscripts of the Sonata in C Minor, K. 457, from 1784 and the Fantasia in C Minor, K. 475, from 1785. In the catalog he kept of his own works, Mozart dated the sonata as "14 October [1784]" and the fantasia as "20 [May 1785]."[6] Although the fantasia was composed seven months after the sonata, and the two works were written at separate times on different paper types, Mozart decided in 1785 to join these two pieces in a single publication, and they are also bound together in a manuscript that was long presumed lost but that resurfaced in 1990 at Philadelphia and is now housed at the Mozarteum in Salzburg.[7]

The fantasia and sonata rank among the greatest achievements in Mozart's piano music. The dissonant chromaticism of both pieces looks back to J. S. Bach's *Musikalisches Opfer* (Musical offering), while in their dramatic concentration they strongly prefigure Beethoven's famous "C minor mood." An impressive feature of the fantasia is the way Mozart unifies the form of the whole, with its several sharply contrasting episodes, through a varied return of the opening Adagio at the conclusion. The bare unison octaves of this opening seem to embody an inevitably objective, immovable, even alien reality confronting the player and listener, a sense heightened here by Mozart's motivic chromaticism, the descent by semitone governing the initial phrases, and his effective use of silence as a rapport of sound with the void. The mysterious opening phrase in unison octaves rises from C and falls back to that pitch, preceding the semitone descent at the outset of m. 2, while the following harmonized phrases and echoes in the upper register convey a quality of bleak melancholy (Ex. 1.1).[8]

The recovery of the autograph manuscript proved most revelatory in relation to the finale of the sonata. As the manuscript shows, the last nineteen measures of the work as we know it were an afterthought. The original final cadence at m. 301 was turned into a deceptive cadence, leading to an astonishing gapped thematic

Datiert: Wien, 20. Mai 1785

Ex. 1.1. Mozart, Fantasia in C Minor, K. 475, beginning.

presentation that soars to high C and E♭ before plunging five octaves to F♯ in the lowest possible register.[9] In the first edition of the sonata, the low F♯ and the five following notes were raised an octave; there are other divergences as well, as are shown in Ex. 1.2. The deep, coiling line played three octaves *under* the accompaniment reaches a tonic cadence five measures later, and another eight measures of cadential flourishes across all these pitch registers prepare the final framing chords.

Mozart sought a culminating gesture here, and the added passage takes on the character of a decisive breakthrough. Furthermore, as Siegbert Rampe has observed, the concluding extension offers evidence of Mozart's attitude toward the pairing of fantasia and sonata.[10] The melody of the added passage—C–E♭–F♯–G–A♭—reshapes the crucial chromatic motive from the beginning and end of the fantasia and then grounds it in the strongest possible way in C minor. The five-octave plunge from high E♭ to low F♯ splits the motive through drastic registral opposition, with its aspiring beginning contradicted and completed in the dark continuation. Robert Hatten writes that "gesturally, although the same hand performs the 'line,' the extravagant cross-hand move marks another voice—fateful in response to the more pleading high register, and implacable as it takes over for an inexorable cadence in the lowest register."[11] One original voice is virtually bifurcated in this majestic and radical reassertion of the motive that had begun the fantasia. Even the understated close of the first movement—tonic chords in the low register set off by rests—seems to be recalled and resolved here in the powerful conclusion of K. 457.

It is unlikely that these close correspondences could be accidental. Since the sonata was composed before the fantasia, it seems probable that the expansion

Mozart's Second Thoughts   19

Ex. 1.2. Mozart, Sonata in C Minor, K. 457, III, conclusion. The upper staves
show the reading in the first edition, the lower staves the reading in the
autograph manuscript.

of the coda to the finale of K. 457 occurred in response to Mozart's subsequent
pairing of these remarkable pieces; his addition begins precisely at the recall of
the seminal motive from the fantasia. The sequence of events in the compositional
process underscores the distinctive aesthetic features of the added passage in the
coda. We catch Mozart's musical mind in action here, casting audible connecting
threads across one of his most imaginative and innovative works.

The present chapter concerns two further instances in which Mozart returned
to a work in progress to make substantial revisions. The Sonata in D Major, K. 284,
is the last of the set of six sonatas completed by early 1775 at Munich. The reworking of its first movement offers insights into Mozart's evolving stylistic language at
a pivotal point in his career. Our second example dates from more than a decade
later, in 1786, when Mozart reshaped the piano entrance in the first movement of
one of his most imposing works for piano, the Concerto in C Major, K. 503.

The Sonata in D Major, K. 284/205b ("Dürnitz"), First Movement

Much of the first movement of the Sonata in D Major, K. 284, composed for Freiherr Thaddäus von Dürnitz at Munich, survives in an original version that was later thoroughly reshaped by Mozart. This canceled first version is preserved as part of the autograph score that contains the final version of K. 284 as well as the other five sonatas of the set dating from 1774–75; this manuscript was formerly part of the collection at the Staatsbibliothek zu Berlin preussischer Kulturbesitz, and it is currently held in Cracow at the Biblioteka Jagiellońska. The rejected draft for K. 284 contains no fewer than seventy-one measures, and it is fully realized, with dynamics and articulation markings. The draft is shown in Ex. 1.3, together with the final version of the passage. When Mozart broke off work on his draft, he was well into the development section. In the revision, the development section was completely reconceived, and extended passages in the first and last sections of the exposition were rewritten as well.

Originally, Mozart employed the opening unison fanfare twice, with an ascent in register and filling out of harmony when the gesture is repeated in m. 6. Against an accompaniment in staccato eighth notes, the right hand is given phrases highlighting two-note sigh figures. These single-voice lines marked *piano* contrast with the more robust texture of the *forte* passages, which suggest the texture of orchestral tutti passages.

In this draft version, short motives tend to be strung together in typical style for the time, and a literal repetition of phrases is more conspicuous, whereas in the revised passage Mozart offers a progression in which each change in the texture seems motivated by what happens before it. However, scholars have not agreed about the relative merits of the two versions. In a study comparing the canceled draft and the final version, László Somfai describes the fragment as "already a masterpiece, probably the best among the six sonatas of the set." He finds a "high level of organic elaboration in the discarded fragment" and regards the early version in this respect as surpassing the finished work.[12]

Let us examine the fragment in detail. It begins with a twofold statement of a six-measure unit,[13] which itself consists of two parts: a unison fanfare leading to a pedal point on the dominant, played *forte*, paired with a rhetorical continuation employing two-note sigh figures, performed *piano*. In his article, Somfai describes the second statement of this dialogical phrase as a "variation" of the first, but that term seems questionable, since apart from new voicing of the initial unison D as a full-voiced chord in m. 6 and a trill on the leading tone in m. 5, there are no other changes; the second phrase is otherwise a literal repetition of the first. The tonic cadence of the two six-measure units overlaps with the ensuing phrase, so that the

Fragment - First subject group

Ex. 1.3. Draft version and final version of the Sonata in D Major,
K. 284/205b, I.

Final form - First subject group

2   Allegro

Ex. 1.3. Continued.

Ex. 1.3. Continued.

Ex. 1.3. Continued.

Fragment - Development section

end of the fragment

Ex. 1.3. Continued.

Final form - Development section

Ex. 1.3. Continued.

full-voiced D major chord in m. 6 serves both as the end of the first phrase and as the beginning of the second.

Melodic continuity acts here as a primary agent of coherence. Hence the opening fanfare figure moves from the tonic note, D, to the dominant, A, and that pitch serves in turn as a repeated pedal point in the following three measures and also in a higher register as the initial pitch of the expressive four-note motive in mm. 2–3. A free inversion of that motive stresses the sigh figure on A–G in m. 4. Mozart then doubles up the two-note phrases in m. 5 as the music moves toward the tonic cadence at the downbeat of m. 6. A stepwise descent through F♯–E and then D–C♯ is outlined in the first and third of the two-note sigh figures in m. 5. Hence the descending line as contained in the two rapid motivic figures of a falling fourth in the opening fanfare motto is outlined in larger note values in the melody as the music moves to the first cadence.

Once the cadence is reached in m. 11, the music of the first version unfolds in steady sixteenth-note figuration outlining turn figures, combined with octaves in the left hand. Beginning in m. 15, this figuration migrates to the left hand as melodic inflections featuring the two-note sigh figure unfold in the treble. This music already assumes a transitional function, and the ensuing mm. 20–24 present a pedal point on the dominant, A, preparing the beginning of the second subject group in A major. These five measures were taken over virtually unchanged into the final version of the sonata.

Let us now examine Mozart's revisions to this first section of the exposition. The change to the initial tonic chord is already arresting and significant. In place of a unison D in three octaves, Mozart now employs a full voicing in the right hand, with added emphasis supplied through an arpeggiation of the chord.[14] At the same time, this initial sonority is curtailed to half its original length, with quarter rests placed on the second beat. Set off by silence, the opening sonority makes a more distinct impression without thereby losing its connection to the gestures that follow.

Another striking change is that the gesture in the second measure now moves to A–F♯–B, creating a dissonance that needs to be resolved, with the second two-measure phrase balancing and resolving the first. When the music reaches the dominant in m. 4, the rhythmic texture in eighth notes—representing a diminution of the quarter notes of the second measure—is continued in the bass motion, while Mozart continues with the following phrases beginning on the D in the octave above middle C. In the second version he has anticipated this progression in the arpeggiation of the opening chord, which lays out the whole tonal space of the opening section.

There is now a gradually increasing rhythmic tension that integrates all of the thematic segments in the first subject group and transition up to m. 21. After the phrases over the dominant pedal point in mm. 4–6, two transitional measures in running sixteenths resolve to the tonic in m. 9. This sixteenth-note figuration employs turn figures similar to those contained in the first version of the movement beginning in m. 11. There, as we have seen, its function was already transitional. Here, by contrast, these two measures of sixteenths (mm. 7–8) have been integrated into the opening theme, which is far broader than before. The original version of the movement displays a relatively loose, blocklike construction, with a double statement of the main subject in mm. 1–6 and 6–11 followed by a transitional continuation in sixteenth notes. By contrast, the final version impressively enlarges the opening theme, which reaches the transition only with the resolution of the augmented-sixth chord to the dominant octave A in m. 17.

The new idea Mozart introduced in mm. 9–12 is connected to the opening measures in tangible ways. Particularly important is the rhythmic correspondence. A half note (or quarter note and quarter rest) followed by five quarter-note impulses and another rest is common to both thematic segments, notwithstanding the sixteenth-note motion in the second half of m. 1 (since each of these motivic groups is identical and is articulated within the space of one quarter beat). Mm. 9–10 can thus be regarded as a rhythmic variation of mm. 1–2, and Mozart carries over a prominent feature of his original mm. 2–5 into the new idea, namely, the steady movement in eighth notes. The newly articulated opening of the sonata, with rests marking off the motivic segments, allows Mozart to postpone the continuous rhythmic motion in eighths until mm. 9–12, when it seems motivated by the preceding acceleration to sixteenth notes in mm. 7–8.

The new subject introduced here has two voices heard above this steady eighth-note pulsation in the bass. In turn, the two-measure unit in mm. 9–10 is intensified as a rising sequence in mm. 11–12. In the ensuing passage, orchestral-style tremolo figures in sixteenth notes are combined with a continuation of eighth-note motion in the bass so that the composite texture is the most animated yet. However, starting at the arrival at the dominant pedal point in m. 17, the rapid sixteenths pass into the left hand while the right hand plays a pattern in eighth notes accelerating to sixteenths. Unlike most of the preceding passages, this music was retained from the original version. This idea represents a variant of the opening motive from m. 1, with the stepwise figure played first in rhythmic augmentation (in eighth notes) and then in sixteenth notes. Mozart thus recaptures the opening fanfare gesture just as the transition comes to an end.

Charles Rosen has singled out the first movement of Mozart's D Minor Concerto, K. 466, from 1785, as manifesting "an important advance in purely musical skill—the art of sustaining an increase in rhythmic motion, that is, the creation of excitement," and isolates no fewer than thirteen steps in the gradual process in the first important climax for soloist and orchestra.[15] Such an advance in creating musical excitement through gradual changes in rhythmic motion is already unmistakably present here, in somewhat simpler form, in the revised first movement of K. 284, a work composed a full decade before K. 466. In fact, the creation of such a dramatic progression through a series of carefully graduated steps was presumably a major factor behind Mozart's decision to rewrite his draft. Another motivation was the effort to recast this sonata on a more imposing level by enhancing its textures and its formal breadth.

Although much of the second subject area was left intact by Mozart, his departures from the draft in the last section of the exposition are revealing. Eight measures from this section were removed and replaced by ten new measures.[16] In turn, this revision was surely bound up with Mozart's dissatisfaction with the ensuing development section of the draft version, for of the original development, virtually nothing remains in the finished work.

In the draft version, Mozart appends a two-measure cadential phrase in *piano* to the end of the exposition, immediately following a pair of robust cadences in *forte*, which sport trills in the right hand and rattling sixteenth-note figuration in the left hand. He then uses the soft two-measure cadential phrase as the motivic basis for much of the development. The motive appears eight times in the first twelve measures, and even the repeated-note figure of mm. 65–67 is derived from the three repeated pitches of the cadential motive, heard in rhythmic diminution.

Curiously, Mozart followed up on this basic compositional idea in the opening Allegro con spirito of his Sonata in D Major, K. 311, from 1777. The end of the exposition in that work incorporates a *piano* phrase featuring two-note sigh figures in parallel sixths, a motive that dominates the first sixteen measures of the ensuing development. Thus Mozart's basic idea in the draft for K. 284 was not completely discarded but found a home in his next piano sonata in this key.

To be sure, the contrast between a powerful, tutti-style scoring and a more intimate, expressive expression is retained and even heightened in the final version of K. 284. The first inserted material near the end of Mozart's exposition features a rhythmic motive employing a dotted eighth and two thirty-second notes (mm. 40, 43), an idea that is expanded into a whole measure of repetitions of this figure in octaves (m. 44) and that reappears in varied form in the penultimate measure of the exposition (m. 50). This thematic material is juxtaposed with arpeggiated chords (mm. 45, 51) foreshadowing the initial chord of the exposition (to be played as this section is repeated), whereas the cadence in A major (mm. 48–49) is now fortified by a trill sustained through one full measure. The more intimate expression in *piano* is nested into mm. 46–47, two measures that sound almost parenthetical in this context, since m. 48 could have followed directly from m. 45.

Why did Mozart completely recast the development of his evolving sonata? Part of the answer may lie in a desire to sustain momentum and rhythmic energy, since the final version of the development unfolds in unbroken sixteenth-note motion until the recapitulation. Another factor is surely motivic. The driving motive that appears in parallel sixths (or thirds) in mm. 52, 54, 56, and 58 deserves special attention in this regard. What is its connection to the exposition? This seven-note figure—with its stepwise move up a fourth and back—is audibly linked to passages in the first theme that Mozart added when he revised the movement.[17] This precise contour is imbedded in the sixteenth-note figuration in mm. 7–8, following the first note of each eight-note group. Furthermore, this general motivic shape, featuring a stepwise rise through a fourth, is also reflected in the important two-measure phrases that Mozart placed at the heart of his rewritten opening section, in mm. 9–12, while the intervallic shape suggests an inversion of the stepwise staccato figures in mm. 17–20. Yet another related passage is found in mm. 33–34 in the second subject group, with its stepwise melodic descent through a diminished fourth heard over an accompaniment in sixteenth notes. These motivic affinities are far-reaching and go beyond the network of motivic correspondences in the first version.

Somfai's claim about the two versions of this movement, that "from a modern analytical point of view, the organization of motives, the rhythm and textures—in general, the phenomenon of 'organic' elaboration—probably reached a higher level in the fragment than in the final form," seems hardly tenable.[18] In its motivic subtlety as well as its forceful rhythmic drive and brilliant textures, the second version of this opening movement of K. 284 represents an important advance. Closer to the mark is Alfred Einstein's observation that "Mozart himself must have had a personal or musical experience that suddenly lifted him to a new and higher level."[19]

The Concerto in C Major, K. 503, First Movement

If the compositional problem in K. 284 related especially to issues of continuity and musical development, the reasons for the revision of K. 503 were specifically associated with the relation of the piano soloist to the orchestral tutti. The evidence of Mozart's compositional process in this case is preserved in the autograph score of the concerto held at the Staatsbibliothek zu Berlin preussischer Kulturbesitz. In an article on this source published in 1953, Walter Gerstenberg isolated and transcribed 127 measures from the beginning of the concerto, describing them as a "particella" or original outline draft of the movement that was later revised when Mozart completed the piece.[20] Gerstenberg's work offers a valuable platform for further study of the genesis of K. 503.

More recently, the studies of Alan Tyson have broadened our knowledge of Mozart's working methods in ways that enrich the interpretation of this source. Tyson's main contribution has consisted in a close study of the papers used by Mozart for composing his music. Since Mozart used a considerable number of different paper types, and he needed to acquire new paper at regular intervals, his use of these papers reflects the chronology of his compositional activity. Furthermore, the investigation of Mozart's original papers has cast new light on a striking aspect of the Mozart sources: the survival of a substantial number of unfinished scores or fragments in various formats. Tyson observes about these sources that "in 1799

Constanze Mozart arranged for a careful catalogue of them to be compiled by the Abbé Maximilian Stadler, and after she had disposed of all the available scores of her late husband's completed works to the publisher Johann Anton André in January 1800, the fate of the fragments, which had not been included in the sale, began to exercise her."[21] Despite the efforts of Constanze Mozart, publishers like Breitkopf & Härtel showed no interest in the fragments, which have long remained obscure. Only in 2002 was a full catalog of these sources with facsimiles published as a volume of the Neue Mozart Ausgabe, edited by Ulrich Konrad.[22]

Tyson's investigation of these fragments and of Mozart's use of music paper led to an important conclusion: that some of his finished works began as fragments that were only completed after a considerable length of time had elapsed. It appears that Mozart's reputation for composing works swiftly was connected in part to his practice of setting aside torsos of incomplete works that could be taken up and finished when an occasion arose, such as a performance opportunity. Such was evidently the case with the first movement of K. 503. Mozart entered this work into his "Verzeichnüss" with the date of 4 December 1786, and he premiered the work on the very next day, 5 December 1786. However, the three double leaves at the beginning of the autograph score of K. 503 differ from the remainder of the score in that they consist of a rare paper type, one that turns up in six other examples. These include parts of the scores of the String Quartet in A Major, K. 464, an aria from *Davidde penitente*, K. 469, and three concertos, the works in F major, K. 459, D minor, K. 466, and C major, K. 467, as well as the whole of a string quartet fragment in A major, K. 464a. All of these works date from between December 1784 and March 1785, a period nearly two years earlier than Mozart's completion and performance of K. 503 in December 1786.

All of this indicates that the particella for K. 503 discussed by Gerstenberg almost certainly dates from the period around late 1784 and early 1785, when Mozart was intensely occupied with piano concertos and brought to fruition three such works, K. 459, K. 466, and K. 467. The fact that one of these pieces—K. 467—was in C major may perhaps have discouraged him from completing another concerto in the same key at that time. In any case, although Mozart composed three further piano concertos during the following 1785–86 season—K. 482, K. 488, and K. 491—it was not until the end of 1786 that he returned to his draft for what became K. 503, which was to become the very last of the great series of twelve Viennese piano concertos that began with K. 449 in E♭ major in 1784.

Mozart's draft is reproduced in Ex. 1.4a, and the final version of the opening solo passage is shown in Ex. 1.4b. The transcription of the draft basically follows Gerstenberg's version, though empty staves have been deleted, and emendations have been made to restore Mozart's strokes as articulation marks. The reconstruction of the draft is made possible through distinct differences in the color of the ink. When Mozart returned to his draft, he filled out the many empty systems in the pages of the draft, rewrote parts of the solo piano passage on folio 5r, and then canceled all of folio 5v. Consequently, he inserted a new leaf, folio 6, into his score. The original folio 6 thus became folio 7, but it corresponds in its paper type to the opening pages of the draft and represents the missing leaf that was paired originally with folio 5.

What did Mozart alter in his draft, and why? The change involved a thorough reshaping of the opening solo piano passage with orchestral accompaniment, which was expanded from fifteen to twenty-one measures. The first measures of the solo, in which the piano responds to soft inflections in the strings, were left unchanged. However, beginning in mm. 96–97, Mozart's refashioning of the piano part involved a fundamental rethinking of the original version. In order to appreciate the revision, it is indispensable to reflect on the challenging context of this solo passage following an imposing and weighty orchestral ritornello.

This Allegro maestoso opens with a pair of weighty orchestral phrases in *forte* rooted on the tonic and dominant, spread across broad registers of pitch and grounded by the taps and rolls of the timpani. In all the Mozart piano concertos, there is no other opening that so much depends on the effect of sheer massive sonority, and indeed, the first four measures of each of these eight-measure phrases involve no harmonic shift whatsoever. Such an opening cannot be effectively transferred to the solo piano by itself, which would sound hopelessly weak by comparison. Presumably for this reason, Mozart decided to introduce the solo indirectly in response to a series of cadential phrases in the strings, played *piano*. As the piano continues, Mozart gives to the soloist a version of another *piano* phrase—the inflection heard twice in the strings in mm. 70–72 of the orchestral introduction.

Thus in K. 503 Mozart faced a special challenge with the opening piano passage, inasmuch as his standard operating procedure in lyrical movements would not apply. It would not do to have the piano initially mimic the opening theme of the orchestral introduction, as occurs in other later concertos such as K. 488, K. 537, and K. 595. Nor was it viable to devise the piano entrance as an expressive recitative-in-tempo passage, as in the two concertos in the minor, K. 466 and K. 491, in which the agitated tension of the orchestral ritornello is reshaped into the more personal utterance of the soloist.

The problem in Mozart's initial attempt at the opening piano passage is twofold: it lacks sufficient stature to enable the soloist to assert himself or herself against the orchestra, and it fails to build a convincing transition in sonority and character to the massive reassertion of the opening theme in the tutti that occurs in m. 106 of the draft, corresponding to m. 112 of the finished work. It is revealing that in his draft, just as in the completed version, Mozart avoids including the solo with the first six measures of this emphatic restatement of the main theme. However, the lighter orchestration of the last two measures of this eight-measure unit offered that

Ex. 1.4a. Draft version of the Concerto in C Major, K. 503, I.

opportunity, and here the solo reenters with sixteenth-note figuration in the high register, a texture of sound heard above the bassoons and oboes and the sustained dominant-seventh chord in the strings.

That distinctive texture of sound—with the rapid piano figuration heard in the high register over the woodwinds—became a key element in Mozart's expansion

Ex. 1.4a. Continued.

of the piano entrance once he returned to the work in 1786. But just as important is the higher degree of articulation given to the phrasing of the passage. In the draft version, the last eight measures of the piano solo unfold continuously, with no articulating pauses in the right hand of the piano. The rewritten version contains several such breaks. An emerging quality of insistence invests the threefold phrases emphasizing the falling dyad F–B in mm. 96–98, and the psychological impression emerges that the soloist will not remain content with understated rhetoric. The richer sonority of parallel $^6_3$ chords and syncopation in mm. 99–100 show an increasing resourcefulness, and the following two-measure phrase, in mm. 101–2, returns to the telltale F with a new twist. In place of the predictable V–I cadences in those rather unimaginative orchestral gestures in mm. 91 and 93, the soloist now harmonizes the F as part of a diminished-seventh chord leading through a deceptive harmonic shift to the sixth degree. Skillful individual innovation thus competes with the massive yet limited resources of the crowd. In the ensuing two-measure

Ex. 1.4a. Continued.

phrase, in mm. 103–4, virtuosity begins to play a role for the first time. This phrase is a variation on mm. 99–100, a variation in which brilliant sixteenth-note scales and broken octaves sweep through registers yet untouched by the piano. Following the same pattern is m. 105, which offers an elaboration of the content of m. 101, accompanied softly by the strings.

The turning point in the entire piano passage comes at m. 106, with the entrance of the horns to articulate the G pedal point in the tonic $^6_4$ chord as the soloist moves into the high register. The flute, oboes, and bassoons join their sonorities with the

CHAPTER 1

Ex. 1.4a. Continued.

piano, with the upper oboe line corresponding closely to that of the piano, though played one octave lower. These orchestral instruments are missing altogether from the early version of the passage in Mozart's particella, which is altogether more placid and less eventful than the final version. In the last three measures of the finished work, the piano's descending figuration is reversed through a rising chromatic scale, followed by restatement of the I_4^6–V^7 progression in a halting rhythm that seems to foreshadow the orchestral chords to come. To a much greater extent than the first version, Mozart's expanded passage for the solo piano conveys a sense of growing

Mozart's Second Thoughts

37

Ex. 1.4a. Continued.

strength and confidence. The solo passage here seems to *lead into* or even help *bring about* the powerful main theme in the tutti rather than merely precede it.

The autograph score of K. 503 thus offers a wealth of insight into the ways in which a single solo piano passage can accomplish a crucial psychological transition while interacting with instrumental groups from the orchestra. But the value of this autograph score for study of the creative process is not confined to this one example. Layers of successive compositional work can be identified throughout the score. As Gerstenberg observes, many passages, especially for the pianist's left hand, were written in a distinct yellowish ink and were clearly filled in later.

Ex. 1.4a. Continued.

Ex. 1.4b. Final version of the piano entrance in the Concerto in C Major, K. 503, I.

It is not surprising that the last part of the musical text to be completed was the piano solo part, and particularly those aspects of the texture that would be realized through patterns of figuration. Indeed, in the autograph score of one of the subsequent concertos, the "Coronation" Concerto, K. 537, Mozart notated little for the left hand in extended passages of the outer movements and in the entire slow movement, even though he performed this piece more than once. Other concertos as well, such as K. 482 and K. 491, contain passages in which Mozart has outlined just a few sustained pitches without realizing the full texture; such passages tend to appear before major cadences, when a sudden interruption of the rhythmic momentum would be especially inappropriate and disconcerting.[23] One reason for the use of such shorthand may have been a reluctance on Mozart's part to fix the text in a single configuration. In specific performances, he could choose among different possibilities of textural realization.

Hence it remains uncertain whether the yellowish ink layer of writing in the score of K. 503 preceded or followed Mozart's first performance of that work on 5 December 1786. In various details, his initial performance of the concerto surely did not coincide with the printed text we know. Some of his late revisions also affect structural features, as with his decision to delete a measure in the slow movement preceding m. 100, which prolonged the diminished-seventh harmony while connecting the piano arpeggios in the high register in m. 99 with the low register at the beginning of the following measure.

With K. 503, as with several of the other great piano concertos from the Vienna years, the greatest gap between aesthetic realization and the preserved text remains the problem of the missing cadenzas. This situation reflects ironically on overly literalist attitudes toward Mozart's musical texts. These texts are not only incomplete but could scarcely ever have existed in one definitive version. It is more appropriate to inquire into the meaning rather than merely the letter of Mozart's musical legacy, recognizing the continuing challenge these works pose for active, imaginative interpretation.

Beethoven's Unfinished
Piano Trio in F Minor from 1816

The subject of this chapter is a piano trio that would have become one of Beethoven's major chamber works had it been completed. On 1 October 1816 the composer wrote to publisher Robert Birchall in London concerning various publication arrangements (see Figs. 2.1–2.2).[1] Beethoven opens the letter with the rather hopeful admonition that "you would not encrease the number of inglishmen neglecting their word and honor, as I had the misfortune of meeting with two of this sort." He returns to the notion of "honor" in his closing paragraph, in which he entreats Birchall to "honor" him "as soon as possible with an answer" regarding his option of purchasing some new compositions. In this regard, Beethoven emphasizes two new major pieces: "A Grand Sonata for the Pianoforte alone 40£. A Trio for the Piano with accomp. of Violin and Violoncello for 50£." The former work is readily identifiable as the Sonata in A Major, op. 101, the autograph score of which was dated the following month, November 1816.[2] This impressive sonata has long been recognized as a pivotal work in Beethoven's creative development, which—along with the two Cello Sonatas, op. 102, and the song cycle *An die ferne Geliebte*—marks the passage to his late style.

The higher-priced item, on the other hand, has long remained almost completely unknown. Few studies of Beethoven mention the Piano Trio in F Minor, which is missing even from the list of fragmentary pieces omitted from the Complete Edition compiled by Willy Hess.[3] An exception is a source study by Nicholas Marston that was published recently, after the present essay first appeared in print. Marston identified an additional sketch leaf related to the main draft of the first movement of the trio, a manuscript that helps confirm the sonata design of the planned movement.[4] The main sources for the F Minor Trio were already given passing mention by the pioneer of Beethoven sketch studies, Gustav Nottebohm, in an article first published in 1876. His essay concerns Beethoven's large-format sketchbook from the years 1815 and 1816, a source that was then held in Vienna but is now part of the library of William Scheide at Princeton, New Jersey.[5] Relying on Nottebohm's comments in his chapter of *The Beethoven Sketchbooks* catalog devoted to the Scheide Sketchbook, Alan Tyson identified twenty-two pages in Scheide as containing sketches for the trio, including entries on leaves originally from that book that are now held in other collections.[6] In a subsequent inventory of sources related to Beethoven's piano trios, Karl Dorfmüller listed the sketches in the reconstructed Scheide Sketchbook in addition to the aforementioned fragmentary draft in full score (Partitur-Entwurf), which is held at the Staatsbibliothek zu Berlin preussischer Kulturbesitz as MS Grasnick 29.[7] In his aforementioned recent study, Marston tabulated a provisional list of sources in addition to the central documents preserving work on the trio: the Scheide Sketchbook and the Grasnick 29 draft. An overview of the manuscript sources for the trio is provided at the end of this chapter.

Within the pages of the Scheide Sketchbook, the entries for the F Minor Trio follow those for the Sonata in A Major, op. 101, indicating that Beethoven worked on the trio in 1816, before he made his offer to Robert Birchall in October of that year. The sketches for the trio follow those for the second movement of the sonata, occupying much of the space between pages 86 and 107. Further evidence for their chronology comes from sketches for other pieces found in the sketchbook. On page 99, interspersed with the work on the F Minor Trio, are entries for the song "Der Mann von Wort," op. 99, which was published in November 1816.[8] Furthermore, at the top of page 87 Beethoven writes the inscription "Variationen aus meinem Jünglingsalter" (Variations from my youth), which presumably relates to his revision of the variations for piano trio on Wenzel Müller's song "Ich bin der Schneider Kakadu," op. 121a, an older project that reached publication only in 1824. In a letter from 19 July 1816 to the publisher Härtel, Beethoven offered this piece, which he described as "Variationen über ein müllersches Thema und von meiner früheren Komposition, jedoch nicht unter die verwerflichen zu rechnen" (variations on a theme by Müller from among my earlier compositions, but not a negligible one). The manuscript paper he used for the revised variations is of the same type employed for the autograph scores of "Der Mann von Wort" as well as the song cycle *An die ferne Geliebte*, op. 98, which was also sketched in the Scheide Sketchbook.[9] Beethoven's interest in revising the Müller variations at this time may have been stimulated by his work on the F Minor Trio, a piece written for the same combination of instruments.[10]

When Beethoven made his offer of the sonata and the trio to Robert Birchall, he had already invested considerable labor in these two pieces. He began composing

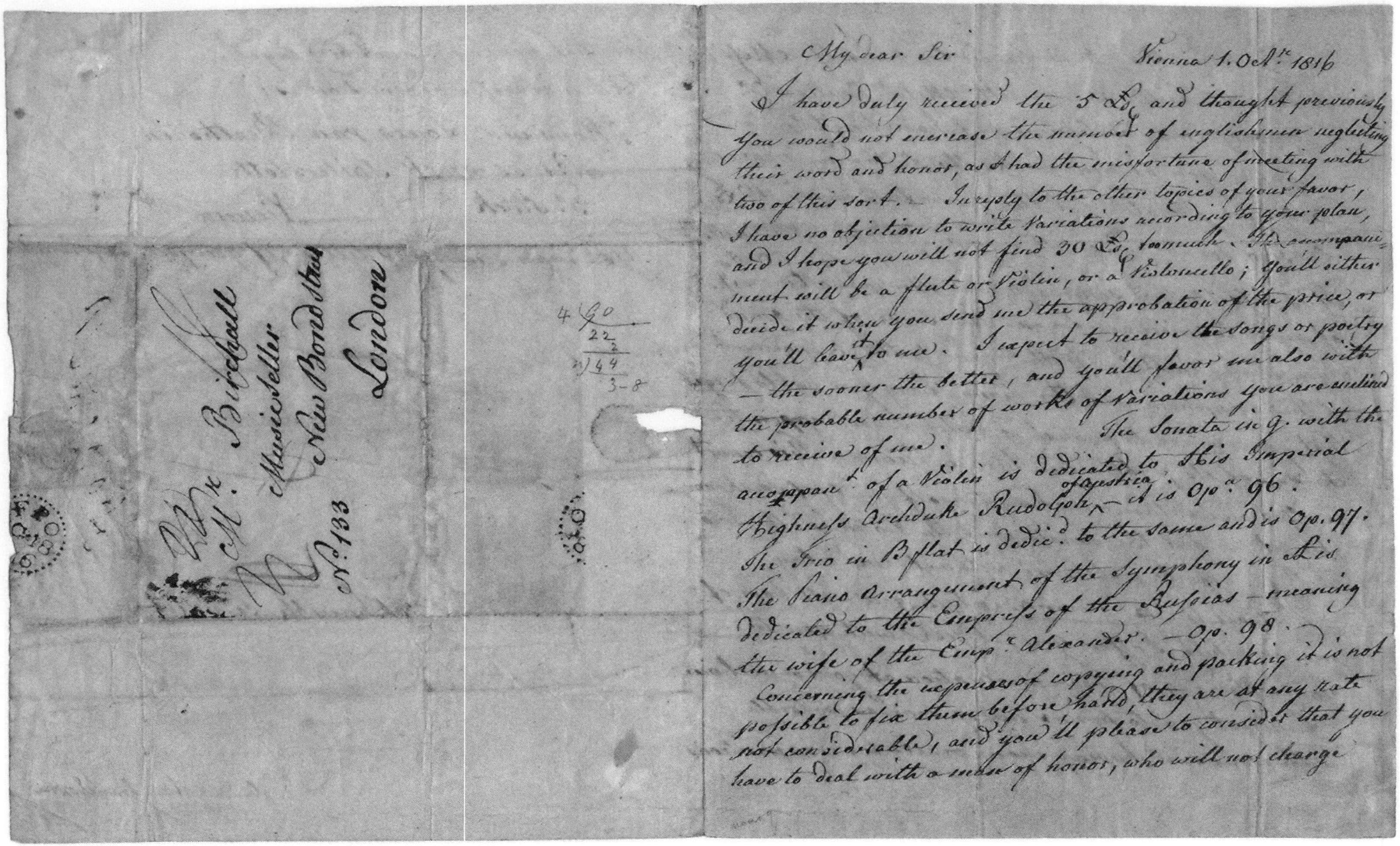

Mr. Birchall
Musicseller
New Bond Street
No. 133
London

My dear Sir   Vienna 1. Oct.r 1816

I have duly received the 5 £ and thought previously
you would not encrease the number of englishmen neglecting
their word and honor, as I had the misfortune of meeting with
two of this sort. In reply to the other topics of your favor,
I have no objection to write Variations according to your plan,
and I hope you will not find 30 £ too much. The accompaniment will be a flute or Violin, or a Violoncello; you'll either
decide it when you send me the approbation of the price, or
you'll leave it to me. I expect to receive the songs or poetry
— the sooner the better, and you'll favor me also with
the probable number of works of Variations you are inclined
to receive of me. The Sonata in G. with the
accompan.t of a Violin is dedicated to His Imperial
Highness Archduke Rudolph of Austria — it is Op.o 96.
The Trio in B flat is dedic.d to the same and is Op. 97.
The Piano Arrangement of the Symphony in A is
dedicated to the Empress of the Russias — meaning
the wife of the Emp.r Alexander. — Op. 98.
Concerning the expenses of copying and packing it is not
possible to fix them before hand, they are at any rate
not considerable, and you'll please to consider that you
have to deal with a man of honor, who will not charge

Figures 2.1–2.2. Beethoven's letter to Robert Birchall of 1 October 1816, from the collection of the Ira Brilliant Center for Beethoven Studies, San José State University. Printed with permission.

one or more than it is charged for himself. Messrs
Fries & Co will account with Messrs Coutts & Co.
The postage may be defrayed at I have told.
I offer good of my works the following new ones;
A Grand Sonata for the Pianoforte alone next
A Trio for the Piano with accomp. of Violin & Violoncello
for 60 £
His Majesty that somebody will offer good other works
of more importance for ex. the Score of the grand
Symphony in A — With regard to the arrangement
of this Symphony for the Piano, I beg you not to forget
that you are not to publish it until I have appointed
the Day of its publication here in Vienna. This cannot
be otherwise without making myself guilty of a dishonor
abroad — but the donate with the Violin and the Trio
in B♭ may be published without any delay.—
With all the new works, which you will have of
me on which I offer you, it rests with you to
name the Day of their publication at your own choice.
I entreat you to honor me as soon as possible
with an answer having many orders for compositions

and that yours may not be delayed.
My address or direction is:
Monsieur Louis van Beethoven
No 1055 &1056 Sailerstette
B. Stock
Vienna

You may send your letter, if you please, direct
to your
your humble servant

Hamburg &c—— Smithson

the sonata during the summer of 1815, but his work was interrupted and delayed repeatedly by other projects. Pages 74–85 of the Scheide Sketchbook contain material for the second movement of the sonata, alongside brief entries for its later movements. Much of the remainder of the sketchbook is devoted to the Trio in F Minor. The sketchbook ends with entries for the march for military band, WoO 24, the autograph of which is dated "3ten Juni 1816."[11] Whereas additional, more advanced sketches for the Sonata in A Major are found in the following large-format sketchbook, Autograph 11/1, all of the extant entries for the Trio in F Minor are found in the reconstructed Scheide Sketchbook together with the draft contained in the Grasnick 29 manuscript. This implies that Beethoven's compositional work on the trio dates from the spring of 1816, following the initial stages of work on op. 101 and preceding the composition of the Military March, WoO 24. That his work on the trio may have overlapped with the march and extended beyond May is implied by the draft of a sentence of a letter to the Archduke Rudolph found on page 95 of Scheide amongst the sketches for the trio. Beethoven refers to having rented an apartment, assuming that Rudolph would help subsidize the cost. Sieghard Brandenburg takes this statement as a reference to the composer's summer lodging in Baden, which began in July 1816.[12]

Beethoven's offer of the F Minor Piano Trio to Birchall in October 1816 was not a freely speculative suggestion but a proposal based on substantial existing work. Yet like some of his other projects from this relatively unproductive period, including the music for Friedrich Duncker's drama *Leonore Prohaska*, WoO 96, and the projected sixth Piano Concerto in D Major, Hess 15, the F Minor Trio was not to be completed. The D Major Piano Concerto offers a basis for comparison. Unlike the manuscripts for the trio, its sources have been examined in considerable detail by Lewis Lockwood and Nicholas Cook.[13] These documents consist of sketches in several manuscripts, of which the Scheide Sketchbook is again especially important, as thirty pages at the beginning of the book are devoted to the concerto. In addition, there is a bulky autograph score for the first movement of the concerto held in the Berlin Staatsbibliothek as Artaria MS 184. This rough preliminary score was written by Beethoven in association with the related sketches, with specific compositional problems in the score sometimes addressed by a return to the sketchbook.

Other studies of Beethoven's compositional process have revealed his tendency to combine initial sketches for a project in a large-format sketchbook with such rudimentary scores or drafts. In his initial labors on the *33 Veränderungen über einen Walzer von A. Diabelli* (33 variations on a waltz by A. Diabelli), op. 120, from 1819, for instance, Beethoven made entries in the Wittgenstein Sketchbook while also compiling an extended draft on loose gatherings of music paper.[14] In view of this compositional procedure, we should be especially alert in interpreting Beethoven's sketches to the presence and interrelationship of work in such dual or multiple formats. The comparison of entries in the large sketchbooks with such contemporaneous drafts or rudimentary scores can be of indispensable value in evaluating the challenging and often enigmatic content of the sketches.

My analysis of the F Minor Trio sources is presented in four parts. The first examines the sketches in the Scheide Sketchbook. The second places these sketches into relationship with the most central document for the trio, the extended draft for the first movement, presented here in facsimile and transcription sound recording at www.press.uillinois.edu/FMinorTrio.[15] The final sections of the chapter assess the place of this major unfinished project in Beethoven's creative development and its affinities with his other, familiar works in this distinctive key.

The Scheide Sketchbook

The commentary on the sources for the F Minor Trio by Nottebohm, "Ein Skizzenbuch aus den Jahren 1815 und 1816," was originally published in volume 7 of the *Musikalisches Wochenblatt* and subsequently reprinted in the collection *Zweite Beethoveniana*.[16] His glancing references to the sketches for the trio are translated in full below. The final musical example from page 67 of the Scheide Sketchbook is printed separately at the end of Nottebohm's article.

> Work now appears for the first and third movements of an incomplete trio in F minor for piano, violin, and cello. The beginning of the first movement finally appears in this form [see Ex. 2.1]:

Ex. 2.1. Theme of the first movement of the F Minor Trio, as transcribed by Gustav Nottebohm in "Ein Skizzenbuch aus den Jahren 1815 und 1816," page 345.

> The main theme of the last movement appears once in this form [see Ex. 2.2]:

Ex. 2.2. Theme of the finale of the F Minor Trio, as transcribed by Gustav Nottebohm in "Ein Skizzenbuch aus den Jahren 1815 und 1816," page 345.

Beethoven later began to write the first movement in score and carried that process rather far toward completion. Then the work was put aside.*

*Of the pages used for the clean copy only a few are extant, and of these the first leaf is missing, which must have contained the beginning of the trio and according to which more specific details could have been obtained. [This statement is printed in Nottebohm's text at the foot of the page.]

(p. 67) a beginning in F minor [see Ex. 2.3] probably intended for the incomplete trio[.][17]

als Deutscher vom letzten Stück

Ex. 2.3. Theme of a German dance intended for the finale of the F Minor Trio, as transcribed by Gustav Nottebohm in "Ein Skizzenbuch aus den Jahren 1815 und 1816," page 348.

Characteristically, Nottebohm did not identify the precise locations of his citations from the manuscript. Comparison of his transcriptions with the Scheide Sketchbook reveals that he selected his examples from the beginning and end of the extended body of sketches. His illustration of the finale theme comes from page 86, at the beginning of the trio sketches. The excerpt from the first movement, on the other hand, is drawn from page 107, the very last page of Scheide devoted to the trio. Nottebohm provides just a teasing glimpse at the material in these excerpts, one that whets our appetite for more.

The large body of sketches for the trio indeed extends from page 86 to page 107, as Nottebohm claimed, and to these pages can be added some entries on the aforementioned leaves that apparently once formed a part of the Scheide Sketchbook, especially folio 5 of MS Grasnick 20a, held at the Staatsbibliothek zu Berlin preussischer Kulturbesitz, and Add. MS 29997, folio 19, held at the British Library in London.[18] Some of these pages in Scheide contain unrelated sketches, such as piano exercises on page 93 ("Scalen für Lernende"), work on the aforementioned song "Der Mann von Wort" on page 99, and sketches for a "Sinfonia" and a "Sonat[e]" on page 106. In addition to the sketches for the trio in Scheide, the ten-page document held in Berlin as MS Grasnick 29 contains a draft for the opening section of the first movement. The overview of sources provided at the end of this chapter lists these and other related manuscripts.

Ex. 2.4. Sketch for the main theme of the finale of the F Minor Trio
(Scheide Sketchbook, page 86).

Nottebohm's uncertainty about attributing the sketch he transcribed from page 67 of Scheide to the incomplete trio can be removed. This entry appears twenty pages before the main run of trio sketches and bears the inscription "als Deutscher vom letzten Stück" (as German dance from the last movement). Beethoven copied this sketch and inscription verbatim onto page 105 of the sketchbook, where it is found among sketches for the first movement of the trio, and there seems to be no question about his intention to use this theme in the finale of the projected work.[19]

What more can we learn about the trio from these extant sources? Examination of the Scheide Sketchbook augments Nottebohm's findings in various ways. For instance, the main theme of the finale in $\frac{6}{8}$ time that Nottebohm transcribed from page 86 actually contains a short introductory preface, and the theme itself is intended to be played in octaves. Beethoven also wrote out indications for an accompaniment to the theme, which have been added to the transcription in Ex. 2.4. The pattern of this accompaniment, with an eighth rest followed by a repeated dyad, relates to the structure of the theme, which employs repeated notes on the second and third beats of each group of three eighth notes. The second of each of these repeated notes is slurred, which highlights the contour of the melody, outlining as it does first the turn figure around the dominant pitch, C, and then the stepwise ascent to the crux of the melody on A♭. In shaping the descent from this melodic peak, Beethoven replaces the stepwise motion by triadic motion, spelling out the chords of D♭ major and F minor.

Here, stress is placed here on the semitone D♭–C in the context of F minor. It is striking how Beethoven employs a pattern of falling motivic thirds that lead to an emphasis on the D♭–C half step. That this is a shared trait of Beethoven's main themes for the first and last movements can be readily appreciated if we juxtapose

Main theme, first movement

Melodic peak, theme of finale

Ex. 2.5. Comparison of the themes of the first and last movements of the F Minor Trio.

the head of the theme for the first movement with the melodic peak of the finale theme (Ex. 2.5). The kinship is hardly accidental, since it represents a familiar feature of other Beethovenian works in this key, such as the "Appassionata" Sonata, op. 57, and the String Quartet in F Minor, op. 95.

Compositional ideas for the finale were clearly the trigger point for Beethoven's work on the F Minor Trio. Sketches for the finale appear before those for the first movement, whereas material for a middle movement or movements is scarce; at the bottom of page 104, under sketches for the first movement and the finale, there is an entry for a syncopated theme in B♭ major labeled "oder 3tes Stück in 3" (or third movement in triple time). By contrast, sketches for the finale are relatively well represented, and the very last page of work on the trio in Scheide, page 107, concludes with what appears to be a transition to its main theme, which is written in $\frac{3}{4}$ instead of $\frac{6}{8}$ and in note values twice as large as in earlier sketches. There are some indications that Beethoven envisioned the finale as a rondo design, in which the "Deutscher" or German dance written on pages 67 and 105 of Scheide might have served as an episode. Motivically, the German dance shares common features with the other main themes, including a prominent emphasis on the D♭–C semitone in its first four measures.

The movement of the F Minor Trio that Beethoven realized most fully is the opening movement, and the surviving torso in score for this part of the work is of extraordinary interest. In the Scheide Sketchbook, Beethoven wrote out the main theme of this sonata-form movement many times in different variants; it appears at the top of pages 88, 92, 98, and 101, at the bottom of page 96, and on pages 102, 105, and elsewhere. As we have seen, the example supplied by Nottebohm is drawn from page 107, at the top of the page, staves 1–2. The version of this theme used in the Grasnick 29 draft differs yet again, but Nottebohm's claim that the final version appears as in his example is based specifically on the position of the entry at the end of the trio sketches in Scheide. We shall return later to the chronology of these entries.

Nottebohm did not include in his transcription the introductory passage on the dominant of F minor, which begins on a downbeat on middle C and gradually rises

Ex. 2.6. Sketch for the beginning of the first movement of the F Minor Trio
(Scheide Sketchbook, page 107).

more than two octaves before reaching a fermata on a sustained E preceding the
onset of the main subject in F minor. This main theme was evidently intended to
begin *forte*, since its continuation at the upbeat to m. 4 is marked *piano* in one of
Beethoven's sketches, on stave 1 of page 101 of the Scheide Sketchbook (shown in
Plate 1). The ensuing motion of the main theme then descends through the same
registral space, reaching middle C in mm. 9–10, before another, more abrupt ascent
of an octave is made in m. 11 (Ex. 2.6).

Although Nottebohm limited himself to illustrating the main themes of the
outer movements of the trio, there are ample indications that Beethoven was also
concerned with issues of tonal direction and larger formal shaping. A notation
below the sketch in Ex. 2.6 specifies the modulatory goal as C major, whereas on
page 100 of Scheide, Beethoven writes "1ter theil in c moll" (1st part in C minor),
indicating that the first section or exposition of the movement was intended to
end in C minor. This raises the matter of the form of the first movement of the F
Minor Trio, a topic best addressed through examination of the Grasnick 29 draft.
Yet before we discuss the draft in detail, we should consider its relationship with
the body of sketch material contained in Scheide.

Beethoven did not always make his sketches in the order in which they appear in
his bound sketchbooks. In the present case, there is reason to believe that the final
notations for the trio on page 107 of the sketchbook are not necessarily the last that
he wrote before breaking off his labors on the project. Beethoven returned to his
sketchbooks at different sittings and often revised or elaborated his earlier work.
When this occurred, his manuscripts could become filled with new entries and
revisions, with a veritable maze of cancellations, additions, and cross-references.
In the sketches for the trio in Scheide, this situation arises on page 101 and to a
somewhat lesser extent on pages 102–3. A glance at page 101 reveals an impressive

density of connective indications in Beethoven's characteristic shorthand; virtually all available space on the page has been utilized (Plate 1).

At the top of page 101, Beethoven has written the main theme of the first movement, the same basic subject that Nottebohm transcribed from page 107. It is especially the lower half of the page that illustrates Beethoven's intense revision process, including many alternative readings signaled by abbreviations. For instance, the two vertical lines with one horizontal stroke seen above stave 8 mark the continuity to stave 12 below, on the left-hand side, while the paired numbers "60" on the right side above stave 12 signal another such connection. Other, similar abbreviations point toward continuities that reach beyond this page, since Beethoven had run out of space. Hence the distinctive large number "800000" seen in the right margin at stave 11 corresponds to another "800000" on page 102, stave 10.

The explanation for the density of revision beginning on page 101 is not immediately self-evident, and if we had access to the Scheide Sketchbook alone, this page would be particularly puzzling. Page 101 represents a part of the sketchbook that was intensely used when Beethoven wrote out the draft on loose papers. Its complexities mirror the process by which he drew upon his sketches in Scheide to create a rudimentary score for the trio. This correspondence between the sketchbook and draft is revealing. As we have seen, Beethoven often used his work in a large sketchbook such as Scheide as a launching pad for such a draft in score on loose papers, and in just this way, the sketchbook is intimately linked to the Grasnick 29 draft. These pages in Scheide mark the point when Beethoven's vision of the new trio had achieved sufficient clarity to enable him to tackle the work in another, more elaborate format, one that in some ways already resembles the score of a completed work.

The Relation between Sketchbook and Draft

The Grasnick 29 draft of the F Minor Trio begins much like an autograph score and includes aspects of notation often omitted in Beethoven's sketches, such as clefs, meter, key signatures, rests, dynamic indications, and pedal markings. The manuscript gradually becomes more schematic and incomplete, yet its first six pages provide a rather clear picture of the evolving work, beginning with a slow introduction and extending to the second subject group of the exposition of the sonata form. Figs. 2.3 and 2.4 show the first two pages of the draft, and Ex. 2.7 provides a full transcription of the first six pages. Although the musical texture becomes thin as the draft unfolds, it is reasonable to supplement this basic text with figuration that is implied by the musical context. For instance, Beethoven surely intended for the initial accompaniment texture in triplet eighth notes to extend across much of the first two pages of the score, but once the pattern was well established, he did not find it necessary to write out all of the notes. In the

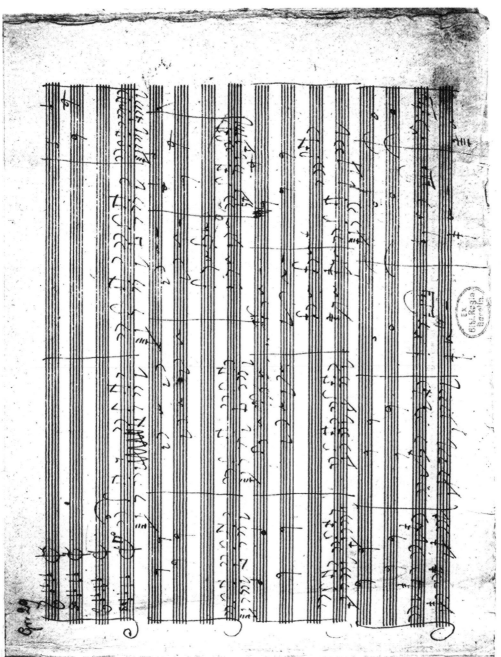

Figures 2.3–2.4. MS Grasnick 29, pages 1–2, Musikabteilung, Staatsbibliothek zu Berlin preussischer Kulturbesitz. Printed with permission.

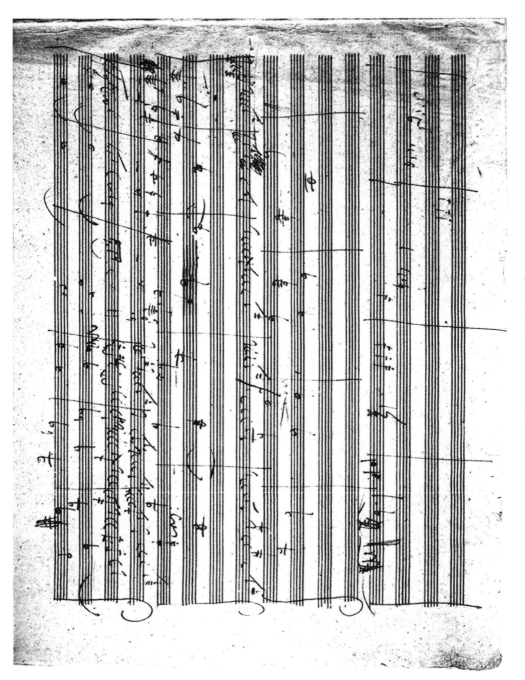

Figures 2.3–2.4. Continued.

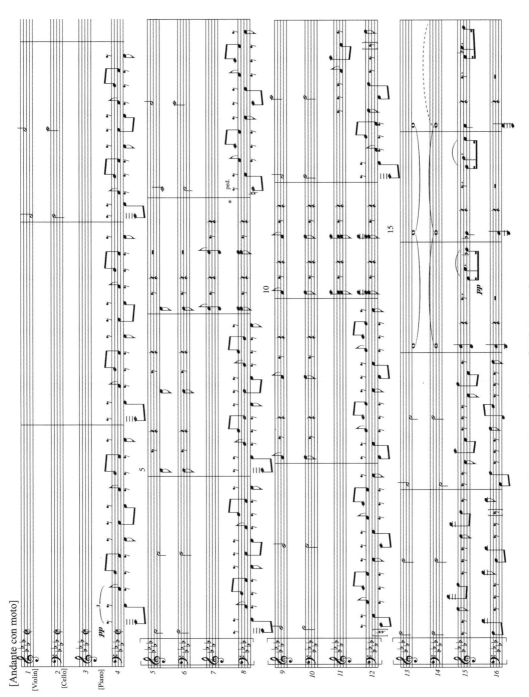

Ex. 2.7. Transcription of MS Grasnick 29, pages 1–6.

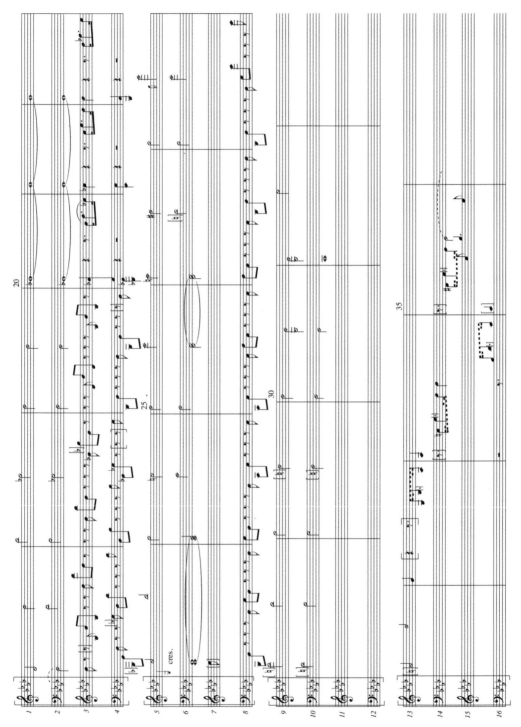

Ex. 2.7. Continued.

Ex. 2.7. Continued.

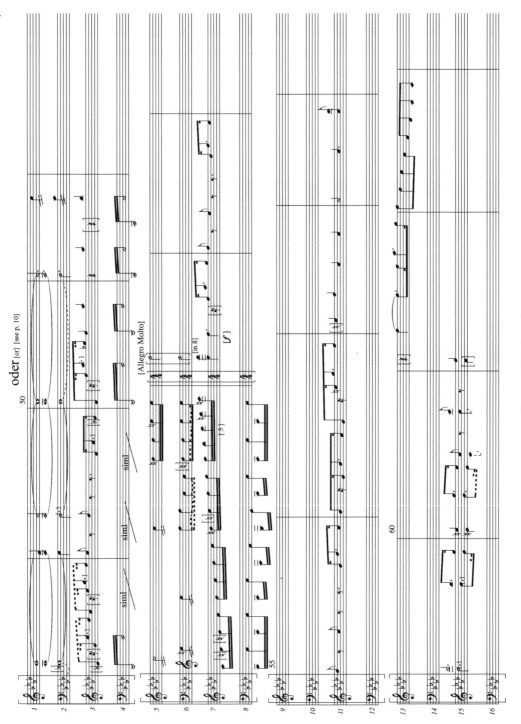

Ex. 2.7. Continued.

Ex. 2.7. Continued.

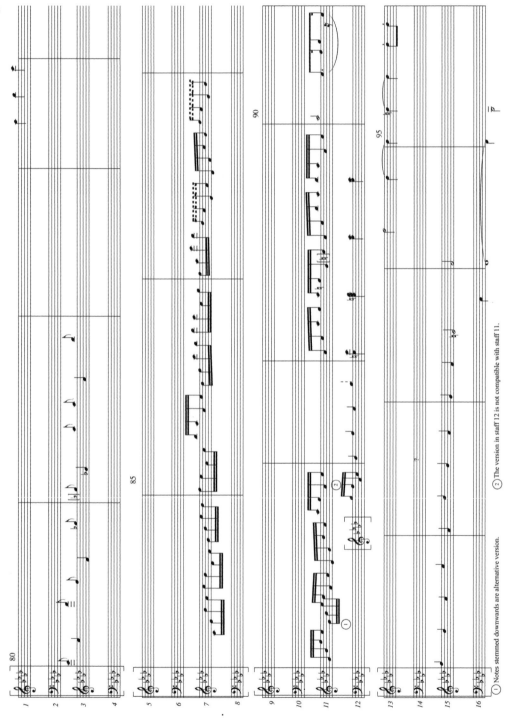

① Notes stemmed downwards are alternative version.

② The version in staff 12 is not compatible with staff 11.

Ex. 2.7. Continued.

audio recording I made with Christina Lixandru, violinist, and Diana Flesner, cellist, in support of this chapter, I have supplied the implied figuration in the piano.

Although Nottebohm evidently knew of this draft, what he writes about it is misleading. Nottebohm claimed inaccurately that the source was missing its first page; the error perhaps arose due to a lack of opportunity on his part to directly compare these sources. In any event, the beginning of this draft shows no signs of being incomplete, although the score does not begin with the main theme that Beethoven had sketched so often. The absence of this theme at the head of the draft is conspicuous and may have surprised Nottebohm. Only in the middle of the second system of page 4, beginning at m. 53, does the main theme appear. The nine-measure statement of the theme in F minor in the piano is followed here by shorter statements by the violin and cello in turn before the piano is given a transition to the lyrical second theme set in the key of D♭ major.

As this draft reveals, Beethoven's plan for the movement features an unusually extended slow introduction, fifty-two measures in length. Wolfgang Osthoff has drawn attention to the general importance of slow introductions in Beethoven's works for piano trio, including the massive, fantasy-like introduction to the aforementioned variations on "Ich bin der Schneider Kakadu," op. 121a, a section of that work that may have been freshly composed in 1816.[20] Osthoff links this tendency to an affinity of the genre to symphonic models. The slow introduction contained in the draft of the unfinished trio from 1816 surpasses all other examples from the genre in its breadth of conception while displaying a fascinating relation to the main theme of the ensuing sonata form.

Important information related to the draft is found in the Scheide Sketchbook. For instance, the tempo indications of Andante con moto for the slow introduction and Allegro molto for the exposition appear next to the corresponding sketch material on pages 101 and 96 of Scheide, respectively.[21] In turn, the Grasnick 29 draft sheds light on many entries contained in the sketchbook. For instance, near staves 4–5 of page 101, under the designation Andante con moto, Beethoven writes "cembal[o]" and "3olen [triolen]," referring to the initial accompaniment texture in triplets in the piano, and beginning in stave 4, he writes out the theme in half notes just as are given to the violin and cello in his draft.

A comparison of page 101 of Scheide with the Grasnick draft demonstrates the close interrelationship of the two sources (see Plate 1 and Figs. 2.3–2.4 as well as the transcriptions in Exx. 2.7–2.8). There are two main layers of work on this page of Scheide. The sketch at the top of the page, which resembles sketches for the main theme on several other pages, was evidently written first. When Beethoven returned to page 101 at a later time, presumably after many sketches for the trio on later pages up to page 107 had been written, he crossed out the preexisting entries on staves 3–4 on the left-hand side of the page and then wrote the aforementioned heading Andante con moto and the words "cembal[o]" and "3olen," designating

Ex. 2.8. Scheide Sketchbook, page 101. Sketch content and measure
numbers correspond to MS Grasnick 29, pages 1–2.

an accompaniment in triplets in the piano. There are two versions of the opening phrase in half notes in staves 4 and 5; the lower version in darker ink is one
measure longer and ties over the half note C. In incorporating this material into
his Grasnick draft, Beethoven chose the version on stave 4. Farther to the right on
this stave, we see a version of the accompaniment figuration in triplets, which was
altered somewhat when he assimilated it into m. 7 of the Grasnick draft.

Other parallels between page 101 and the Grasnick draft can be identified as follows. The second phrase in half notes, corresponding to mm. 7–10 of Grasnick 29,
is crammed into stave 4 of Scheide; the third phrase in the sketchbook begins with
a D♭ instead of an A♭, as in Grasnick 29, and shows the accompaniment written in
sixteenth notes instead of quarter notes. The continuation of this phrase also exists
in two versions in Scheide; Beethoven selected the version in stave 6 to be used in

the Grasnick draft. This stave contains the musical continuity corresponding to mm. 12–20 in Grasnick 29, reaching page 2 of the draft; the whole note G♭ in the string parts of m. 20 of Grasnick 29 is contained in stave 7 of Scheide. Stave 8 of page 101 corresponds to mm. 20–27 of Grasnick 29; at the sign with one horizontal and two vertical lines, Beethoven sketched a variant continuation on stave 12 below. However, what he absorbed into Grasnick 29 was not this version but another variant written directly below, in stave 9, which reaches yet another shorthand sign at the margin. The passage sketched in stave 8, with the sequence of the figure B♭–G–E–F to C–A–F♯–G, corresponds to Grasnick 29, mm. 23–27, while stave 9 corresponds to Grasnick 29, mm. 27–31, up to the final system of page 2 of the draft.

Ex. 2.8 extracts the content from page 101 of Scheide that corresponds to the first two pages of Grasnick 29, up to m. 33 of the draft. (Since the transcription from page 101 begins directly with the theme and lacks the introductory measures, it starts at m. 3.) The unraveling of the complexity of page 101 uncovers compositional decisions that lie behind the creation of the draft. Most of the content of Beethoven's further continuation in Grasnick 29, from mm. 33 to 42, is found on Scheide page 101, stave 12, to the right of the second "60" mark; to the far right, he writes the terse main motive in dotted rhythm in the low bass octave on C, writing "$\frac{6}{4}$" above it to specify the second-inversion position of the chord. The abiding role of this low pedal point on the dominant is confirmed on stave 13, left side, as Beethoven indicates a repetition of the B–D♭–C pattern with the abbreviation "sim[i]l," followed by tied whole notes on low C to signal a further continuation. Whereas page 101 served as the model for the Grasnick draft up to the pedal point on the dominant, the striking upward shift in the bass from C to an octave tremolo on D♭ is found on page 102, stave 10, a few measures after the number "800000," which marks the connection from page 101, stave 11. This sketch on page 102 corresponds to the passage in Grasnick 29 beginning in m. 45; Beethoven here adds the meter signature for cut time, which applies in the draft to the entire slow introduction.

Scrutiny of pages 102–3 shows that Beethoven continued to use these parts of Scheide in support of his efforts to write out the Grasnick draft. Stave 11 of page 102 contains sketches for the beginning of the exposition, and the passage for the first violin at mm. 61–62 of Grasnick 29 is found at the bottom right-hand corner of page 102, with a shorthand continuation leading across the spread of pages to stave 10 of page 103. Comments below this sketch seem to relate to the tonal structure of the slow introduction: "1ter Theil in g schließt in c moll 2ter Theil" (1st part closes in G [minor,] 2nd part in C minor), referring to the cadences in these keys in the Grasnick draft for the slow introduction, mm. 32 and 37, respectively. Furthermore, stave 11 of page 103 includes sketches for the D♭ pedal point section of the introduction, and both pages contain work on the second subject of the ensuing exposition of the sonata form, which is marked "m.g." (for *Mittel-Gedanke*) on stave 14 of page 103 and is also sketched on staves 12–13 of page 102.

Recognition of the close link between the sketches on pages 101–3 of Scheide and the Grasnick 29 draft provides an important clue to the chronology of Beethoven's entries in the Scheide Sketchbook. The sketch transcribed by Nottebohm from the top of page 107, as shown in Ex. 2.6, seems strangely placed in view of Beethoven's intensive labors on the work several pages earlier in the sketchbook. In this sketch, the descending third motive from the main subject is treated as the basis for rising sequences in an introductory passage. This introduction, however, is a mere five measures long—quite a difference from the massive fifty-two-measure introduction contained in the Grasnick 29 draft! Could this relatively simple sketch, placed as it is at the end of Beethoven's sketches for the trio in Scheide, signal a repudiation of the elaborate slow introduction that we have discussed in detail?

A more persuasive interpretation takes account of the layers of writing contained on pages 101–3 of Scheide. It appears that all of the pages up to page 107 already contained sketches when Beethoven began to write out the Grasnick draft but that many of these pages were not yet full. We should note in this regard that Beethoven wrote out a sketch virtually identical to the one in Ex. 2.6 already on page 102, stave 6. This sketch surely predated all of the entries we have discussed in connection with the Grasnick draft, as is implied by the fact that Beethoven's work connected to that draft is found on the lower parts of these pages, whereas none of the sketches found at the tops of the pages are directly connected to the draft. The explanation seems clear: in the initial phase of work, Beethoven partially filled the pages up to page 107 with sketches placed mainly on the upper parts of pages. Only later did he return to pages 101–3 to try out more advanced ideas while entering the corresponding material into Grasnick 29. The intimate correspondence between the entries on pages 101–3 and the draft offers proof of this sequence of events.

In view of this chronological sequence, it seems likely that Beethoven's final work on the F Minor Trio in Scheide in conjunction with the Grasnick draft stems not from the spring of 1816 but from a time closer to his letter to Birchall, perhaps during the summer or early fall of that year. A further indication that the compositional work bound up with the Grasnick draft may postdate the main work in Scheide is the paper type of the draft itself. For Grasnick 29 is not written on paper bearing the "Kiesling" watermark as used in Scheide but rather on 16-stave paper of the same type used in the next standard-format sketchbook, Autograph 11/1, in which Beethoven continued his labors on the op. 101 sonata during the latter half of 1816. This paper stems from Bohemia and bears the watermark "Welhartiz" with a lily and coat of arms.[22] Certain sketches for Beethoven's next major project after op. 101, the "Hammerklavier" Sonata, op. 106, are also written on this paper type.[23] In view of the way in which Beethoven returned to his preexisting sketches for the trio while tackling the first movement as an extended draft in score, it seems reasonable to extend the period of use of the Scheide Sketchbook beyond Tyson's end date of May 1816.[24] Beethoven's last use of Scheide was bound up with Grasnick 29, and it seems probable that this occurred after his entries for the Military March, WoO 24, found at the end of the sketchbook.

Nottebohm's casual judgment about page 107 that "the main theme of the first movement finally appears in this form" is thus wide of the mark. Entirely apart from its incomplete rhythmic notation, the theme is not yet represented here in its larger musical context. The main theme of the movement finds its final form not in Scheide at all but in the Grasnick draft, which is the most important and revealing outcome of Beethoven's labors on the F Minor Trio.

The Significance of the Grasnick 29 Draft of the First Movement

The draft itself begins with two measures of soft piano accompaniment before a series of four-measure phrases unfolds in the strings above this texture in triplets in the piano. In this initial section, the main subject of the Allegro molto is absent; yet Beethoven soon alludes to features of this theme. As we have seen, the main theme is characterized by falling thirds that emphasize the lowered-sixth degree in F minor, D♭. Similarly, the framework of falling thirds in mm. 3–5 of the draft lays stress on the flat-sixth degree, and a D♭ harmony anchors the end of the first phrase as well in mm. 4–5. The pattern of repeated short notes that closes the first phrases in the strings and is echoed in the piano foreshadows the pattern of eighth notes similarly set off by rests in the main theme of the Allegro. The second of these four-measure phrases closes on the tonic in mm. 9–10. In the third phrase, however, Beethoven again emphasizes the flat-sixth relationship while elongating the motive by spreading it across the D♭ triad in two octaves, reaching a long-held D♭ octave in the strings from mm. 14 to 16.

At this point, Beethoven first introduces the dotted rhythmic motive that forms a key element in the main theme of the ensuing sonata form. This dotted rhythmic figure calls to mind a similar motive in another work involving piano, violin, and cello—Beethoven's Triple Concerto, op. 56, from 1804. In the trio, this motivic figure is heard in the piano after the unison octave on D♭ in m. 14 and again following the unison octave on G♭ in m. 20. The following phrase then extends the basic four-measure pattern of the earlier motivic units, employing a modulating sequence that carries the music in the direction of the dominant, C minor, where a strong cadence is affirmed in m. 37 at the top of page 3 of the draft. Now Beethoven incorporates imitations of the terse rhythmic motive in all three instruments, leading, in mm. 41–45, to a four-measure unit characterized by exchanges of this motive between the strings and piano as a rhythmic ostinato figure. Although Beethoven avoids placing the root of the tonic chord at the beginning of m. 41, a tonic pedal point is affirmed through the ensuing repetitions of the four-note motive, alternating between the strings and the piano.

Since the rhythmic motive places such stress on the half step D♭–C, Beethoven can effectively reverse this relationship in mm. 44–45. The extended platform of the C pedal point becomes the springboard for the upward shift to the D♭ harmony in m. 45, which is prolonged over seven measures. This expands the C–D♭ relation enormously, projecting the terse motivic half step onto the harmonic structure of a passage a dozen measures long. Having reached this harmonic goal on D♭, Beethoven now for the first time extends the four-note motive into a larger thematic unit in the right hand of the piano. Two sequential restatements of that idea bring a return to the pedal point on C in the bass of the piano part in m. 52, and Beethoven writes a fully scored emphatic cadence resolving into the long-delayed main subject of the exposition in F minor, which is played in octaves beginning in m. 53. To further dramatize the connection between the introduction and exposition, he writes a rapid rising scale in the piano that culminates on high F, and this note in turn forms the starting point of the main theme.

The transformational character of this lengthy slow introduction deserves attention. Beginning with a complete absence of tension, as the rumbling accompaniment figure is heard by itself, Beethoven gradually introduces consequential musical elements that foreshadow the main theme of the ensuing Allegro molto. The short notes that conclude the opening phrases of the Andante already foreshadow the rhythmic structure of the main subject of the Allegro. Its characteristic dotted rhythmic motive, moreover, first appears pianissimo, at the upbeat to m. 15 of the introduction, and by stages this motive is developed through imitation and finally emphasized as an ostinato pedal point and then as part of a thematic unit of breadth and verve. In its evolving rhythmic intensification and motivic concentration, the passage invites comparison with some features of the introduction to the first movement of the Seventh Symphony. Taken as a whole, this weighty introduction in the trio offers a gradually unfolding intensification or crescendo that leads with a sense of inevitability to the emergence of the main theme.

Beethoven did not realize the exposition in as much detail as the introduction, as is seen in pages 4–6 of the draft. The nine-measure statement of the main theme in the piano is followed by abbreviated statements in the violin and cello in turn. In mm. 63–64 and again in mm. 67–68, he adapts the figuration in rising thirds first heard in the D♭ section of the introduction as a transitional element, and three explicitly transitional measures (68–70) lead to the *Seitensatz*, the beginning of the second subject area.

On pages 102–3 of the Scheide Sketchbook, as we have seen, Beethoven makes entries for a second subject, or *Mittel-Gedanke*, marking these sketches with his typical abbreviation, "m.g."[25] Like the second subject area of his draft, these sketches display prominent G♭s, pointing to the key of D♭ major. Use of the key of D♭ major in the overall context of F minor is another compositional strategy familiar from

Beethoven's other works in this key. In the first movement of the "Appassionata" Sonata, for instance, Beethoven emphasizes D♭ major in the development of the first movement, and he also employs it as tonic of the slow movement, collapsing D♭ major into F minor at the transition to the finale, as the serenity of that Andante con moto is shattered with tragic force. In the present instance, the continuation of the second subject assumes a rather schematic appearance, and Beethoven would certainly have made changes and refinements in the material had he completed the piece. Nevertheless, the main thrust of his compositional approach is well defined. Whereas the first theme of the exposition has a largely descending contour, this second subject displays an ascending contour as a conspicuous feature. Its character is lyrical, with a melodic shaping emphasizing the rising semitone F–G♭ (mm. 71, 75) intensified by ensuing upbeat figures in sixteenths (mm. 72, 76, 78). Mm. 75–79 develop the motive of the rising step, outlining an ascending melodic progression from F through G♭, A♭, and B♭ to C.[26] From this point, Beethoven doubles the rate of upward movement, so that the next three measures outline further rising steps up to A♭ and B♭. This ascending motion provides basic scaffolding for a theme that has not yet been conceived in much detail.

The middle systems of page 6 show Beethoven developing this schematic framework through a type of figurative variation guided by pervasive rising motion. In this pattern, each dyad is followed by a rising counterpart, so that the texture of sixteenth notes drifts upward by step. Hence the rising third C–E♭ in stave 7 is followed later in that measure by D♭–F, whereas the falling step B♭–A♭ is immediately lifted to C–B♭. This is a decoratively enhanced variant of the schematic ascent found at the top of the page. After the second subject area, Beethoven's draft for the trio becomes increasingly fragmentary and skeletal, and its final page revisits the end of the slow introduction, exploring alternative ways of shaping the big, emphatic cadence in F minor that marks the outset of the exposition.

Marston writes concerning the second subject of the sonata design in the Grasnick draft that "what does seem fairly certain is that Beethoven did not envisage a 'textbook' lyrical *Seitensatz*: the only passage that might fulfil this particular formal role is the one beginning at measure 90, and repeated in a varied and expanded form from measure 103 onward."[27] He thereby overlooks this lyrical second subject sketched in mm. 71–83, which is set apart from the first subject by its key of D♭ major and its pervasive ascending linear motion. Beethoven did not envisage "textbook" themes, but he nevertheless displayed a tendency to employ contrasting subjects of lyrical character in the key of D♭ major in works with an overall tonic of F minor. In the present instance, the expressive character of the sketched theme can be recognized from the repeated short-long rhythmic pattern that typically marks each upbeat leading to the downbeat of an ensuing measure, a pattern that in combination with the rising melody lends an imploring or pleading tone to the musical discourse. The concentrated gestural quality of the theme is sustained through its series of rising sequences moving toward an implied cadence in m. 84 on high D♭, a pitch Beethoven did not notate in his draft.

How does the surviving torso of the opening movement of the trio in the Grasnick draft relate to Beethoven's outstanding series of compositions in F minor? One thinks in this regard not only of the "Appassionata" Sonata but of the String Quartet in F Minor, op. 95, as well as of the *Egmont* Overture and the dungeon scene in the second act of *Fidelio*. All of these works assume a dark, tragic character, which is conveyed in part through heightened harmonic dissonance, with special motivic stress placed on the semitone from the lowered sixth to the dominant, or D♭–C. In *Fidelio* and in the "Appassionata," Beethoven also treats the flat-sixth degree, D♭, as the platform for a new key area or a contrasting movement whose sudden collapse can signal the destruction of dreams or ideals through the intrusion of grim reality. Thus, in the Grave orchestral introduction to the dungeon scene, the emphasis on the expressive half step D♭–C in F minor prepares the consoling tonal shift to D♭ in m. 21 and, more importantly, the Adagio cantabile in A♭ major in Florestan's ensuing aria, a passage reached through the pitches D♭–C–A♭ at his words "steht bei dir." In the "Appassionata" Sonata, on the other hand, the pathos of the outer movements relies heavily on the semitone D♭–C, while D♭ major serves as the key for the lyrical second subject in the development of the first movement and as the tonality for the entire second movement—those parts of the sonata that are distanced or protected from the tragic character of the work as a whole. In Beethoven's compositions in F minor written after 1810—the quartet and overture as well as the final version of Florestan's aria in *Fidelio*, with his delirious vision of Leonore as an "angel of freedom"—the device of a modal shift from F minor to F major is used with remarkable effect to embody the sudden overturning of the tragedy through the power of an idealistic vision.

In returning to the key of F minor for this major chamber-music work in 1816, Beethoven drew on this rich context of expressive and structural relationships. In a sense, the opening of the trio, with its quiet unfolding of piano accompaniment, is reminiscent of the opening of the *Egmont* Overture, if only by negation. The overture begins with a powerful prolonged unison F, an elemental gesture that opens the tonal space for the ensuing discourse. In the trio, by comparison, the two rumbling measures of soft piano accompaniment, without harmonization apart from the dominant note C sounding within the spare texture of octaves on F, convey the sense of a preexisting background of sound that is heard before the main musical material is introduced at all. In a rather different way, he experimented with such a tentative opening in the Sonata op. 101, in which the music begins delicately poised on the dominant, in medias res.

At the other end of the transformational progress embodied in the slow introduction of the trio, Beethoven chooses as the principal subject of the exposition

Ex. 2.9. Comparison of themes from the exposition of the Piano Trio in
F Minor and the opening of the String Quartet in F Minor, op. 95.

a theme that displays strong similarities to the terse opening gesture of his String
Quartet in F Minor, op. 95. Ex. 2.9 provides a comparison of the two themes.
Each of these subjects begins *forte* on the tonic F, rises to the third (A♭), and then
descends stepwise through the fifth from G to C, whereby the pitch D♭ is emphasized by being placed on a strong beat. Beethoven shaped the main subject of the
trio out of the same complex of pitches contained in the opening of the quartet. In
the trio the motivic shaping gives prominence to a structural chain of falling thirds.
This chain of thirds begins as A♭–F and F–D♭ and then continues in the following
measures as D♭–B♭, B♭–G, and G–E, leading to a harmonic platform on the dominant, C, and a very striking affirmation of the crucial half step as the ascent C–D♭
before the falling chain of thirds is reiterated, leading to the tonic cadence in m. 61.

In yet other ways, Beethoven draws upon established compositional strategies
of his "F minor mood" in the trio from 1816. The placement of the lyrical second
subject in the *key* of D♭ major recalls the "Appassionata," and especially the development section of its first movement, in which the lyrical second theme appears
in this tonality.[28] The Grasnick sketch of this second subject displays with clarity Beethoven's intention to employ consistent *ascending* melodic motion in this
subject, as opposed to the descending motion characteristic of the first theme.
The schematic nature of this subject is apparent, catching Beethoven in the act
of working out the basic concept of the melody before fleshing it out in detail,
yet the content of the draft is not less interesting on that account. There is even
a specific point of motivic connection between the two main themes: the rising
semitone from leading tone to tonic, C–D♭. Beethoven singles out this half step in
mm. 58–59 of the main theme, where it is treated as part of a phrase closing in F
minor. The reinterpretation of this motive becomes a guiding idea in the second
subject, exerting increasing dominance as the theme unfolds.

At another juncture—the last eight measures of the slow introduction—Beethoven
enlarges this semitone motive into a pivotal and dramatic musical event. The upward shift of the sustained pedal point in the bass from C to D♭ recalls the similar

treatment at the outset of the recapitulation of the first movement of the "Appassionata" Sonata, and the tension of the passage is heightened by the expansive rising sequences of phrases in the piano, which rigorously develop the four-note motivic cell with the descending thirds. Beethoven was sufficiently interested in this passage as to virtually complete the scoring, quite unlike the following draft for the exposition, which reverts to one voice at a time.

The relative proportions of the Grasnick draft invite comment. If Beethoven had returned to the work, the exposition of the sonata form would have required considerable extension; such structural expansion can often be observed in his compositional process.[29] Less clear is how the last section of the Grasnick draft might have evolved, since this part is heavily revised with alternative continuations.[30] On the other hand, the basic plan for the expansive slow introduction seems viable and indeed markedly original in its gradual building of tension, culminating in the decisive cadence that marks the beginning of the exposition. The generous scale of the introduction implies that the movement would have been of substantial length had it been completed.

In characterizing the Grasnick draft, Marston describes "Beethoven's tendency to begin writing out a potential final version at an often hopelessly early stage in the compositional process," but this judgment fails to do justice to the artistic content of the document. Marston does not acknowledge how Beethoven derived and elaborated his draft from pages 101–3 of the Scheide Sketchbook; he finds the musical content of the Grasnick draft "detailed, indeed literally performable," only in "the opening 25 or so bars."[31] The transcription and sound recording illustrating this chapter show that Beethoven's concept of the opening movement is significantly more developed; the implied continuation of figuration in the piano part in the slow introduction is supplied in the recording, which extends up to the second subject of the sonata form, and includes more than eighty measures.

Beethoven's incomplete trio displays affinities with certain of his later pieces and helps fill out the picture of his artistic development during this crucial yet relatively unproductive phase of his career. The F Minor Trio belongs to an exploratory dimension of his creativity, anticipating compositional strategies used in future works as he forged the elements of his late style. His next major composition after the completion of op. 101 was the "Hammerklavier" Sonata, op. 106. Charles Rosen has described Beethoven's op. 106 as "an extreme point of his style," claiming that "he never again wrote so obsessively concentrated a work."[32] As Rosen has shown, nothing is more characteristic of the "Hammerklavier" than chains of descending thirds, which are embodied on different levels of structure, ranging from motivic detail to the sequence of modulations in the opening Allegro. Beginning with the tonic B♭, a modulatory chain of thirds moves through G and E♭ to B, setting up a powerful tension against the tonic B♭ major that resonates through much of the remainder of the movement. The other movements of op. 106 also display such patterns. As Rosen observes, both the Adagio sostenuto and the transition Largo preceding the finale begin with such descending third-chains, which pass through the tonic triad in minor and continue by falling another major third. In the Adagio, this spells out the pitches C♯–A–F♯–D; in the Largo, F–D♭–B♭–G♭.[33]

The introduction of the Trio in F Minor adumbrates this procedure, beginning as it does with the falling third-chain C–A♭–F–D♭ in mm. 3–5. The main theme of the Allegro, moreover, displays a motivic concentration on falling thirds that is quite as obsessive as the "Hammerklavier." The process, so characteristic of pages 106, whereby descending third-chains and semitonal conflicts are combined, is found at the end of the slow introduction of the trio, with its surprising yet logical shift to the D♭ pedal point in the bass.

Hence, it appears that some of Beethoven's compositional deliberations in his work on the trio came to fruition in the biggest of all his sonatas, a work completed two years after the trio was set aside. Furthermore, the use of a theme unfolding in half notes through a chain of descending thirds brings to mind the fugue subject for "Et vitam venturi saeculi Amen" in the Credo of the *Missa solemnis*, a theme that occupied him for an extended period beginning in 1819.[34] Nor do these examples exhaust the analogies that might be drawn between the trio draft and certain of Beethoven's other later compositions. Particularly noteworthy in the slow introduction of the trio is the overall psychological progression, leading from a tensionless beginning to a highly dramatic culmination. One might think in this regard of the extraordinary concluding section of the penultimate Piano Sonata in A♭ Major, op. 110, beginning with the hushed *una corda* appearance of the fugue theme in inversion and leading through many closely interrelated stages to the ecstatic culmination on the final tonic sonority seventy-seven measures later. There is no similarity in the thematic material of these two pieces, yet the kind of graduated psychological process that is outlined in the abandoned trio seems to be richly achieved in the sonata.

Conclusion: The Biographical Context

Other important questions remain. Why did Beethoven leave the F Minor Trio unfinished, and what other projects occupied his attention when he set the trio aside? The main series of entries in the Scheide Sketchbook dates from the spring of 1816, probably from no later than May of that year, whereas the draft made in Grasnick 29 in conjunction with Scheide perhaps dates from somewhat later, as we have seen. Along with the Sonata in A Major, op. 101, the trio occupied Beethoven soon after the completion of the song cycle *An die ferne Geliebte* in April 1816, and it evidently remained a current project through much of that year. Yet unlike the sonata, which was completed by year's end, Beethoven failed to resume sustained work on the trio, despite having thoughts in that direction. An entry in his diary or

Tagebuch, presumably from September 1816, shortly preceding the letter to Birchall, contains the memo to himself to "finish the sonata and the trio."[35] During 1816, at least, Beethoven intended to complete this major work. Although Beethoven's sketches for much of the projected work remained rudimentary, his plans for the slow introduction to the first movement are highly distinctive, and it does not appear that the project was dropped because of any lack of artistic potential.

Several factors may have played a role in Beethoven's inability to finish the work. He experienced difficulties with his health, especially during late 1816, but these troubles did not prevent him from completing some other projects, such as folk-song settings for George Thomson in Edinburgh and the Sonata op. 101.[36] Barry Cooper has suggested on the basis of a letter that Beethoven wrote the trio out of affection for Marie Erdödy's three children, one of whom died suddenly in the spring of 1816, yet the context of the letter in question is ambiguous, and it is clear from his *Tagebuch* entry and letter to Birchall that Beethoven still planned to complete the trio in October.[37] More pertinent is the reply Beethoven received to his letter of 1 October from Birchall's partner, Christopher Lonsdale, on 8 November 1816.[38] As this letter states, Birchall turned down the offer of both the sonata and the trio. While Birchall's own failing health seems to have been an issue, Beethoven's own aggressive business practice in arranging simultaneous publications of works played a role.[39] His rather condescending tone in writing of "inglishmen neglecting their word and honor" while failing to promptly acknowledge the receipt of payments from Birchall cannot have helped endear him to the British publisher.[40] Without a publication agreement in place, Beethoven would have felt less urgency to complete the trio. At the same time, an impressive series of publications of major works had appeared beginning in 1815 with Beethoven's new Viennese publisher, Sigmund Anton Steiner. The Steiner publications of 1816 included *An die ferne Geliebte*, the Seventh Symphony, the Sonata for Violin and Piano, op. 96, the String Quartet in F Minor, op. 95, and the "Archduke" Trio, with the last two of these works appearing in September at about the time the composer reminded himself in his diary to "finish the trio." Perhaps this flood of new publications, including the long-delayed appearance of the quartet and the "Archduke," whose autograph scores both date from several years earlier, undercut his motivation to complete the Trio in F Minor.[41]

Yet another, perhaps more telling reason for Beethoven's lowered artistic productivity around this time was his preoccupation with his nephew Karl, who was then ten years old. Beethoven had assumed the guardianship of his nephew following the death of his brother Kaspar Anton Karl van Beethoven in November 1815. The process was messy and complicated, and Beethoven was especially concerned to curb the influence and access to her son of his sister-in-law Johanna Reiss, toward whom he was antagonistic and whom he dubbed the "Queen of the Night." The documents from this period contain abundant evidence of Beethoven's overriding

Lebhaft. Marschmäßig
Vivace alla Marcia

Ex. 2.10. Beethoven, Piano Sonata in A Major, op. 101,
beginning of second movement.

concern for his young relative, including an inscription in the Scheide Sketchbook itself on page 55 that reads "Bücher für Karl" (books for Karl). Even Beethoven's reminder to himself in his diary to finish the trio is paired with a memo to obtain medicine for his nephew, who underwent a minor operation on 18 September. His ability to remain focused on artistic projects was surely taxed by the sudden demands of the guardianship. A week earlier, on 12 September, the Giannattasio del Rio family had visited Beethoven in Baden, bringing with them nephew Karl, who was enrolled in Cajetan Giannattasio del Rio's private school for boys; it was on this occasion that Beethoven confessed to Giannattasio del Rio that "he was unhappy in love" and implied that he would never marry.[42] In one of the adjacent diary entries from September 1816 Beethoven exhorts himself to "live only in your art. . . . This is the *only existence* for you."[43] The reality was otherwise, and the fate of the unique and promising but unfinished Trio in F Minor reflects Beethoven's difficulties in balancing the simultaneous demands of life and art.

As 1816 drew to a close, Beethoven's compositional impulses moved in other directions. A pocket sketchbook used at this time records his completion of the finale of the op. 101 Sonata. As this source implies, Beethoven's date on the autograph score of the sonata, "1816 im Monath November," probably refers to the beginning rather than the completion of that score; the first edition appeared in February 1817. The chronological proximity of Beethoven's completion of op. 101 with his abandonment of the piano trio project is suggestive. The rhythmic outline of the sonata's second movement, marked Vivace alla marcia, corresponds closely to the main theme of the Allegro molto in the trio, with its pattern of dotted figures in duple time (Ex. 2.10). In each case, a strong downbeat at the outset of the theme is followed by phrase units containing the dotted rhythmic figure, which are treated in a pattern of increasing compression. Consequently, the two themes conspicuously resemble one another. Since his almost obsessive preoccupation with this rhythmic idea found a realization in the marchlike sonata movement in the major mode of F, this connection might also have played a role in his loss of interest in the F Minor Trio.

Advanced sketches for the coda of the finale of op. 101 are juxtaposed with entries for the songs "Ruf vom Berge," WoO 147, and "So oder so," WoO 148.[44] "So oder so" was published in February 1817, and Beethoven gave a printed copy to the two Giannattasio del Rio daughters, Fanny and Anna.[45] "Ruf vom Berge" was written for Anna in mid-December; the long-lost autograph score of this song, which has recently resurfaced, confirms Nottebohm's report that it dates from 13 December 1816.[46] According to an account given by Anna's daughter Anna Pessiak-Schmerling to Alexander Wheelock Thayer in 1881, Beethoven wrote out the melody of this short strophic song for Anna on an excursion with the Giannattasio der Rio family to the Himmel, a lookout point near Vienna.[47] The text by Friedrich Treitschke, in six stanzas, beginning "Wenn ich ein Vöglein wär' und auch zwei Flüglein hätt', flög' ich zu dir. Weil's aber nicht kann sein, bleib' ich allhier" (If I were a little bird and had two little wings, I would fly to you. But because it can't be so, I remain ever here), is filled with yearning tinged with resignation, a mood that must have resonated strongly for the composer around this time.

In the context of Beethoven's career aspirations, a yearning for remote destinations not to be reached calls to mind his important connections to Britain, where Haydn had enjoyed such success a generation earlier. If Beethoven's contact with London publishers like Birchall and Lonsdale came to an end in late 1816, England continued to play a key role for him in the immediately ensuing period. The most intriguing of his sketch leaves on the "Welhartiz" paper common to Grasnick 29 and the Autograph 11/1 Sketchbook, a source presumably dating from the period in question, is a page with a draft for the beginning of the Ninth Symphony. This single sketch leaf sold at Sotheby's 2002 auction in London for a record-breaking £1.3 million—quite an increase from those prices fetched previously for his sketch leaves or that he received for his completed works during his lifetime.[48] Nottebohm knew the leaf in question and inscribed it as "die allererste Skizze der Sinfonie No IX" (the very first sketch for the Ninth Symphony). Yet even if this sketch dates from 1816–17, as seems most likely, Nottebohm's assessment is not strictly correct, since the earliest sketch used in the Ninth Symphony is the notation for the second movement, marked "fuge," found at the top of page 51 of the Scheide Sketchbook.[49] To judge from its context in Scheide, that sketch probably dates from December 1815 or January 1816.

Furthermore, there exists a related sketch leaf held in Weimar containing sketches for the first and second movements of the Ninth together with entries for the canon "Das Schweigen," which are closely associated with sketches found on page 55 of Scheide, the same page containing Beethoven's reminder to himself about "books for Karl."[50] Beethoven wrote the two canons, "Das Schweigen" (Silence) and "Das Reden" (Talking), WoO 168, into the album of the English pianist Charles Neate on 24 January 1816, preceding Neate's departure for England. In 1815 Neate had traveled to Vienna to spend eight months there, motivated by his admiration for Beethoven. He was one of the original members of the London Philharmonic Society, and his connection to Beethoven formed part of the context for the invitation from the Philharmonic Society the following year, on 9 June 1817, according to which Beethoven was to compose two symphonies. The composer accepted the terms in a letter of 9 July 1817, declaring his intention to compose the symphonies and travel to London by January 1818.[51] Even though Beethoven's relationship with the Philharmonic Society was not always smooth, the journey never took place, and the completion of his last symphony took until 1824, the symphonic plans for London nevertheless exerted an impact on his creative activities during the period in question.

The Scheide Sketchbook already contained the first entries for what eventually became the Ninth Symphony, and this project, along with the "Hammerklavier" Sonata, continued to tap Beethoven's creative energies after he had finished the op. 101 Sonata and set aside the F Minor Trio.[52] His thoughts of leaving Vienna with a new symphony while still hoping to collect the annuity conditional on his Austrian residence were vividly expressed in his diary in early 1817: "There is no other way to save yourself except to leave here, only through this can you again lift yourself to the heights of your art, whereas here you are submerged in vulgarity. Only a symphony—and then away, away, away. Meanwhile collect the salary, which can still be done for years."[53]

Commentators on Beethoven's stylistic development have often pointed to a sharp reduction in Beethoven's creative output during 1816–18. Martin Cooper describes these years as "the most unproductive of his life," and Maynard Solomon finds his productivity during 1816 and 1817 "extremely low."[54] The point should not be overstated, in view of the importance of works like *An die ferne Geliebte* and the Sonata op. 101, both completed during 1816. Relevant as well to the assessment of Beethoven's productivity at this time are compositional projects that evolved over many years, like the Ninth Symphony, and other projects that remained unfinished. Foremost among the unfinished works at this time is the Piano Trio in F Minor. The fortunate survival of the Grasnick 29 draft in Berlin and related material in the Scheide Sketchbook at Princeton allows us insight into one of Beethoven's most original ideas for a chamber music work. Although it remained a fragment, this project nevertheless belongs to the mainstream of Beethoven's creative development. The unfinished Trio in F Minor is deeply grounded in compositional strategies found in the cluster of F minor pieces reaching back to the "Appassionata" Sonata, the *Egmont* Overture, and the String Quartet in F Minor, op. 95, while anticipating features of Beethoven's next masterpieces: the Sonata in A Major, op. 101, and the "Hammerklavier" Sonata, op. 106.

Music Manuscripts for the Piano Trio in F Minor

Scheide Sketchbook, fifty-six leaves, Library of Mr. William Scheide, Princeton, New Jersey. Material for the unfinished Piano Trio in F Minor is found on pages 67, 86–91, 94–98, 100–105, and 107. Three leaves containing sketches for the trio that were presumably once part of Scheide belong before page 93 of the sketchbook. These are folio 5, Grasnick 20a, Musikabteilung, Staatsbibliothek zu Berlin preussischer Kulturbesitz, and folios 19 and 37, Add. MS 29997, British Library, London. The paper of the Scheide Sketchbook and these three leaves contains sixteen staves and bears the watermark "G. Kiesling" with three moons. It is classified as type 42 in *The Beethoven Sketchbooks* by Douglas Johnson, Alan Tyson, and Robert Winter.

The Grasnick 29 MS, Musikabteilung, Staatsbibliothek zu Berlin preussischer Kulturbesitz, contains ten pages of sixteen-stave paper bearing the watermark "Welhartiz" with a lily and coat of arms. It is classified as type 33 in *The Beethoven Sketchbooks* by Johnson, Tyson, and Winter. Two additional sources on this paper type are related to this draft: folio 20, Add. MS 29997, British Library, London, and page 9, A 46, Gesellschaft der Musikfreunde, Vienna. The first page of this bifolium in Vienna contains material for the trio.

Other manuscripts related to the piano trio include folios 15–18 ("Welhartiz" watermark, type 33), Add. MS 29997, British Library, London; and pocket sketches, MS 103a, Bibliothèque nationale, Paris, and Mendelssohn 2 MS, Biblioteka Jagiellońska, Cracow. The pocket gathering Paris MS 78 and MS 103 is supplemented by the leaves identified in Cracow by Sieghard Brandenburg, as described in *The Beethoven Sketchbooks* catalog, pages 344–45. For a provisional list of pages from these pocket leaves that may be related to the Trio in F Minor, see Nicholas Marston, "In the 'Twilight Zone': Beethoven's Unfinished Piano Trio in F Minor," *Journal of the Royal Musical Association* 131 (2006): 236.

Schumann, Beethoven, and the "Distant Beloved"

We turn now to a much-discussed composition by Robert Schumann, a piece that lies at the center of his innovative cluster of piano works from the 1830s and that was conceived in 1836 at the stressful nadir of his struggle for the hand of Clara Wieck, the brilliant young pianist who became his wife four years later. Perhaps no other work by Schumann underwent a more fascinating genesis. As originally conceived, the composition in question was an offering to Beethoven, who had died almost a decade earlier, in 1827. The call for a monument to Beethoven at his birthplace, Bonn, went out on the composer's birthday, 17 December 1835, whereupon Schumann proclaimed his passionate support for the project in an essay in his journal, the *Neue Zeitschrift für Musik*, entitled "Monument für Beethoven" (Monument for Beethoven), published in early 1836. Almost a decade later, in 1845, the Beethoven monument was finally erected on the Münsterplatz at Bonn (Fig. 3.1), thanks largely to the strenuous efforts and financial contributions of Franz Liszt. In 1836, when the efforts to raise this monument to Beethoven were at an early, formative stage, Schumann decided to create a musical work, the proceeds of which were to be a contribution toward building the Beethoven monument at Bonn.

What we are describing is the project that eventually became Schumann's Fantasie in C Major, op. 17, first published in 1839. Like the *Davidsbündlertänze*, op. 6, the Symphonic Études, op. 13, and other works, Schumann's fantasie underwent an involved compositional evolution.[1] Stages of this process are reflected in the various descriptive titles for the work that he contemplated between 1836 and 1839. Already in 1836 Schumann had devised a detailed set of titles for a three-movement work:

Obulus
auf
Beethovens Monument
Ruinen, Trophaeen, Palmen
Große Sonate
für das Pianoforte
von
Florestan u. Eusebius
op. 12[2]

According to a letter by Schumann to Clara Wieck, the three-movement sonata was completed except for details in June 1836.[3] The Greek word "Obulus" designates a small coin, meaning in this context a modest contribution to the cause of Beethoven's monument. The authors of this op. 12 version, "Florestan" and "Eusebius," refer, of course, to the two sides of Schumann's artistic personality: the extroverted, impulsive, energetic persona is Florestan, while the dreamy, reflective, introverted side is Eusebius. This dualistic psychological framework, in turn, is modeled on the literary practice of the imaginative writer Jean Paul Richter, who often used such pairs of characters, such as the twin brothers Vult and Walt in his novel *Flegeljahre*, a work Schumann admired and read many times over. If the marchlike second movement of the fantasie displays the passionate, Florestan side of Schumann's musical temperament, and the slow final movement is suggestive of the Eusebius character, the opening movement blends the two, interweaving slower, introverted passages with the stirring opening music, marked "Durchaus phantastisch und leidenschaftlich vorzutragen" (To be played in an entirely fantastic and passionate manner).

A separate *Arbeitsmanuskript* (autograph working manuscript) of the first movement of the fantasie carries a title in French:

Ruines
Fantaisie pour le Pianoforte
dediée
à
[crossed out and illegible]
par
Robert Schumann
op. 16a.

This source has encouraged speculation that Schumann first conceived the work in one movement, but that conclusion seems unwarranted.[4] The higher opus number, but especially the replacement of "Florestan u. Eusebius" by "Robert Schumann," indicates that this title followed the op. 12 version, since Schumann discontinued at this time his earlier practice, as with his Piano Sonata in F♯ minor, op. 11, of listing Florestan and Eusebius as the authors of his works.

CHAPTER 3

Figure 3.1. Beethoven monument, Münsterplatz, Bonn.

At a still later stage in the genesis of the fantasie, Schumann described the three movements as *Dichtungen* (poems), and at this point he resolved to dedicate the piece to Franz Liszt. Although Schumann was initially pleased with the title "Dichtungen," he again changed his mind. The revision of this title page can be seen in a manuscript held at the National Széchényi Library in Budapest (MS Mus. 37).[5] This source is the corrected copy that served as the *Stichvorlage* (engraver's copy); it contains numerous notations and emendations in Schumann's hand. The title page of the Budapest score is shown in Fig. 3.2. It will be seen that the title "Dichtungen" is canceled and replaced by "Fantasie" and that yet another opus number has been specified, the now-familiar op. 17. The former movement title is also obliterated at the head of the first page of the score, as shown in Fig. 3.3. The canceled titles of the three movements appear in this score as "Ruinen—Siegesbogen—Sternbild" (Ruins—triumphal arch—constellation); these designations were not included in the published composition. Schumann indicated that instead of the movement titles three stars should be printed before each of the three movements—a direction that was not followed when the work was published. At the foot of this page, Schumann wrote "Ueber die Anfänge der drei verschiedenen Nummern bitte ich jedesmal drei Sterne zu setzten" (At the head of each of the three different movements I ask for placement of three stars).

Schumann's changes in this score are not confined to titles and opus numbers. At this late stage in composition, he added many directions related to performance, such as pedal and dynamic markings, and altered some expressive indications. At the beginning of the "Im Legendenton" section in C minor in the first movement, Schumann originally included the more specific performance direction "Erzählend im Legendenton" (Narrating in the manner of a legend), a formulation that sheds light on his attitude toward the narrative possibilities of instrumental music.

A startling musical revision made in this source is the removal from the end of the third movement of a variant of the close of the first movement, in *adagio* (Plate 2).[6] If this passage had been retained, this intermovement thematic recall would have established an obvious musical link between the close of the first movement and the end of the entire work.

Although suppressed, this thematic recall stretching across the fantasie is strongly suggestive, drawing attention both to the expressive import of the *adagio* passage and to its affinity with a composition by Beethoven: his song cycle *An die ferne Geliebte*, op. 98, from 1816. Since Hermann Abert made the suggestion a century ago that Schumann quoted Beethoven in the fantasie, Beethoven's song cycle and Schumann's fantasie have often been compared, but the precise nature of the connection is worth revisiting.[7] It is often said that Schumann quotes Beethoven in this *adagio* passage, heard as the first movement draws to a close. As Charles Rosen puts it, "the beginning of the last song of Beethoven's cycle *An die ferne Geliebte* (a setting of the words 'Take these songs then, my love, that I sang') is clearly quoted at the very end of the first movement of Schumann's work but also hinted at throughout the movement."[8] Rosen cites in this connection two passages to which we will return: part of the reflective second subject in the subdominant, F major; and the aforementioned miragelike passage found in the central section of the fantasie, marked "Im Legendenton" (In the manner of a legend). The second of these passages may be bound up with yet another of Schumann's discarded titles for the movement, *Fata Morgana*, which refers to a miragelike vision.[9]

As other commentators have observed, however, Schumann's reference to Beethoven in his fantasie is not a straightforward quotation, as occurs in the "Florestan" piece in *Carnaval* with its wandering butterfly, or "Papillon," or with the

Figure 3.2. Title page, corrected copy of Schumann's Fantasie in C Major, op. 17, National Széchényi Library, Budapest (MS Mus. 37).

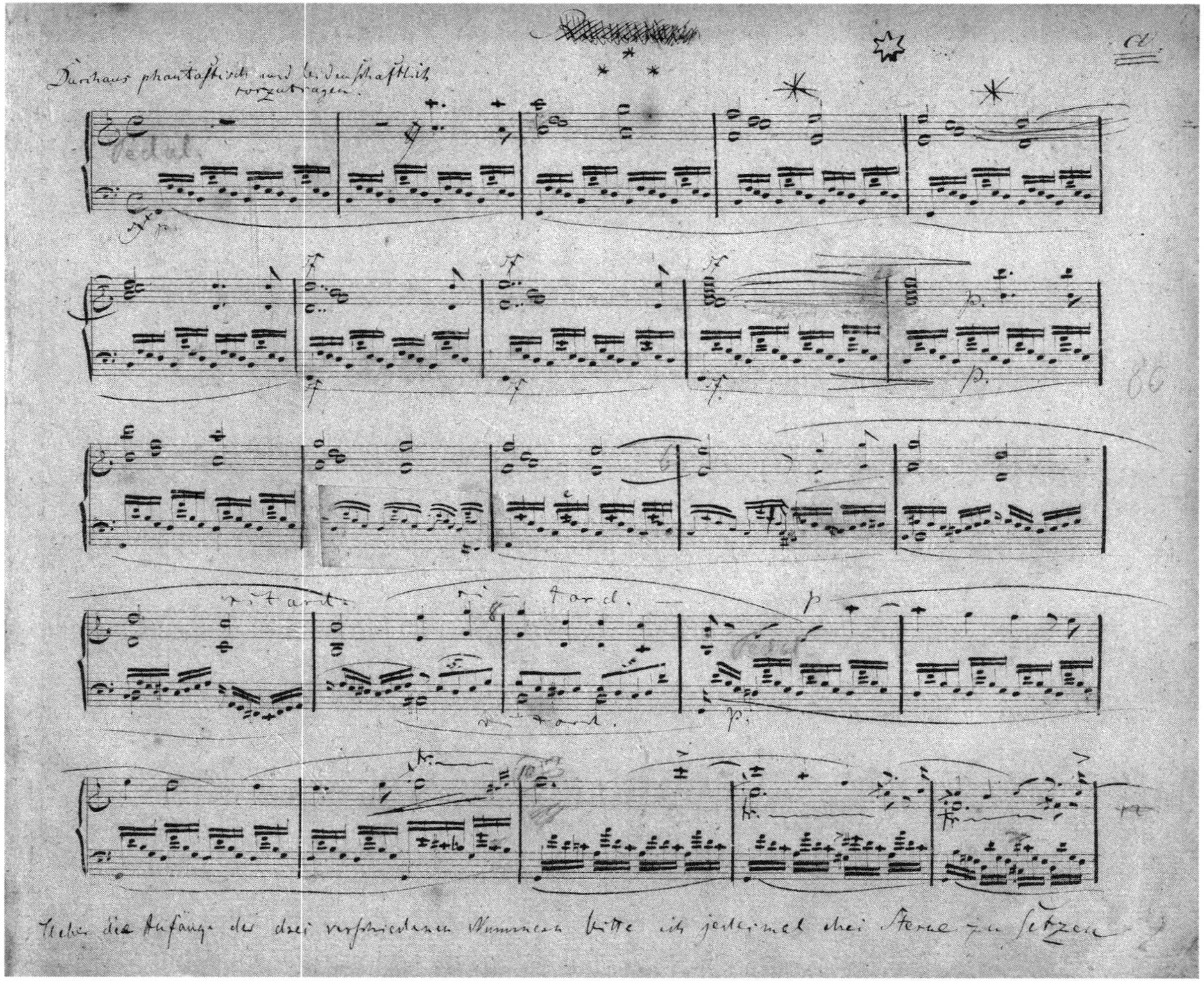

Figure 3.3. Corrected copy of Schumann's Fantasie, op. 17, National Széchényi Library, Budapest (MS Mus. 37), page 1.

"Stimme aus der Ferne," or "voice from afar," in the last of his Novelettes, op. 21, in which he quotes a piece by his beloved, Clara Wieck (the "Notturno" from her *Soirées musicales*, op. 6). The Beethoven allusion in Schumann's fantasie is more pervasive and far-reaching than these other examples. To appreciate Schumann's approach, we would do well to consider not only his compositional preoccupations and ongoing engagement with Beethoven's music but also Beethoven's own treatment of the theme of a distant beloved in several works, pieces that in turn became sources of inspiration for Robert Schumann and Clara Wieck during their difficult periods of separation in the later 1830s.

The *ferne Geliebte* as Metaphor:
from *Fidelio* to *Egmont*

The archetype of the *ferne Geliebte* had wide currency, with its presence in Beethoven in no way confined to his song cycle or individual strophic songs such as "An den fernen Geliebten," op. 75, no. 5, and "Ruf vom Berge," WoO 147. Perhaps the most arresting Beethovenian examples appear in his music to Goethe's *Egmont*, op. 84, from 1810, and in the dungeon scene of his opera *Fidelio*, particularly in the expanded version of Florestan's aria that was prepared for the performances of the opera in its final incarnation in 1814.

Schumann for his part was intimately familiar with Beethoven's *Egmont* music and with *Fidelio* as well as with Beethoven's song cycle, which he had heard in performance already as a teenager. In a detailed study of Schumann's Beethoven reception, Bodo Bischoff documents Schumann's initial acquaintance with *An die ferne Geliebte* as beginning in November 1828. When Schumann first heard *Fidelio* is uncertain, but his first surviving reference to the work dates from 1834, and numerous performances of the opera took place at Leipzig during these years.[10] Schumann may have heard Beethoven's *Egmont* music, op. 84, as early as August 1832 and gone to performances of the *Egmont* overture on other occasions. He was powerfully moved by the performance of the *Egmont* music with poetic interpolations by Friedrich Mosengeil, given at Leipzig on 4 December 1837. During the period in question, he engaged intensely with all three of these works.

As in Beethoven's *Egmont* music, the "distant beloved" idea is combined in *Fidelio* with symbols of an ethical and political cast. The roots of this conception reach back to the original French libretto that was translated and remodeled to serve as the basis for Beethoven's opera. Beethoven and his librettists made very significant departures from the original French text for Florestan's aria in the dungeon. The names of the principal roles were retained, however, and Beethoven's Florestan, an imprisoned freedom fighter, clearly influenced Schumann to choose this name to represent the extroverted side of his own artistic persona.[11] In the French original, the prisoner sought consolation by staring at a small portrait of his wife, and he later expressed a suicidal death wish. In Beethoven's *Fidelio*, the death wish is deleted, and the vision of the beloved is transformed in a manner rich in symbolic overtones. In *Fidelio*, moreover, the music assumes an indispensable role at this point, conveying Florestan's inward bond with the distant beloved.

Florestan's aria in *Fidelio* embodies a complex psychological progression, culminating in his delirious vision of his wife, Leonore, as an angel leading him to freedom—the passage added to the work in 1814. In this F major section, Beethoven uses an oboe melody soaring into the high register to symbolize the angel Leonore. The association is made explicit at Florestan's words "ein Engel, Leonore" (an angel, Leonore), which mimic the preceding oboe phrase, engaging in a dialogue with the miragelike presence of the "angel of freedom." In its contour, Florestan's expressive line becomes indistinguishable from the soaring oboe melody.

Nowhere else in the opera are the boundaries between imagination and reality so challenged as here. The final section of this aria is one of Beethoven's most significant monuments to the romantic tenet that the current of subjectivity, of spiritual activity, of the individual's apprehension of *value*, is more real than external reality.

The immediately ensuing melodrama—with spoken text for Leonore and the jailor Rocco accompanied by orchestral music as they descend with a lantern into the dungeon—sheds further light on Florestan's spiritual condition. As the prisoner comes into view in the gloom, Leonore comments that he seems motionless. Rocco replies dryly, "Vielleicht ist er todt" (Maybe he is dead). At that point Florestan makes a movement just as we hear the expressive oboe line in F major, a fragment of that same music that dominated the conclusion of his aria. This is a highly suggestive artistic device. The citation from his aria in the melodrama encourages us to regard the content of Florestan's aria as fundamentally a spiritual state, a sustaining vision that prolongs his life under circumstances of extreme adversity. In this context, one might regard the conclusion of Florestan's aria with his vision of Leonore as angel of freedom as *coinciding* with Leonore's descent to his cell. We might even toy with the notion that Florestan conjures up the object of his devotion or, at least, that his intense vision of Leonore enables him to endure, keeping him alive up to the moment of his rescue.

In extending Florestan's aria in 1814, Beethoven built upon the closely related dramatic composition that he had finished in 1810: the *Egmont* music, op. 84. Florestan's direct counterpart here is Count Egmont, another imprisoned freedom fighter who is similarly inspired by his beloved, Klärchen. Like Florestan, Egmont falls victim to oppressive forces, while Klärchen, unable to rouse the populace to rescue Egmont, eventually takes poison. Although neither Egmont nor Klärchen survives the action, as do Florestan and Leonore in *Fidelio*, the parallels are unmistakable. In his cell awaiting death, Egmont falls asleep, whereupon he is visited by an apparition of freedom in the shape of Klärchen. Egmont's head is crowned with laurels by the apparition, preparing the powerfully stirring *Siegessinfonie* (victory symphony), whose F major music had already capped the overture. The key symbolism of a dark, tragic F minor yielding to a luminous F major is common to both works, and an expressive use of the oboe to symbolize the heroine also appears in the *Egmont* music at the outset of no. 5, the third "Zwischenakt," following their scene together.[12]

The importance of *Fidelio* and the *Egmont* music for Schumann and Clara Wieck during the 1830s was inextricably bound up with their personal situation, especially the severe challenges to their relationship beginning in 1836. During 1837, in response to an electrifying performance of the opera with Wilhelmine Schröder Devrient as Leonore, Schumann wrote in his diary "*Fidelio* über Alles" (*Fidelio* above everything). The motive of conjugal devotion from the opera struck home, as expressed in a comment by Schumann from October of that year that "der eine Gedanke der Treue überwiegt aber Alles" (the one thought of faithfulness looms above everything). Soon thereafter, on 28/29 November, he closed a letter to Clara as follows: "Ich küße Dich in inniger Liebe.—Addieu, mein Fidelio in Gestalt v. Julius Kraus und bleib so treu wie Leonore ihrem Florestan" (I kiss you in heartfelt love.—Good-bye, my Fidelio in the form of Julius Kraus and remain as faithful as Leonore to her Florestan). ("Julius Kraus" refers to the male name that Clara Wieck asked to be put on Schumann's letters to her in order to keep their correspondence from being intercepted by her father.)[13] The symbolic identification of Schumann with Florestan and Clara with Leonore continues in a letter from 2 January 1838, in which he slips in the statement that "die Lenore bist Du, mein geliebtes Mädchen, und die Pizarros wollen wir schon aus dem Weg räumen" (you, my beloved girl, are Leonore, and we will clear the Pizarros out of the way), which carries the clear implication of assigning Clara's father, Friedrich Wieck, to the role of Beethoven's villain.[14]

Even before Schumann wrote this last letter, he had assimilated the heroic symbolism of *Egmont* to their situation as well in response to a performance on 4 December reinforced by a late-night reading of Goethe's play. Schumann writes:

"Clärchen," was ich eigentlich niemals leiden konnte, wenn man Dich so nannte, heiße ich Dich heute zum ersten mal. Und warum denn? Weil ich neulich die Musik zum Egmont gehört hatte und darauf den Göthe'schen noch einmal las. In meinem ganzen Leben bin ich noch nie von Musik so ergriffen worden, als an jenem Abend—ich schämte mich beinah, als ich merkte, daß mir die holden Tränen immer über die Backen liefen. Aber welche Musik auch—kennst Du sie genau?

["Clärchen," a name that I could never before tolerate for you, I call you today for the first time. And why? Because I have again heard the music to Egmont and then read Goethe once more. In my whole life I have never been so gripped by music as on this evening—I was ashamed to see that noble tears flowed down my cheeks. But what music—do you know it well?]

Later that year, he wrote a poem to Clara Wieck including the following lines:

> Egmont's Geliebte Klärchen hieß—
> O Namen wundersüß!
>
> Klärchen Schumann
> Ein Engel den Namen ersann.[15]
>
> [Egmont's beloved was called Klärchen—
> Such a wonderful name!
>
> Klärchen Schumann
> An angel thought up the name.]

And on 31 May 1839, after going to a performance of Goethe's play, Schumann again wrote to Clara in the same vein:

> Egmont sah ich vorgestern; aber ich war gebeugt von Schmerz "hättest Du doch auch solch ein tapferes Klärchen dacht' ich. Und nun hab' ich's wieder. Nichtwahr, Du gingst mit mir in die Schlacht, an meiner Seite.[16]
>
> [I saw Egmont yesterday, but was burdened by pain. I thought, "Might you too have such a courageous Klärchen?" And now I indeed have her, don't I? You're going with me into battle, on my side.]

As these sources show, Beethoven's double pair of protagonists and their music became assimilated into the personal mythology of Robert Schumann and Clara Wieck during the later 1830s. The quintessential Beethovenian narrative of overcoming adversity helped them to deal with their painful separation and maintain confidence in a shared future.

In this context, we shall reevaluate the impact during this same period of another Beethovenian work on Schumann's fantasie: the song cycle *An die ferne Geliebte*.

Reaching the *ferne Geliebte*: A Transcendence of Space and Time

In 1816, two years after the revival of *Fidelio*, Beethoven composed his song cycle *An die ferne Geliebte*. An innovation of this work consists in the way the music and text of the opening song, beginning "Auf dem Hügel sitz' ich spähend" (On the hill I sit gazing), are recalled at the conclusion of the whole cycle. Joseph Kerman has convincingly suggested that Beethoven added the last stanza to the opening strophic song in order to promote this long-range cyclic connection.[17] The fifth stanza of "Auf dem Hügel" contains a closing couplet identical to the end of the last song, preceded by two lines that may stem from Beethoven himself.

Denn vor Liedesklang entweichet
jeder Raum und jede Zeit
und ein liebend Herz erreichet,
was ein liebend Herz geweiht.

[For the sound of song transcends
all space and time
that a loving heart receive
what a loving heart has consecrated.]

The import of these lines resists literal translation; what is involved is a communication from one soul to another, overcoming spatial and temporal constraints. Much the same message is conveyed in the dedication Beethoven wrote over the Kyrie of his *Missa solemnis*: "Von Herzen—möge es zu Herzen gehen!" (From the heart—may it go to the heart!).

The beginning of the final song, "Nimm sie hin denn, diese Lieder, die ich dir, Geliebte, sang" (Take to your heart these songs that I sang to you, beloved), is surely one point of reference for Schumann in his *adagio* at the end of the first movement of the fantasie, yet it is not the singular nor perhaps the most fundamental point of connection. A later strophe sets this same music to words that signal the overcoming of "space and time" through artistic means, as the beloved sings back the songs that have penetrated to her. Beethoven emphasizes this moment through a slowing of tempo to *molto adagio*, just as the sun disappears behind the mountains that physically block the lovers from one another. As Beethoven restores the basic tempo at a repetition of the crucial words "und du singst, und du singst, was ich gesungen" (and you sing, and you sing, what I sang), it seems that an artistic communication succeeds. Despite formidable physical barriers, a message is carried forth that, according to the text, displays an awareness not of artifice but only of *Sehnsucht* (yearning). It is precisely at this point, marked "Ziemlich langsam and mit Ausdruck" (Rather slowly and expressively), that Beethoven recalls the opening song of the cycle and dwells passionately on the notion of a heart-to-heart communion, even stammering on the word "was" (what), which stands for that inexpressible essence of what a loving heart has consecrated.

Writing more than a century ago, Beethoven's distinguished American biographer Alexander Wheelock Thayer gave expression to what many have felt in commenting that "there is something more in this music than the mere inspiration of the poetry."[18] The poignancy of these songs surely derives in part from Beethoven's personal experience, and we know that his famous letter to the "Immortal Beloved" stems from 1812. It seems possible, as Maynard Solomon has claimed, that this beloved was Antonia Brentano, a married woman with children who was compelled to leave Vienna for Frankfurt that autumn.[19] If so, Beethoven's last and most serious chance for personal fulfillment through marriage was foreclosed in late 1812.

Consequently, Kerman writes about the song cycle that "it seems likely that this music helped Beethoven to bring his emotional conflicts to rest; by bringing his feelings into the open, he was renouncing or abandoning them."[20]

In this connection we should consider some of Schumann's and Clara Wieck's thoughts about the fantasie immediately after it was published, in April 1839. In a letter dated 10 June 1839, Schumann asks Clara leading questions about how she likes the first movement, and he cites one particular excerpt as his favorite. He adds playfully that "he almost believes" that she is the "tone" in the poetic motto from Friedrich Schlegel that he had decided to place at the head of the score.[21] The motto refers to "Ein leiser Ton gezogen / Für den der heimlich lauschet" (A soft tone being drawn [through the music] / For those who listen secretly).[22] The passage from Schumann's letter with its musical excerpt drawn from the exposition of the opening movement is shown in Ex. 3.1. In response to these hints, Clara Wieck declared to Robert that "es ist doch sonderbar, daß meine Lieblingsstelle im ersten Satz der Fantasie auch die Deinige ist!" (it is very strange that my favorite passage in the first movement is the same as yours!).[23] Their favorite passage in question is drawn from the second subject area, and its continuation is bound up with an imitative echoing of musical phrases. Ex. 3.2 shows this passage in the recapitulation of the first movement of the fantasie.

We are reminded here perhaps of the echoing effect in Florestan's delirium scene, in which he imitates the tones of the oboe to the words "ein Engel, Leonore." But there is a possible further significance to the ensuing passage of the fantasie, which slows to a reflective *adagio*, the same slow tempo as is employed at the very end of the movement. Berthold Hoeckner has suggested that this passage harbors a second quotation from Beethoven's *An die ferne Geliebte*, one that relates specifically to the end of the cycle.

It is in this last stanza of his closing song that Beethoven recalls the music from "Denn vor Liedesklang entweichet" in the first song:

> Denn vor diesen Liedern weichet,
> was geschieden uns so weit,
> und ein liebend Herz erreichet
> was ein liebend Herz geweiht!
>
> [Then the distance that so divides us
> dissolves through these songs,
> that a loving heart receive
> what a loving heart has consecrated!]

It is the stammering on "was" (what)—"and you sing, what I sang" and "what a loving heart has consecrated!"—that drew Hoeckner's attention.[24] Schumann's version is quieter, more inward and reflective rather than ecstatic, but the melodic outline stressing B–C at the pianissimo passage leading to the *adagio* in Schumann

Ex. 3.1. Musical excerpt in Schumann's letter of 10 June 1839.

Ex. 3.2. Continuation of passage in second subject area, recapitulation
of first movement, Fantasie, op. 17.

corresponds closely to the *molto adagio* at "und du singst" in Beethoven (Ex. 3.3).
Schumann's conspicuous use of silence suggests a rapport of music with that which
lies soundlessly beyond.

It is striking that Schumann's passage, drawn here from the second subject area
in the recapitulation of his movement, *can* correspond so closely with Beethoven's
coda. For the fantasie is in C major, and this parallel involves Schumann's use
of E♭ major for a recapitulation of the second theme, a highly unusual, quite un-
Beethovenian procedure. Yet in terms of the musical symbolism of Schumann's
works of the 1830s, this tonal procedure makes sense. From *Carnaval* in particular, we know how alert Schumann was to the relation of E♭ to *S*, the first letter of

Ex. 3.3. Beethoven, *An die ferne Geliebte*, op. 98, setting of "und du singst."

his name. Clara's symbolic key, on the other hand, tends to be C major, and it is also remarkable, in view of Schumann's personal situation at the original time of composition, in 1836, how the tonic key of C major is handled in the entire first movement of the fantasie.

During 1836, as we have seen, Clara was indeed a "distant beloved" and seemingly an unattainable or lost beloved to Schumann. For more than a year, all contact between the two was broken off. In June 1836, under pressure from her father, Clara and Robert returned their letters to one another. In this context, Schumann later described the first movement of the fantasie as a "deep lament" for Clara, one that reflected his melancholy and despair from the summer of 1836. Consequently, Nicholas Marston, in his book on the fantasie, has argued that the initial creative impetus for the fantasie was not Beethoven but the crisis over Clara Wieck and that Schumann's title, "Ruins," refers to his own deep emotional pain. As Marston puts it, "His life must have seemed to him to be quite literally in ruins."[25] Without underestimating the depth of Schumann's crisis that summer, it is perhaps more persuasive to regard the Beethoven allusions and Schumann's own close personal identification with his work as closely interwoven strands that cannot be separated from one another. This seems all the more the case if we reflect on Schumann's own reciprocal definitions of "ruin" and "monument" in documents from these years. For Schumann, "ein Denkmal ist eine vorwärts gedrehte Ruine" (a monument is a ruin directed forward) into the future.[26]

How, then, can we best grasp the overall narrative and formal design of the first movement of the fantasie, a work that is so rich in sudden contrasts, changes in tempo, and abrupt shifts in mood? How too are we to understand in relation to the whole the slower sections, the *adagio* passages in the second subject area, the central C minor section beginning "Im Legendenton" (which was originally labeled "Romanza"), and the concluding *adagio* in C major, which Schumann considered using as well at the end of the third movement? Here again, Beethoven's music provides valuable clues. But a revealing perspective emerges from one of Schumann's earlier letters sent to Clara in Dresden in July 1834. In this letter, Schumann writes that he would gladly talk, chatter, or laugh with her but that the best communication would instead be musical, if he sat at the piano and sounded rich sonorities such as an eleventh chord, a C minor sonority including D♭ and F♭ (Ex. 3.4).[27]

Ex. 3.4. Chord in Schumann's letter of 10 July 1834.

This raises the general issue of the relationship of harmony to expressive emotional states. Sonorities suitable to express or embody states of yearning will tend to be more complex than a triad. Hence, in Beethoven's setting of "Nur der Sehnsucht sich bewußt" (Conscious only of its longing), he draws out his phrase to rest upon an arpeggiated dominant-seventh chord. As an historical tendency, composers sought richly ambiguous harmonies to convey yearning, such as the minor triad with added sixth used by Berlioz in his love music to *Roméo et Juliette* from 1839 and by Wagner in his *Tristan und Isolde* from 1859, the so-called Tristan chord. The family of sonorities alluded to in Schumann's letter and illustrated in many works by Beethoven and Schumann involves a stacking up of thirds, which often build upon and enrich the harmony of the dominant.

A comparison of the harmonic practice of Beethoven and Schumann in this regard is revealing. For instance, the climactic sonority of Beethoven's great *Leonore* Overture No. 3, at the triple fortissimo climax in the Presto coda, is a minor ninth chord on the dominant whose resolution generates the powerful momentum and jubilant character of the end of the overture. In Beethoven's later works, on the other hand, it is often the *major* ninth chord on the dominant that receives emphasis.

Let us consider in this context two of Beethoven's last piano sonatas, each of which elaborates and transforms a lyrical utterance in unforgettable fashion. The finale of the E Major Sonata, op. 109, from 1820, unfolds as variations on a heartfelt theme that Beethoven described in his sketches as a *Gesang* (song). Beethoven dedicated this sonata to Maximiliana Brentano, Antonia Brentano's daughter. The lyric culmination of the theme comes in its final phrase and is placed on the harmony of a major ninth chord involving the pitches B, D♯, F♯, A, and C♯ (Ex. 3.5). Beethoven emphasizes this melodic peak through arpeggiation of the chord, spreading out the notes of the sonority, and he thereby lingers briefly on the C♯–B step, a motive that later assumes special importance.

Most extraordinary is the final, sixth variation of this theme, which gradually transforms its textures through a rigorous process of rhythmic diminution or acceleration. Beethoven develops the emphasis on the dominant, B, in the theme itself by placing this note above the melody as an upper pedal point, and he then gradually increases the rhythmic motion as the theme unfolds. Thus, through a rigorous process of rhythmic acceleration and registral expansion, the slow cantabile theme virtually explodes from within, yielding, through a kind of radioactive breakup, a fantastically elaborate texture of shimmering, vibrating sounds.

Another example is the Arietta and variations that form the finale of Beethoven's last sonata, op. 111, in C minor. In this work, Beethoven enlarges the procedure of progressive rhythmic diminutions from the sixth variation of op. 109 so that it shapes the development of each of the variations of the lyrical Arietta. The melody of the Arietta emphasizes the dominant note G of the last measure, a note marked with an accent. In the climactic recapitulatory fifth variation near the end of this movement, Beethoven sounds G and A together as part of a major ninth chord. This culminating gesture is then sustained and concentrated in the ensuing trill, which sounds G and A together as a simultaneity (Ex. 3.6). Even more than in op. 109, this music resonates into the silence beyond itself, saturating the tonal space as it does with the sonority of the trill, and it is no wonder that Thomas Mann, whose character Wendell Kretzschmar gives an Adorno-influenced lecture on the sonata in the novel *Doktor Faustus*, writes movingly of the effect of "ein Ende auf Nimmerwiederkehr" (an end without any return).

Now, at long last, we return to Robert Schumann's Fantasie in C. What is so arresting about Schumann's opening to this work is how he begins at once in the agitated left-hand accompaniment with the rich major-ninth harmony that had served as the culmination of the Arietta movement of Beethoven's op. 111 (Ex. 3.7). Indeed, the presence of C in the right-hand chords supporting the melody enriches the sonority into a chord of the eleventh, one similar to the sonority through which Schumann had sought to send his tidings through the ether to Clara in distant Dresden. The first movement of the fantasie unfolds as a series of waves, sustained by a passion that yields intermittently to reflection. But what is consistently avoided throughout is any firm settling onto the stable tonic sonority of C major. The repose and profound serenity of Schumann's conclusion owes much to this long-delayed

Ex. 3.5. Beethoven, Sonata in E Major, op. 109, theme of finale (mm. 11–16).

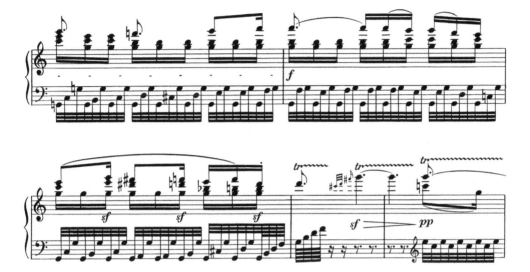

Ex. 3.6. Beethoven, Sonata in C Minor, op. 111, transition to coda (mm. 157–61).

affirmation of the missing tonal foundation of C major, with cadences and root-position triads supplied only as the movement nears its conclusion.

Thus we can see that Schumann in his op. 17 Fantasie has *inverted* Beethoven's aesthetic framework. Schumann's musical monument to Beethoven arises out of the ruins of Beethoven's tonal architecture, infusing the climactic sonorities immediately with intense subjectivity. The work's import as a "deep lament" for Clara seems bound up in several ways with the archetypal framework of the distant beloved. Motivic variations or premonitions of the *ferne Geliebte* theme are scattered about, with some of the most direct allusions taking the form of miragelike visions, as in the phrase of the "Im Legendenton" section. The sensitive dialogue passages, on the other hand, strive to break the isolation of the lament, conjuring up the presence of a responding voice. In the concluding passage of the movement, as Rosen has claimed, "Schumann makes Beethoven's melody sound as if it were derived from its new context, as if Schumann's music could expand organically to produce a scrap of Beethoven," but there is also an important shift in

Ex. 3.7. Schumann, Fantasie, op. 17, beginning.

the musical discourse at this point, as what was long withheld is granted.[28] In this context, we may regard the concluding *adagio* as alluding above all to Beethoven's setting of "and you sing, what I sang" rather than merely to the opening of the sixth song of the cycle, with the words "Take these songs then, my love, that I sang." The actual appearance of the concluding *adagio* in C major corresponds to Beethoven's strategy of allowing the concluding music to stand for an answering voice as the melody is sung back, transcending space and time. Freed from physical constraints, the music achieves what is seemingly impossible, anticipating the fulfillment of yearning.

The Symbolism of Schumann's Beethoven Allusion

Some commentators have remained skeptical about Schumann's apparent allusion in the fantasie to Beethoven's *An die ferne Geliebte*. Failing to find confirmation of the allusion in documents from Clara Wieck Schumann or other nineteenth-century sources, Anthony Newcomb suggested that this Beethoven allusion may actually have arisen from "a more recent critical tradition." He asks, "Might it be that for Schumann and for the musical culture of the nineteenth century, the quotation was not there—or at least . . . it was not for them part of the content and meaning of the piece, as we now understand it?"[29] In response to Newcomb's argument, Marston sought to broaden the critical context in a different way by suggesting possible Schubertian allusions in the fantasie.[30] R. Larry Todd, in yet another assessment, asked whether such connections were "generic resonances, covert allusions, or nothing more than coincidental resemblances."[31]

In the context of Schumann's serious ongoing engagement with Beethoven and his circumstances during 1836, when the fantasie was conceived, it may be hard to maintain such skepticism. The double allusion—to the distant beloved archetype as embodied in *An die ferne Geliebte* and to Clara Wieck as his own *entfernte Geliebte*—resonates just too well with the Beethovenian aura of their personal mythology as an embattled couple, as Florestan and Klärchen. The shift of perspective in the musical narrative, implying the "singing back" of the songs, supports Hoeckner's perception of a broadened range of allusion to Beethoven in the fantasie. Even Schumann's notion of a monument as a ruin turned toward the future lends itself well to the interpretation of this unique movement.

The lack of a documented reference to the Beethoven allusion from Clara Wieck is surely connected to its private associations for Schumann. In a letter to Clara from January 1839, he alludes to the imminent appearance of the fantasie in print, "die Phantasie (von der Du nichts kennst) die ich während unsrer unglücklichen Trennung schrieb und die übermelancholisch [ist]" (the fantasie [which you don't know at all] that I wrote during our unhappy separation and which [is] overly melancholy).[32] This comment implies that Schumann felt that the fantasie was bound up with an unhappy phase in his life that he had left behind. His telling parenthetical remark—"you don't know [it] at all"—indicates that he had shared little about the work during its original period of composition in 1836, an impression that receives further confirmation from their subsequent correspondence. After receiving the published work in May 1839, Clara wrote enthusiastically about the marchlike second movement. In response, Schumann asked her about her impression of the first movement and the motto from Schlegel. As we have seen, these comments are rich in implications, even if they offer no specific confirmation of the connection to Beethoven's *An die ferne Geliebte*.

What sheds further light on the concluding *adagio* passage of the first movement is the revelation that Schumann originally planned to recall this same music at the end of the entire work. In the finale, the melodic note that introduces the *An die ferne Geliebte* allusion is the same high A first heard at the beginning of the opening movement. Shifted down an octave near the close of the first movement, this A triggers the beginning of the entire fourteen-bar *adagio* passage, complete with its interludes and the threefold cadential gestures, whereby the final cadence is enhanced through rhythmic augmentation and textural means (Ex. 3.8). Subtle changes in harmony subtly modify this large-scale thematic recall, casting a unifying poetic thread over the work as a whole.

Ex. 3.8. Schumann, Fantasie, op. 17, ending of first movement.

Scrutiny of Schumann's finale shows that its concluding gateway gesture has been elaborately prepared from the outset. Beginning softly and weightlessly, the music is initially marked "Durchweg leise zu halten" (Kept soft throughout) (Ex. 3.9). Within the opening bars of arpeggios, the second measure shifts to an A major chord, and the arpeggios of the third measure unfold on A with the harmonic support of an F major chord. The expressive melodic crux that emerges out of these arpeggios is heard in m. 4, as a prolonged A is marked by a *ritardando*, while a resolution of this pitch to G occurs at the last group of three eighth notes.

Taken as a whole, Schumann's concluding slow movement displays a highly directional character, no less than the opening movement. It is characterized by extended passages of quiet restraint that build with gradual inevitability to reach a pair of fortissimo climaxes: in F major at m. 68 and in the tonic C major at m. 119. Schumann also incorporates prominent deceptive cadences, which bring a varied recall of the mysterious opening arpeggios, played pianissimo. The first of these deceptive cadences takes place in m. 30, with a turn to A♭ major; the second such passage, at m. 87, carries the music into D♭ major. Consequently, any strong cadential articulation of C major, such as could have been expected at m. 32, is avoided and delayed until the concluding passages after the C major climax.

Within this unusual formal design, Schumann repeatedly juxtaposes the mysterious arpeggios from the outset with a melodic phrase marked "Etwas bewegter" (Somewhat more animated); this segment highlights the scale step from the fifth to the sixth degrees. First heard in mm. 34–35 in A♭ major, the "Etwas bewegter" phrase is the first gesture to rise above a dynamic level of *piano*. Its stress on the 5–6 scale step, as well as the juxtaposition of this phrase with the texture of quiet arpeggios, links this idea to the fourth measure of the movement. Beginning in m. 38,

CHAPTER 3

Ex. 3.9. Schumann, Fantasie, op. 17, beginning of last movement.

Schumann restates the "Etwas bewegter" motive in the keys of F major and G minor in a developmental, modulatory context. Then, beginning in m. 44, we hear a new, more extended melodic variant of this idea, with a gently lilting rhythmic swing, beginning with a motivic ascent from 5 to 6, or C to D in the key of F major. This gesture initiates the passage that gradually builds to the fortissimo climax twenty measures later. As this occurs, we can recognize that the climactic fortissimo outburst is actually a transformation of the "Etwas bewegter" idea, involving a quickening of its rhythm and an enhancement of its texture into a series of full-voiced chords.

Impressive as it is, the first climax lacks staying power; it fades to pianissimo within four measures, and the shift to a seventh chord on A in m. 71 takes on the character of another deceptive cadence. In this context, the later, high-register recapitulation of the twenty-measure passage, beginning with ethereal tenderness on the dominant of C major in m. 99 and leading to the long-withheld, definitive C major cadence in m. 122, carries much weight. Schumann's overall formal plan is shaped as a double cycle, whereby the inconclusive character of the earlier F major climax is supplanted by the much more satisfying and emphatic arrival in C major before the original texture of arpeggios returns in m. 122.

Following the cadence, the concluding passage takes on a character of reminiscence through its return to the original arpeggios, now heard over a tonic pedal point, as well as its recall of the gentle lilting theme, heard first in the middle register in the right hand and then in the bass. The gradual descent of this subject prepares its disappearance, as both hands take up the arpeggiated texture, just as at the beginning of the entire movement. Marked "Nach und nach bewegter und schneller" (More and more animated and faster), the music of this coda seems to strive toward a further climax.

This last manifestation of directionality raises intriguing questions. In its familiar published version, the coda is twenty measures long, precisely the same length as the earlier passages of gradual intensification. But what is the goal of this final passage? Melodically, the peak is reached at the accented notes A and G, eight and six measures before the end, respectively. In the final moments, music slows to *adagio*, as the plagal cadence is confirmed by three soft sustained tonic chords played in the lower registers. The A to G scale step recalls once more the expressive gesture from m. 4. The serene close of the movement signals a return to its origins, with this quality confirmed through a cessation of the slow, wavelike motion of arpeggiation. As this cessation occurs, three measures from the end, we hear a C major chord with E as highest tone that corresponds in its registral placement to the initial arpeggiated sonority of the finale. The later chord represents the a priori condition, as it were, for the beginning of the entire movement.

Yet as we have seen, Schumann originally intended a more extended and complex ending to the work, one in which the crucial high A would serve as the springboard for a recall of the end of the first movement of the fantasie (Ex. 3.10). As Charles Rosen puts it, "The manuscript ending of the finale, in spite of the careful way it is prepared by the opening bars, creates a momentary break in the form of the last movement, only to imply the greater unity of the work as a whole."[33] The sense of a break is more palpable because of the all-embracing continuity in the sound of the movement up to this point; when the original manuscript version is performed, the rests at the beginning of the *adagio* passage should not be drowned by the pedal. Following the silence, those pitches of the diminished-seventh chord supporting high A on which the earlier music broke off now serve to convey the slightly varied recall of the closing *adagio* of the first movement.

Schumann of course suppressed this ending, but is the artist himself always the best editor of his own work? Rosen comments: "If an editor had made this change, we would call him a vandal."[34] Nor is this an isolated instance. In the case of Schumann's Symphonic Études, for example, the manuscript version reveals five outstanding pieces that were rejected by Schumann but whose restoration arguably enhances the piece. Alfred Brendel observes that "their withdrawal caused almost the entire Eusebius to be deleted from a work whose original title had read 'Etüden im Orchestercharakter von Florestan und Eusebius.'" Commenting as a performer, Brendel continues: "After many years of working with Schumann's 'symphonic' version, I would not want to go any longer without the five posthumous pieces; it is their inclusion that makes Schumann's Op. 13 one of his finest compositions."[35]

Seeking a broader context for some of Schumann's questionable revisions of his own works, Rosen has pointed to other examples in which "what is most idiosyncratic in his musical invention is erased by Schumann in an apparent attempt to make his work sound like everybody else's."[36] Although the familiar published ending of the fantasie is hardly perfunctory, the manuscript version is most inspired.

Ex. 3.10. Schumann, Fantasie, op. 17, original ending of last movement.

As originally conceived, the striving character of the music here overreaches itself, just as the emblematic memory of the earlier *adagio* reveals a hidden affinity between the outer movements, casting a unifying thread across the entire composition. Furthermore, Schumann's repetition of the Beethoven quotation at the end of the final movement echoes Beethoven's own procedure in *An die ferne Geliebte*, where the last song brings a return of the music and words of the first. Perhaps this very parallel to Beethoven's cyclic procedure might have played a role in Schumann's second thoughts, were he concerned to veil the "soft tone" sounding through the whole, ensuring its "secrecy" for the listener who "hears furtively." Presumably because of its "overly melancholy" personal associations, he did not wish for Clara to experience the piece in the way he evidently conceived it.[37] For us, however, insight into the genesis of the fantasie is not a burden but only adds to the fascination of this uniquely impressive composition.

In a recent interpretation of Schumann's allusion to Beethoven's *An die ferne Geliebte* in the C Major Fantasie, Christopher Reynolds downplayed the connection to Clara Wieck, arguing that "Schumann may have fulfilled the instruction to sing the poet's own song back to him as a way of achieving a musical—if not spiritual—union with Beethoven."[38] At the same time, the suppression of the second allusive passage as well as the apparent removal or concealment of yet another Beethovenian reference in the finale—to the slow movement of the Seventh Symphony—indicate a process of retrenchment on Schumann's part.[39] Furthermore, any direct reference to Beethoven in the title of the work, such as Schumann had originally intended, was removed in the published composition. In the work as we know it, the relation to Beethoven is no longer an allusion in a "public sense," as Reynolds contends, but the allusive context remains inextricably bound up with the personal connection to Schumann's own "distant beloved" at the original time of composition.

To conclude, let us return briefly to the year 1845, the year the Beethoven statue at Bonn was finally unveiled. The Schumanns, then in their fifth year of marriage, did not make the journey to the celebrations, which were colorful and even rowdy. The dignitaries present took offense at Beethoven's bad manners, since they had been seated behind the statue and saw only the composer's back when he was unveiled. The French contingent took offense when Liszt failed to acknowledge their donation, and Liszt's alleged mistress, Lola Montez, enlivened the dinner party by dancing on the tables.[40]

Schumann, for his part, returned to the theme of the distant beloved in another way. Precipitated by the stressful tour of Russia with Clara during 1844–45 and perhaps also by his withdrawal from editorial involvement with his journal, the *Neue Zeitschrift für Musik,* he suffered a serious psychological breakdown, an ominous foreshadowing of the suicide attempt of 1854 that resulted in that grim period in the Endenich asylum leading to his death in 1856. Rebounding from this depressive phase, Schumann immersed himself during 1845 in the composition of a symphony in the same key as the op. 17 Fantasie, a work that became the Symphony in C Major, op. 61.

The C Major Symphony remains a relatively neglected work of Schumann's, but it deserves more recognition. Its parallels to the C Major Fantasie include a prominent role of the key of E♭ as well as conspicuous motivic allusions to the "distant beloved" complex in the third and fourth movements. An important outcome of its overall narrative trajectory lies in the theme heard beginning at m. 394 of the finale (Ex. 3.11). The music displays an obvious melodic similarity to the sixth song of Beethoven's *An die ferne Geliebte* in its rise of a third, drop of a fourth, and descent to the sixth. Detailed analysis of the symphony lies beyond the scope of the present discussion, but Erik Horak-Hult has commented sensitively about the character of these allusions, which seem to relate once more to the "singing back"

Ex. 3.11. Schumann, Symphony in C Major, op. 61, theme in finale.

of the songs. Horak-Hult concludes that "in its retrospective, inclusive character, the symphony seems to transcend not only Beethoven's experiential model, but Schumann's own earlier experience."[41]

One wonders what remained of all of this in Schumann's awareness during those final bleak years at Endenich near Bonn, knowing as we do now that a favorite destination for his frequent walks with the personnel from the asylum was Beethoven's statue on the Münsterplatz. The trip to Beethoven's statue that Schumann had been unable to make a decade earlier became a routine of his life in its last, declining phase.

A final point relates to the strangely tangled history of the C Major Fantasie after Schumann's death in 1856. The tensional relationship between Clara Schumann and Liszt resulted in her attempt, when the fantasie was prepared for republication, to cancel the dedication to Liszt and substitute her own name. Complicating this situation is the likelihood that Clara indeed had been intended as the original dedicatee. Neither Clara Schumann nor Liszt promoted the work in public performances to any extent, although Brahms played the work in public concerts in the 1860s, and Liszt taught it in his Weimar master classes. Alan Walker has observed that when the fantasie was finally taken up in a big way, it was by Liszt's pupils.[42] Schumann himself in the later years seems to have undervalued the work, but it remains one of his most innovative and imaginative creations, not least on account of its enduring response to Beethoven's legacy.

Aesthetics of Integration in Mahler's Fifth Symphony

The intertwining of song and symphony so characteristic of Gustav Mahler's *Wunderhorn* years did not end with his purely orchestral Fifth Symphony but assumed another form. Unlike the preceding three symphonies, which include both song quotations and texted movements, the Fifth Symphony contains no vocal setting; instead, an entire orchestral movement virtually stands in place of a song. The fourth of five movements, the Adagietto, bears a strong affinity to Mahler's song on Friedrich Rückert's poem "Ich bin der Welt abhanden gekommen" (I've become lost to the world).[1] Through its use in Luchino Visconti's 1971 film *Death in Venice* (*Morte a Venezia*), based on Thomas Mann's novella of the same title, the Adagietto's popularity suddenly soared. As a result, discussions of the symphony have become curiously unbalanced. Visconti's interpretation of Mahler's music has affected the symphony's reception even more than the report of the Dutch conductor Willem Mengelberg, who maintained that the Adagietto served as Mahler's love offering to Alma Schindler at a formative stage in their courtship. Yet both have encouraged an isolated view of the Adagietto, which has tended to be lifted out of its original context in recent commercial recordings and some critical studies.[2] In the symphony, the Adagietto leads directly into the concluding Rondo-Finale, with which it is bound thematically. Mahler himself designated these final two movements as subsections of the third part of the symphony. Both the intermovement connections and the Adagietto's backdrop of "Ich bin der Welt abhanden gekommen" yield an uncommonly rich interpretative field, drawing together formal as well as symbolic issues.

The questions of aesthetic meaning and biographical context raised by the Adagietto are complicated by the fact that the finale of the Fifth Symphony has generated its own share of controversy since the appearance in 1960 of Theodor Adorno's classic study *Mahler: Eine musikalische Physiognomik*.[3] Translated into English in 1992, Adorno's work continues to exert influence, and his comments on the Fifth Symphony have resonated widely in the secondary literature. For Adorno, "the Adagietto of the Fifth, despite its important conception as an individual piece within the whole, borders on genre prettiness through its ingratiating sound; the Finale, fresh in many details and with novel formal ideas like that of the musical quick-motion picture, is undoubtedly too lightweight in relation to the first three movements."[4] Adorno unpacks his critique of the finale as follows:

> The positivity of the *per aspera ad astra* movement in the Fifth . . . can manifest itself only as a tableau, a scene of motley bustle. . . . Mahler was a poor yea-sayer. His voice cracks, like Nietzsche's, when he proclaims values, speaks from mere conviction, when he himself puts into practice the abhorrent notion of overcoming on which the thematic analyses capitalize, and makes music as if joy were already in the world. His vainly jubilant movements unmask jubilation, his subjective incapacity for the happy end denounces itself. . . . His successful final movements are those that ignore the radiant path *ad astra*.[5]

The "radiant path" to which Adorno refers leads to a celebratory brass chorale in D major heard in mm. 711–49. Although a variant of the same passage in the second movement receives his endorsement, as a "chorale vision that saves the movement from circularity," it is the quality of affirmation or "positivity" in the finale that Adorno rejects, quite apart from his accusation of its being "too light-weight." For Adorno, Mahler's "special tone" is that of "brokenness": "Aberrations are of [the] essence" in his music as he "tracks down meaning in its absence."[6] In his dismissal of the chorale in the finale, Adorno's judgment resonates curiously with Alma Mahler's initial response. She related that when Mahler first played the symphony for her at the piano in the autumn of 1902, she told him the chorale at the conclusion was "hymnal and boring" and that he was "not . . . at his best in working up a church chorale."[7] This critical stance has been echoed more recently, notably by Bernd Sponheuer, but without becoming a dominant view.[8] As Donald Mitchell writes, "Adorno's notorious adverse judgement has already achieved wide currency," yet "the assumption that Mahler was incapable of affirming a humane belief in humanity, that he was unequal to the task or uninterested in it . . . has the ring of ideological intolerance—an ideologically rooted pessimism—about it."[9]

The following analysis begins with a study of these paired final movements of the Fifth Symphony and explores the nature of their interrelationship. In the final section of this essay, Mahler's techniques of integration are assessed in light of the influence on his style of Bach and Wagner as well as his interest in the aesthetics of polarity as articulated by one of his favorite writers, Jean Paul. In this context, we will return to Adorno's conviction that "brokenness" is the key to Mahler's music.

The Adagietto as a "Song without Words"

"Ich bin der Welt abhanden gekommen" and the Fifth Symphony absorbed Mahler's compositional energies during the latter half of 1901. The genesis of the song is especially well documented due to the survival of Mahler's rough drafts for the piece, which are held in the Pierpont Morgan Library in New York, together with the original autograph score of the Fifth Symphony.[10] The source that captures Mengelberg's description of the song as a declaration of love is the conductor's own score. In that score, Mengelberg wrote words that fit closely to the melody heard at the outset of the movement, beginning as follows: "Wie ich dich liebe, Du meine Sonne, ich kann mit Worten Dir's nicht sagen" (How I love you, you my sun, I cannot tell you with words) (Plate 3).[11] Mengelberg, who claimed to have received confirmation of the musical love message from both Mahler and Alma, comments at the bottom of the score: "Wenn Musik eine Sprache ist, so ist sie es hier—*er* sagt ihr alles in *Tönen* und *Klängen*, in: Musik" (If music is a language—as it is here—*he* tells her everything in *tones* and *sounds*, in music).

Mengelberg's report cannot be dismissed lightly, and it is well supported by the chronology of Mahler's compositional activities at Maiernigg on the Wörther Lake during August 1901. According to Natalie Bauer-Lechner's account, "Mahler had just finished his holiday work for this year, wanting to devote the last few days to relaxation, when he was suddenly seized with the urge to set the last of the Rückert poems that he had originally planned to do, but set aside in favour of the symphony. This was 'Ich bin der Welt abhanden gekommen.' He himself said that this song, with its unusually concentrated and restrained style, is brim-full with emotion but does not overflow. He also said: 'It is my very self!'"[12] The next piece to command Mahler's attention was the Adagietto, written presumably after he met Alma Schindler in November. As Stephen E. Hefling has claimed, "there seems no reason to doubt the essence of Mengelberg's testimony."[13]

In his film *Death in Venice*, Visconti's rather different reading of the Adagietto involves isolating the movement as he uses it to portray psychological isolation. *Death in Venice* is a fictional construction in which the controlled recurrences of the music of the Adagietto underscore the yearning and sagging vitality of the ailing composer Gustav von Aschenbach, whose extreme detachment from the world around him foreshadows his death. Visconti's film bears a complex tensional relationship to both Thomas Mann's novella and Mahler's life and music.[14] Mann's story about the writer Aschenbach was already linked to Mahler, since its conception was influenced by the news of the composer's death in 1911, and Mann described how he gave his hero, "who succumbs to lascivious dissolution,"

Mahler's first name as well as his facial features, placing the "mask" of the great musician on Aschenbach.[15] Mann presents Aschenbach as the "poet-spokesman" for a "new type of hero"; this ideal "was beautiful, it was *spirituel*, it was exact, despite the suggestion of too great passivity it held."[16] In Visconti's interpretation, this passivity receives an emphasis that is pointedly associated with Mahler's Adagietto. Visconti rewrites Aschenbach as a composer (as opposed to a writer) while incorporating episodes from Mahler's life as flashbacks within the film, with Aschenbach's friend Alfred standing for Arnold Schoenberg. In this cinematic context, Aschenbach is the very source of the music of the Adagietto, and it is *his* music that represents an ideal of serene beauty that in his "lascivious dissolution" becomes identified with the Polish boy Tadzio.[17]

Some critics have responded dismissively to the languid interpretations the Adagietto has received in performances, especially since the appearance of Visconti's film. Henry-Louis de La Grange writes that "Mahler certainly did not anticipate, nor would he have wished for, the excessive sentimentality which most conductors today indulge in when playing this short piece. The slowed-down tempo at which they take it completely distorts its tender, contemplative character and changes it into a syrupy elegy."[18] This interpretative trend does seem connected to the detachment of the Adagietto from its symphonic context, even though Franco Mannino's recording of the movement with the Orchestra dell'Accademia Nazionale di Santa Cecilia on the soundtrack of the film is not particularly slow, at nine minutes and twenty-eight seconds. The static visual effects and absence of dialogue in much of the film lend an emphasis to the music that may have influenced some orchestral performances.

For de La Grange, the Adagietto's similarity to the song "Ich bin der Welt abhanden gekommen" casts doubt on Mengelberg's account of the symphonic movement being used as a love offering. He argues that "it is improbable that Mahler could have written two pieces so related in every way with such different meanings."[19] But perhaps Mengelberg's account does not restrict the scope of meaning as narrowly as de La Grange perceives. As de La Grange himself points out, Mengelberg's tempos for the Adagietto, with total durations of seven minutes and four seconds in his first recording and eight minutes and twenty seconds in his second, are quite flowing and far removed from the slowest available, which are longer than thirteen minutes.[20] This presumably has to do with Mengelberg's sense of the Adagietto as a medium of utterance or "song without words" rather than as primarily a static or timeless sound-space removed from the outer world. This brings us to a consideration of the Rückert song, in which Mahler set text to music that bears a striking affinity to the Adagietto.

The psychological core of the Rückert poem resides in the increasingly intense subjectivity, or *Innigkeit*, of its three stanzas. The first stanza culminates in the thought that from the perspective of the outside world, the protagonist has become lost and has even ceased to exist. In the middle stanza, the poet-artist fully confirms this perception by stating: "Ich kann auch gar nichts sagen dagegen, / denn wirklich bin ich gestorben der Welt" (I can say nothing against it, / since I really have died in relation to the world). The notion of being cut off or of dying carries in this context some strongly positive connotations that reach their climax in the last of the three stanzas:

> Ich bin gestorben dem Weltgetümmel
> und ruh' in einem stillen Gebiet!
> Ich leb' allein in meinem Himmel,
> in meinem Lieben, in meinem Lieben, in meinem Lied.
>
> [I have died to the turbulence (tumult) of the world
> and rest in a still realm!
> I live alone in my heaven,
> in my love, in my love, in my song.]

Two drafts of this song have been preserved, the second of which is dated "16. Aug. 1901." These manuscripts document Mahler's changes in Rückert's original poetic text, such as the alternation of the penultimate line "Ich leb' in mir" (I live in myself) to "Ich leb' allein" (I live alone). The use of "Weltgetümmel" (worldly tumult) in place of "Weltgewimmel" (worldly throng) derives from Mahler, as does the repetition of the words "in meinem Lieben" in the last line.

Especially striking are some of the changes Mahler made in his first draft of the last stanza. For instance, the registral and melodic climax of the song on high A, at the repetition of the phrase "in meinem Lieben" (in my love), was first written for the voice. The final page of Mahler's first draft is shown in Fig. 4.1, where the passage in question appears on the right-hand side in the first system. Mahler subsequently returned to this passage, entering the abbreviation "ob" for "oboe" in pencil while crossing out the words "in meinem Lieben," and in his next draft he incorporated the soaring oboe line familiar from the final version. The revision of the passage in the second draft is shown in Fig. 4.2. This interpolation for the oboe has the effect of broadening and sustaining the entire passage, which forms the expressive peak of the last stanza and of the entire song. As Hefling has noted in his detailed discussion of these drafts, this oboe ascent to a sustained A has a close parallel at the conclusion of the Adagietto, the passage shown at the end of Ex. 4.1.[21] In the song, this entire instrumental phrase is foreshadowed in turn in the important instrumental introduction to the lied, reminding us of the extent to which the symphonic conception helps embody and enhance the quality of serenity and suspended time suggested by the words.

Adorno regarded the Adagietto as "actually a song without words . . . linked to 'Ich bin der Welt abhanden gekommen.'"[22] Mitchell describes it as "another Rückert setting," that is, as essentially one more Rückert song that is paradoxically

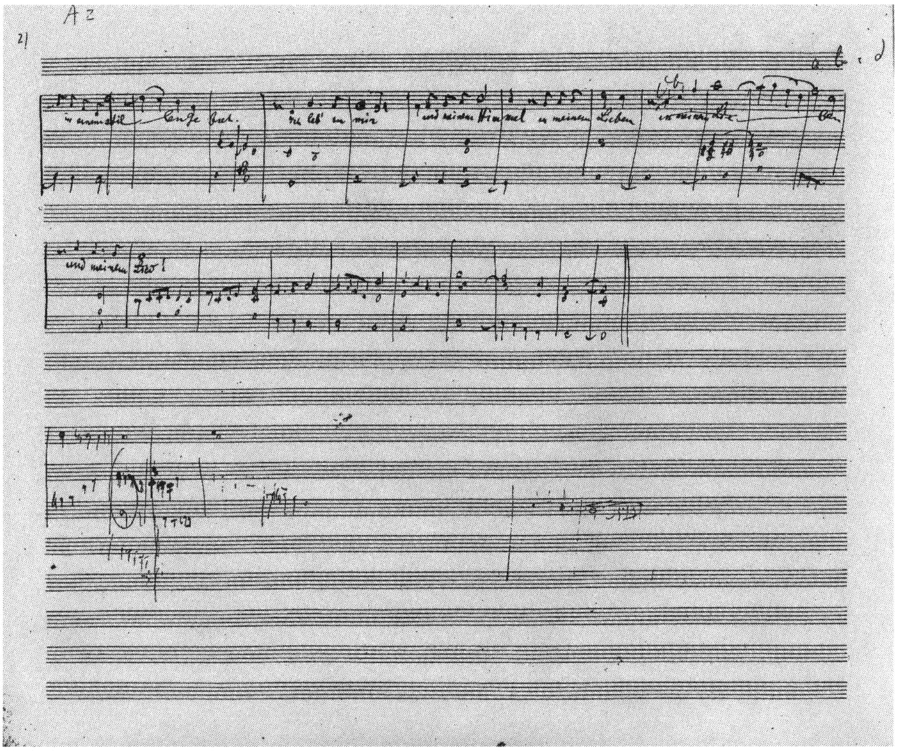

Figure 4.1. Draft of the end of "Ich bin der Welt abhanden gekommen,"
Mary Flagler Cary Music Collection, Pierpont Morgan Library. Used by permission.

Figure 4.2. Later draft of the end of "Ich bin der Welt abhanden gekommen,"
Mary Flagler Cary Music Collection, Pierpont Morgan Library. Used by permission.

Ex. 4.1. Mahler, Fifth Symphony, Adagietto, mm. 56–103.

Ex. 4.1. Continued.

Ex. 4.1. Continued.

Ex. 4.1. Continued.

Ex. 4.1. Continued.

Ex. 4.1. Continued.

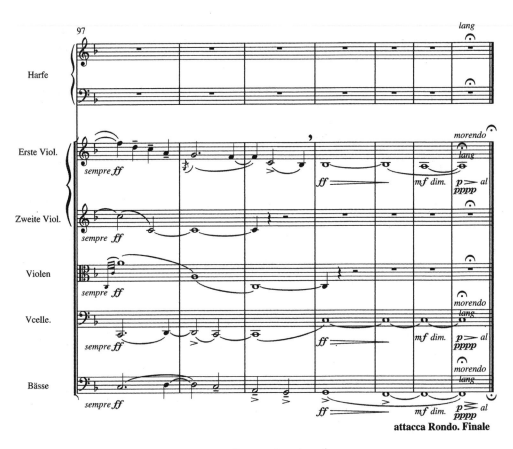

Ex. 4.1. Continued.

written for orchestra alone.[23] The parallels between the Adagietto and "Ich bin der Welt abhanden gekommen" are numerous and include not only the meter, basic tempo, and motivic material but also the ternary design of each piece, with a more fluent character in the middle section, the suggestive, almost bardic use of the harp triplets as accompaniment, and the expressive use of appoggiatura figures and of harmonies blending third-related triads. Significant, too, may have been the original F major tonality of Mahler's drafts for the song, since this is the tonic key of the Adagietto movement. Only later to accommodate the singer Friedrich Weidemann did Mahler lower the key of this Rückert setting to E♭ major.

While acknowledging the close affinities between these two roughly contemporaneous works, it is profitable to consider their differences. In timbre and texture, the Adagietto is more homogeneous than its sister setting on account of the absence of the voice and of any orchestral wind sonority and the soft, highly sustained quality of the string writing. The place of the vocalist is filled by the continuous violin line, creating the effect of a song without words whose breathing points for the hypothetical singer are marked by no fewer than thirty-two commas punctuating the flow of melody. Can the expressive and narrative implications of the music be further specified here, in spite of the absence of words? Here the analogy to "Ich bin der Welt abhanden gekommen" can be fruitful and suggestive.

In the Adagietto, as in the song, Mahler intensifies the reflective, contemplative character not only through performance indications such as *seelenvoll* (soulful) but through rhythmic means as well. Thus, in the second, larger phrase of the Adagietto, Mahler employs a rhythmic augmentation of the basic motivic unit, with the expressive upbeat figure of a rising third, C–E, repeated in quarter notes leading to half notes in the tenth measure instead of in eighths leading to quarters as in the second and third measures. This quality of holding back, of reposing in a suspended psychological state, is enhanced by extended pedal points and by an ambiguity of tonality and a certain tendency toward pentatonicism that may have roots in the Oriental flavor of Rückert's poetry. The suspended sonority at the outset is a third, C–A, that can belong to either of two triads, F major or A minor, and it is between these two keys that the music shifts in its first two extended phrases. The lyric climax on high A in m. 30 seems to celebrate the reaffirmation of F major after this key is put into question through the move to A minor.

Throughout this opening section of the ternary form, there is little sense of discrete dramatic events: even the changes of key from F major to A minor and back seem more like pivots within a basically static tonal field. However, this effect changes in the middle section of the form, containing as it does several clear modulations to contrasting keys: C minor, G♭ major, D♭ major, A♭ minor, E major, and D major, leading to the reprise of the main theme in F major. A sense of action, or restless yearning, is conveyed here through the replacement of the stepwise melodic motion of the first section by an initial rising motion of a third and then by increasingly wide melodic turns and leaps.

This intensification in the middle section of the Adagietto involves a probing of real depth and magnitude. Such restless striving contained within the soul of the implied protagonist can seem to strain against the boundaries of artistic form; there are ample models in the artistic tradition to which Mahler was a self-conscious heir. Among purely instrumental musical works, one thinks perhaps of earlier slow movements of pensive character in which an abrupt discontinuation or interruption can seem to imply the intrusion of the world beyond, sometimes with tragic implications, as at the end of the slow movement of Beethoven's "Appassionata" Sonata or in the disruptive central episodes of slow movements by Mozart and Schubert.[24] Yet differently from these examples, the inward lyricism of Mahler's Adagietto is juxtaposed with the bright and richly diverse character of the surrounding symphonic movements, the Scherzo and Rondo-Finale, with their polyphonic vigor and almost bewildering range of contrasts. Mahler himself, borrowing vivid poetic images from Jean Paul, wrote about his Scherzo as follows:

"And the public—heavens!—what kind of face will they make when they are confronted with this chaos out of which a world keeps being born, only to fall apart again moments later, at these primeval jungle sounds, this rushing, roaring, raging sea, these dancing stars, these breathtaking, scintillating, flashing waves?"[25]

As we move through the symphony, from the Scherzo to the Adagietto and then the Finale, we can note Mahler's special efforts to integrate this contrasting slow movement. The connection of the Adagietto to the rondo is signaled by the direct transition in sonority between these movements, with the final note A from the Adagietto carried over into the D major of the finale and, most importantly, by the prominent motivic and thematic connections that exist between these last two movements. This brings us to a dimension of the symphony that reaches beyond the context of the Rückert lieder. Mahler's slow movement in the Fifth Symphony raises issues of expressive meaning that require the examination of several related passages in other parts of the symphony.

Solitude and the Collective: The Adagietto and Rondo-Finale

Overarching the relationship between the Adagietto and the Rondo-Finale is a larger network of thematic connections, involving for the most part the first two and last two movements. Rather conspicuously, as we have said, the emphatic D major brass chorale heard near the end of the second movement returns in this key in the finale. An outline of thematic and formal relationships in the symphony is shown in Fig. 4.3 (the reuse of thematic material is indicated by arrows). Especially relevant in this context is the threefold appearance of the upward-striving melodic material from the middle section of the Adagietto in the finale. These lively grazioso passages in the Rondo-Finale are so prominent that they might be regarded less as reminiscences of the Adagietto than as music foreshadowed in the preceding movement. The striking change in character provokes basic questions of interpretation. Is the sublime, reflective, lyric theme from the Adagietto transformed or even parodied here, or is it, rather, liberated from constraints, revealing some more fundamental essence?

Perhaps both interpretative spheres can be entertained at once. Mahler's handling of the music in "Ich bin der Welt abhanden gekommen" casts the sanctuary of the inner self—distanced from the outside world—in a largely positive light. Being "dead to the world" appears here as a kind of achievement, and the preoccupation of the inner subject with love and art— "Lieben" and "Lied"—seems entirely compatible with Mahler's reported use of the related symphonic movement as an offering to Alma Schindler at a formative stage in their relationship. The emphasis on solitude—as represented in the song particularly at the line "Ich leb' allein," as altered by Mahler in the Rückert setting—may have represented a private solici-

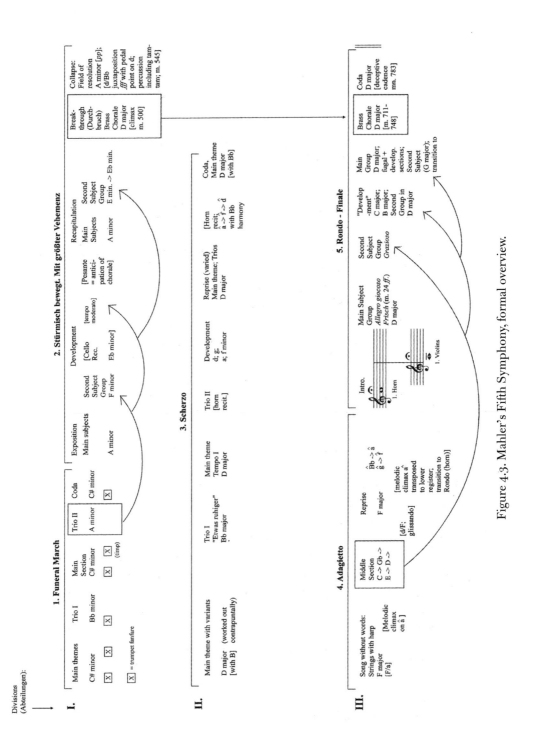

Figure 4.3. Mahler's Fifth Symphony, formal overview.

tation for a response enabling Alma to share paradoxically in this isolation from the outer world. Her response to receiving the Adagietto, according to Mengelberg's inscription on his score, was to urge Mahler to join her: "Er soll kommen!!!" (He should come!!!). This line of interpretation also receives support from Alma Schindler's intense response to Mahler's comparison of their relationship to that of Hans Sachs and Eva Pogner in Wagner's *Die Meistersinger*, a matter to which we shall return and that is richly documented in his letters and her diary entries from early December 1901.

In the biographical context of his engagement to Alma, the Adagietto could offer Mahler what his vocal settings and most of his symphonic movements could not: a song without words of a suggestive nature that encouraged her to join him in—or perhaps even save him from—his resigned, self-willed isolation. A key to the possible narrative significance of the Adagietto in the larger context of the symphony may lie, above all, in its middle section, whose restless modulations and twisting chromatic ascent to the high D at the reprise have no counterpart in "Ich bin der Welt abhanden gekommen."[26] This is precisely the part of the Adagietto that Mahler recalls so prominently in three passages of the rondo finale. The melody appears in the grazioso sections, the last one of which is used as a springboard for the climactic D major chorale.

Sponheuer, following Adorno's characterization of Mahler as a failed "yea-sayer," has described Mahler's secularization of the affirmative brass chorale closing the finale as "the logic of effect rather than the thing itself" and as an "illusion" or "phantasm" (*Phantasmagorie*). Like Adorno, Sponheuer approves of the chorale at its first appearance near the end of the grim and turbulent second movement. Here, the chorale functions as what Adorno liked to describe as a *Durchbruch*, or "breakthrough."[27] This initial manifestation of the triumphant music seems either premature or unreal, and although it marks the first appearance of the central tonality of the symphony as a whole—D major—the passage is anything but integrated into its context. The coda to this movement reasserts A minor and takes on a character of desolation and bitter sarcasm, completely negating the affirmative message of the chorale with its majestic quality and its connotations of the sacred and sublime. This failed teleology is what makes the chorale palatable to Adorno.

As Sponheuer and especially Carolyn Baxendale have shown, the same chorale in the finale assumes a very different and more integrated position in the movement as a whole.[28] Its key of D major has now become the tonic key, and, even more importantly, its motives provide much of the thematic substance for the rondo. In a manner somewhat reminiscent of Wagner's *Die Meistersinger*, where the march theme of the mastersingers is playfully and comically allocated to the apprentices in rhythmically compressed form, Mahler here employs individual motives used in the majestic chorale to serve as basic building blocks for a range of shifting contrapuntal episodes of energetic and sometimes humorous character.

If we weigh the possibility that the final part of the symphony forms an integrated pair of movements, one parallel deserves special attention: the different outcomes reached by the melodic unfolding first heard in the restless central section of the fourth movement. In the Adagietto, this passage eventually reaches the registral stratosphere as the peak of a protracted melodic ascent over a sustained pedal point on A, leading to the melodic goal on high D in the violins in m. 72, as shown in Ex. 4.1. In turn, this melodic arrival becomes the moment of recapitulation, a formal turning point within the movement, representing a retreat from activity in favor of a renewed sinking into a more static form of contemplation. It is as if the more active music of the middle section leads here into a kind of vast deceptive cadence, as the implied tonal goal of D major is replaced by F major at the recapitulation.

The approach and entry into the recapitulation bring a series of rhythmic and motivic augmentations, slowing the pace of the unfolding music, as the direction *zurückhaltend* (holding back) at m. 67 enhances this sense of restricted motion. In a study of motivic relations in the Adagietto, Allen Forte has drawn attention to the ascending-fourth relation that is so prominent in the melodic structure of the movement as an elaborated element in the "middleground" voice leading of the ten-measure passage leading to the recapitulation.[29] The unfolding of this ascent embraces more than his analysis can indicate. Forte marks the ascent as beginning on A in m. 63 and finds that the rising pattern through B and C♯ to D is spread over the following nine measures. The ascent from high A in the first violins begins audibly one measure later, in m. 64, marked *pianissimo* and *espressivo*. The melody of mm. 64–68 outlines a stepwise ascent through the rising fourth from A to D, one, moreover, that is given important support by the second violin line moving in parallel a sixth lower. The second violins reach C♯ at the end of m. 64, and these two parts move upward in sixths during the next two measures. However, in m. 67 the second violins fail to support the rising line, and the undulating eighth notes of the melody lead, at the designation *zurückhaltend*, to a meditative dwelling on the motive of a falling seventh, either as B–C♯, as in mm. 68 and 70, or as B–C, as in m. 69. Hence these measures do guide a motivic augmentation of the rising line to its peak, as Forte's analysis implies, but they also chart a retreat from such goal-directed motion.

Constantin Floros draws an analogy here to the so-called gaze or glance motive in Wagner's *Tristan und Isolde*. Floros relates the falling-seventh interval in the Adagietto to Wagner's work, and he even writes that Mahler "quotes" and "paraphrases it several times."[30] Some scholars, such as Mitchell, have expressed skepticism about Floros's claim, yet the musical affinity deserves consideration, particularly in view of the deep interest in Wagner shared by Mahler and Alma at this time.[31] In the discussion of "Liebst du um Schönheit" in her memoirs, Alma recalled that "I used to play a lot of Wagner" and mentioned that Gustav inserted this song in a Wagner score, expecting her to discover it there. It was the last of

Mahler's individual Rückert songs and the only one written explicitly for her, "the only love song he ever wrote."[32] If we assume, as seems reasonable, a detailed knowledge of *Tristan und Isolde* on the part of both Mahler and Alma, the affinity of the middle section of the Adagietto to this motive does not seem far-fetched. After all, this particular motive gains specific dramatic meaning in Isolde's narrative (act 1, scene 3) when she describes how Tristan's deep gaze into her eyes touched her and caused her to drop the sword with which she had intended to exact vengeance. The musical gesture that embodies this original moment of their love bond involves an upward melodic ascent leading to a prominent falling interval—an octave at her word "Augen" (eyes) and a seventh at the ensuing echo in the violas, marked *sehr ausdrucksvoll u. zart* (very expressively and tenderly).[33] The conspicuous slowing of tempo in this passage, which is marked *sehr zurückhaltend* leading to *langsam* at Isolde's dropping of the sword, contributes to its expressive affinity with the central section of Mahler's Adagietto.

Even if we set aside the matter of a specific allusion to *Tristan und Isolde*, there is no question about the importance in the middle section of the Adagietto of the prominent falling interval adjoined to the characteristic ascending motion. There is a delicate balance here between the predominantly rising linear motion of the passage and the larger falling intervals of sevenths, themselves inversions of the rising second. Yet the most miraculous effect is reserved for the deceptive shift at m. 72, at the beginning of the reprise. The return to F major is sudden; instead of preparing its dominant, Mahler has emphasized the dominant of D, the key indicated by his signature of two sharps, and the attainment of the melodic peak coincides with a juxtaposition of the D minor and F major triads enhanced by a delicious glissando in the violins through two octaves.[34] A prolonged moment of tonal ambiguity and retreat from the goal-directedness of the melodic ascent thus characterizes the onset of the recapitulation. The interval of descent through the glissando is a major ninth plus octave displacement, reaching from the high D of the first violins to the long dominant pedal point on middle C that will be sustained through six measures. The falling gesture itself could be considered a magnified version of the descent akin to Tristan's "gaze"—an astonishing enhancement of those many expressive falling sevenths leading up to the reprise.

In assessing the role of this thematic material in the grazioso sections of the finale, we should first consider the overall form of that movement. Although Mahler identified it as a rondo, this formal label has prompted much debate. For Sponheuer it is questionable, and he regards the movement mainly from the perspective of a sonata-form design.[35] Floros also emphasizes its "sonata traits" and distinguishes an exposition, development, and recapitulation while regarding the passage following the chorale as a coda.[36] Among the difficulties in imposing a sonata-form design on the movement is the appearance, in the so-called development, of the theme drawn from the Adagietto in D major, the tonic key. It seems more convincing to accept Mahler's designation of a rondo while acknowledging the presence of two main complexes of thematic material, one of which is motivically related to the chorale and the other to the middle section of the Adagietto, with the latter assuming an increasingly central role as the movement unfolds. In the episodic and developmental sections of the finale, Mahler explores contrapuntal and fugal procedures in particular.[37] In the grazioso sections of the finale, the violin line from the Adagietto contributes to the forward-driving flow of the rondo, and by stages it becomes a wholehearted player in the kaleidoscopic sound-world of the Allegro finale.[38]

One possible analytical approach to Mahler's treatment of this thematic material in the larger formal context of the finale is what Warren Darcy has termed "rotational form." In his study of the slow movement of Mahler's Sixth Symphony, Darcy regards rotational form as "a cyclical, repetitive process that begins by unfolding a series of differentiated motives or themes as a referential statement or 'first rotation'; subsequent rotations recycle and rework all or most of the referential statement, normally retaining the sequential ordering of the selected musical ideas."[39] Darcy continues: "It sometimes happens that a brief motivic gesture or hint planted in an early rotation grows larger in later rotations and is ultimately unfurled as the telos, or final structural goal, in the last rotation. Thus the successive rotations become a sort of generative matrix within which this telos is engendered, processed, nurtured, and brought to full presence. As a result of this process of 'teleological genesis,' the rotations may be construed—within the aesthetic of the time—as growing successively more 'revelatory.'"[40]

Processes of this kind are indeed at work in the finale of Mahler's Fifth. Two main thematic areas are initially presented as distinctly contrasting, with aspects of their polarity subsequently bridged and overcome through their recurrences. In this instance, however, indispensable elements belonging to this so-called teleological genesis originate already in the chorale vision heard in the second movement and in the Adagietto. If the chorale vision has the character of a miragelike, long-range anticipation, the middle section of the Adagietto takes on an even more essential role in the narrative design of the finale. This theme seems bound up with the subjective quest of the isolated self. Thus it seems fitting and significant that the three appearances of this theme in the finale become progressively more integrated with the sound-world of the final movement.

Mahler takes care to remind the listener of the Adagietto when he first recalls its thematic material in the finale. At the first recall at the upbeat to m. 190, he distinctly replicates the character, register, and orchestration of the beginning of the Adagietto. However, the new tempo lends to the theme an animated, dance-like, even carefree quality. Beginning at the grazioso, the orchestration is limited to strings, marked *zart, aber ausdrucksvoll* (tenderly but expressively), with the pizzicato writing for the low strings reproducing the texture of the double bass part at the outset of the preceding movement. Only sparingly does Mahler introduce bassoons and flutes near the end of the grazioso passage, and only after the *a tempo* marking at m. 233 does he allow phrases drawn from the middle of the Adagietto to be placed in the horns and oboes. When the Adagietto theme returns in the midst of the central developmental region of the movement, it appears at once in polyphonic dialogue with the woodwinds and in the higher register characteristic of its placement in the preceding movement. Its key is now D major, and Mahler replicates some of the same turns of phrase in the first violins on the identical pitches used in the Adagietto. The falling sevenths B–C♯ in mm. 389–90, for instance, recapture the highly expressive *zurückhaltend* passage heard just before the Adagietto's reprise. Mahler dwells on this gesture while blending woodwinds with the strings. The B–C♯ inflection recurs as part of the five-note phrase in mm. 406–7, leading into a serene cadential gesture in D major that closes in m. 415. A soft transitional postlude with descending string chords acts as a codetta to this section, just as it had at the end of the first such passage in the finale based on material from the Adagietto.

At its final appearance, the theme from the Adagietto is more thoroughly worked into the larger orchestra, as phrases are played by the woodwinds and horns, with quirky touches added in the clarinets. In the first measures shown in Ex. 4.2, the characteristic five-note motive from the Adagietto is played fortissimo in the winds, and the sequential phrases that have an intensely subjective, searching quality in the Adagietto (mm. 57 and 67 of Ex. 4.1) are given a jaunty presentation in the horns. By m. 674 the rising melody is placed in a duet with the bassoons and contrabassoon, and in the following measures of Ex. 4.2, preceding rehearsal number 31, the woodwinds assume leadership in completing an astonishing transformation in character: by m. 684 the languid upbeat motive from the Adagietto, with three rising notes leading to an appoggiatura, has become the means to initiate a dynamic, upward-driving dramatic ascent, supported by full orchestral forces, rising from C♯ to C, D♯, and E, then to F and F♯, G, G♯, and A. This linear ascent is then repeated in a higher octave, eventually reaching high A to give emphatic dominant preparation for the ensuing climactic appearance of the brass chorale beginning at the upbeat to m. 711. In this passage, unlike in the second movement, the chorale emerges gradually out of the preceding music. The relation of the chorale to the main body of the finale remains complex and will be considered further in the context of Mahler's compositional and aesthetic models.

The formal unfolding of Mahler's finale shows how an initially contrasting element—the recall of the Adagietto—becomes increasingly integrated and finally indispensable to the symphony's conclusion. By its second appearance, this section affirms D major; in its serene tonic stability, it stands in place of one of the main thematic returns in the rondo design. Already at this juncture, the passage realizes an implication that was left unfulfilled in the Adagietto, when the sound-space of

Ex. 4.2. Mahler, Fifth Symphony, Rondo-Finale, mm. 666–89
(transition to the chorale in D major).

Ex. 4.2. Continued.

Ex. 4.2. Continued.

Ex. 4.2. Continued.

Ex. 4.2. Continued.

Ex. 4.2. Continued.

D major was suddenly left behind at the very moment when the first violins attained their linear goal of high D at the threshold of the recapitulation. By placing the final statement of this theme in the finale in G major, Mahler follows classical precedent in shifting the tonal balance in later stages of a movement toward the subdominant. The alliance of these two themes with tonal associations to D major and origins in earlier movements will cap the finale. Recalling the symbolic backdrop of the Adagietto material, we could propose a reading of these compositional strategies as implying the ultimate insufficiency of solitary withdrawal and the need for reengagement with the collective, a notion that is evidently bound up with the "teleological genesis" or "revelatory" trajectory of the whole.

Means of Integration: Bach, Bruckner, Wagner, and Jean Paul

Mahler himself regarded the Fifth Symphony as marking a new stage in his development, a stage in which polyphony assumed a greater role. Several witnesses attest to his intense interest in the works of J. S. Bach around this time, an interest that is confirmed as well by his acquisition by 1901 of the then recently completed Bachgesellschaft edition in forty-six volumes.[41] According to Bauer-Lechner, Mahler stated in 1898 that "in its highest form, as in its lowest, music reverts to homophony. The master of polyphony, and of polyphony alone, is Bach. The founder and creator of modern polyphony is Beethoven. Haydn and Mozart are not yet polyphonic. Wagner is really polyphonic only in *Tristan* and *Die Meistersinger*."[42] In this connection, Hans Redlich has written that Mahler's "growing predilection for strict polyphony had something to do with his tendency to avoid the excessive chromaticism and over-seasoned harmony of the late romantics," and he observed that "fugal writing crops up for the first time in his work in the finale of Symphony V," with a "great variety of texture" provided by "the more polyphonic manner of the middle symphonies."[43]

A synthesis of Bach and Wagner is especially relevant to the polyphonic style of the Fifth, the finale in particular. Another work that deserves consideration in this context is Anton Bruckner's Fifth Symphony in B♭ Major, from 1876, a piece that Mahler conducted in February 1901, albeit in a version containing substantial cuts.[44] The finale of Bruckner's Fifth combines fugue with aspects of chorale while recalling earlier movements in the service of the teleological trajectory of the whole. Despite these parallels, the character of Mahler's work seems closer to Wagner than to Bruckner. We should recall Mahler's intense preoccupation with Wagner's *Die Meistersinger* during the years immediately preceding his composition of the symphony. During late 1899 he was obsessed with *Die Meistersinger* as he prepared the first run of uncut performances of that work ever given in Vienna. The first performance took place on 26 November, and Mahler commented to

Bauer-Lechner with relief that "my fear that I might weary of this work after hearing it too often has fortunately proven groundless." He continued enthusiastically that "if the whole of German art were to disappear, it could be recognized and reconstructed from this one work. It almost makes everything else seem worthless and superfluous."[45]

A comparison of Mahler's Fifth Symphony with *Die Meistersinger* is revealing. Wagner employs two different chorales at conspicuous moments in the drama. As the curtain goes up in act 1, we witness the congregation singing in Saint Katherine's Church in Nuremberg, and Wagner foreshadows the opening phrase of their chorale at the end of his overture, even devising a parallel melodic contour that links the chorale to the mastersingers' theme first heard at the beginning of the overture. More impressive still is the "Wach auf!" chorale sung by the assembled citizens of Nuremberg to honor Hans Sachs in the closing scene of act 3. In its dramatic context, this chorale represents an overwhelming public acknowledgment of Sachs. In his more private sphere, the cobbler-poet experiences conflicts and sorrows that are made abundantly clear elsewhere in the work, particularly in his "Wahn" monologue, in which he muses over the folly and delusion in human existence.

Mahler's own heightened awareness of the conflicted state of Sachs's soul is reflected in documents from the crucial period of his courtship of Alma Schindler in late 1901. "Remember our beloved Evchen and Hans Sachs!" he wrote pointedly to her at the close of his letter of 5 December.[46] The reason for heeding Sachs's cautionary lesson was the disparity in their ages; Mahler was almost twice as old as Alma. In this situation, art and real life became uncomfortably close. In act 2 of *Die Meistersinger*, in reply to Evchen's leading question, "Could a widower not succeed?" Sachs tells her: "My child, he would be too old for you." And in act 3, to the quotation of the *Tristan* music, Sachs says, "My child, I know a sad story about Tristan and Isolde. Hans Sachs was smart and wished to avoid King Marke's fate." Mahler's pointed allusion to Hans Sachs and Evchen triggered an intense response in Alma. After reading his letter, Alma confessed to her diary that "I keep thinking of him more and more," continuing:

> His dear, dear smile, I've actually kissed this man, and what is more, he's kissed me. I'm beginning to think that I really do love him. . . . I really do want him [Mahler] now. I think about him all the time—His dear, dear eyes. . . . If only I see Mahler before he leaves! . . . Evening, this letter—I could cry! I have the feeling that I've lost him—and I was already thinking he was mine—a marvellous stroke of luck! I feel utterly miserable. I must see him—before he leaves—I've got to see him. He doesn't want me, he's abandoning me—that last sentence, that terrible last sentence! I realize now how much I love him—I suddenly feel so empty. I must go to him tomorrow. My longing knows no bounds. Evchen and Hans Sachs—an empty subterfuge—it's just not possible![47]

CHAPTER 4

Just two days later the two were secretly engaged, as Mahler's Sachsian resignation collapsed in favor of passionate commitment. On 23 December they were officially engaged; the marriage took place on 9 March. The genesis of the Fifth Symphony framed their entire courtship, and it was during the summer of 1902 that the draft score of the symphony was completed.

The paired Adagietto and finale of the symphony correspond to the double perspective of Hans Sachs in *Die Meistersinger*, with its division into private and public spheres. Like the last act of the opera, the third part of Mahler's symphony begins in a contemplative mood of subjective isolation. "Ich bin der Welt abhanden gekommen" could well apply to Sachs in his melancholy detachment, sorely tempted as he is by "Wahn" in the form of the opportunity to sing for Eva's hand in the song contest on Saint John's Day.[48] Yet the public side of the opera, relating to Sachs's status as a mastersinger and his key role within the Nuremberg community, also finds a prominent place. Here humor is crucial in differentiating the musical material to reflect the diversity of a social community. Just as Wagner's pompous march theme for the mastersingers is sped up to represent the skirmishing apprentices, the violin theme from the Adagietto is accelerated "like a musical quick-motion picture," in Adorno's words, as it begins to be taken up by the multiplicity of other orchestral voices that inhabit the symphony.

Mahler was closely familiar with two outstanding comic operas that use fugal technique to depict dramatic unfoldings and a variegated social fabric. Giuseppe Verdi's unique closing fugue on "Tutte nel mondo è burla" (All the world's a joke) in *Falstaff* forms a masterful culmination in which all of the principal characters participate and are rendered more or less equal. Mahler admired *Falstaff* and conducted it at Hamburg in 1894 before leading the first performances at the Vienna Opera a decade later. The other fugal example is found once more in *Die Meistersinger*, in the "Polterabend" scene closing act 2, following Sachs's "Cobbler's Song" and Beckmesser's serenade. This fugue shows "Wahn" at work, as imitations of Beckmesser's ill-fated wooing song mirror the disturbance spreading throughout the community. The logical framework of imitative polyphony paradoxically depicts social chaos, as the outwardly ordered Nuremberg society runs amok.

Adorno's description of the symphony's finale as "a tableau, a scene of motley bustle" captures its colorful diversity while not acknowledging its polyphonic ambition, spiked as it is by elaborate contrapuntal combinations that remind us of Mahler's study of Bach. The movement's introduction harbors yet another allusion—to a singing contest of a very special kind. Following the transitional echoes on A carried over from the end of the Adagietto and a brief "summons to the 'real world'" issued by the horn, four successive and striking phrases in the solo bassoon, oboe, and horn present much of the thematic material on which the movement will be based.[49] These are the phrases that contain the motivic components not only for many episodes and fugal adventures of the finale but also for the climactic brass chorale in D major. The humorous dimension of the passage is confirmed through Mahler's ironic self-quotation of his *Wunderhorn* song "Lob des hohen Verstandes" (In praise of lofty intellect), which is cited in the first phrase in the bassoon. In this song, a donkey serves as judge for a competition between a nightingale and a cuckoo, and he chooses—of course—the cuckoo. A parallel to Beckmesser's role in *Die Meistersinger* may be fortuitous, but Mahler's allusion to the song as a swipe at his critics is likely, given its original title, "Lob der Kritik" (In praise of critics). Mitchell regards this reminiscence as "a sardonic reference in the context of a highly sophisticated and artfully contrapuntal Finale to a song which was aimed at those with long ears, and of lofty intellectual equipment, who prefer the cuckoo's song to the nightingale's." Mitchell continues: "Mahler was not free from sensitivity about his contrapuntal technique . . . and I fancy there was something of a deliberate gesture of defiance in his recollection of the *Wunderhorn* song in the Finale of the Fifth, as if he were daring the donkeys to fault his contrapuntal art—and half expecting them to do just that, at the same time."[50]

What is the point of this sharply contrasted treatment of the thematic material, which is dissected into scraps played by the bassoon and built up into an impressive, majestic chorale for the full orchestra? Insight into the guiding aesthetic attitude behind such compositional strategies may lie in Mahler's lifelong enthusiasm for imaginative writers such as E. T. A. Hoffmann, Laurence Sterne, and especially Jean Paul, the author of several novels and the voluminous aesthetic treatise of 1804, the *Vorschule der Ästhetik* (Introduction to aesthetics).[51] It is in the context of Mahler's love of Jean Paul's works that Bruno Walter reported the composer as often saying that "without the purification of life through humor he could not have borne the tragedy of human existence."[52] Relevant in this connection is Jean Paul's idea of "die vernichtende oder unendliche Idee des Humors" (the annihilating or infinite idea of humor).[53] Jean Paul refers specifically to the music of Haydn as embodying the boldness of "annihilating humor," whereby, as he puts it, "ganze Tonreihen durch eine fremde vernichtet und zwischen Pianissimo und Fortissimo, Presto und Andante wechselnd stürmt" (whole configurations of notes can be negated through opposing gestures that storm through the music as a contrast between pianissimo and fortissimo, presto and andante).[54] Here, as elsewhere, Jean Paul draws attention to the aesthetic importance of heightened contrasts embodying polar opposites. For Jean Paul, humor is "das umgekehrte Erhabene" (the inverted sublime). Another of his sly definitions of humor is that of a kind of divorce merchant, a "person disguised as a priest who marries the most unfitting of partners."[55] Therein lies his central argument related to the sublime and the humble, the great and the small, whereby each perspective is a critique of the other. What is annihilated is the appearance of complacent self-sufficiency of either perspective.

In this context, let us return to the disputed brass chorale and to Adorno's characterization of Mahler as a "poor yea-sayer." For all its outward impressiveness, this affirmative gesture is also surely critiqued within the work itself. On the one hand, hints of parody in the preceding music drawn from the Adagietto introduce a sense of ironic distance. The gestures of the woodwinds in mm. 641–42 are somewhat uncouth but are nonetheless juxtaposed with a pianissimo continuation of the melody in the first violins. In the ensuing transition to the chorale, as the horns take up the Adagietto's phrases in mm. 670–72, there is a reduction of nuance and coarsening of expression or "dirtying lyricism" that is ultimately bound up with the collective utterance manifested in the chorale.[56] It is also noteworthy that Mahler does not allow the chorale to have the last word. The breathless, accelerating coda that begins in m. 749 contains not just jubilation but overt comic touches, as when the orchestra lands on a powerful deceptive cadence with a jolt on B♭ in m. 783, recalling similar gestures earlier in the movement. Last but not least is the final cadence itself, as the horns and trumpets blare out the stepwise falling fourth D–A: this is none other than an emphatic version of the motive first played by the bassoon in the introduction—the motive coyly derived from the praise of the donkey's wisdom in "Lob des hohen Verstandes"—which now drops a fifth into the closing tonic unison.

While Adorno's critique accurately targets a quality of overextension in the chorale, it underestimates Mahler's resourceful integration of musical resources. Even if, as Leon Botstein has recently claimed, "Mahler's discontinuities . . . underscore the function of the listener as creator of coherence," many aspects of this music encourage us to explore the implied meanings of "integration into a complex, multilayered whole."[57] Important here is Mahler's linking of the contrasting sections of the finale through their elemental motivic content; these shared motives and phrases actually sound early in the movement as part of the "motley bustle." Before we first hear the recall of the Adagietto in the grazioso sections, we have already heard formative aspects of this music. In the robust "Sempre l'istesso tempo" and "Nicht eilen" sections (mm. 167–86), he already highlights the motive of the stepwise rising fourth and then the characteristic sequential figure from the Adagietto in the woodwinds. We first hear an emphatic, accented falling fourth, followed by the motives using the stepwise rising fourth with vigorous detached articulation, before these very same phrases are heard in the gentle string presentation in the B major grazioso passage.

On the largest level of the symphonic design, Mahler employs analogous anticipatory strategies that embrace even the most astonishing contrasts and discontinuities. In the second movement, the chorale is anticipated at the end of the development section in the passage that carries the same expressive direction, *pesante* (mm. 316–22). This potentially uplifting shift into the sphere of the triumphant major mode is brutally negated in the *Tempo I subito* beginning in m. 323, leading into the imminent recapitulation. Hence what Mahler prepares in this passage is not the "chorale vision" in isolation but the larger narrative pattern, including the negativity that will culminate in the grim coda of the movement, with its taking back of the promise of the utopian vision of the chorale.

Large-scale foreshadowing of the chorale is more extensive in the finale. This includes a massive preparation in the heart of the movement that grows out of the D major presentation of the Adagietto theme, with passages of transparent three-part counterpoint joining contrasting subjects. The expressive falling gesture from the Adagietto, heard as a slurred C–D in the violins in mm. 461–62, is rendered in free inversion as the insistent rising motive A–F in m. 471 and A–F♯ in m. 473; the crescendo beginning in m. 475 then reinforces the chromatic expansion of these two-note figures until the octave A is reached in m. 479, while an immense pedal point builds in the lower instruments. The triple fortissimo passage over the dominant pedal point beginning in m. 483 corresponds to the arrival of the chorale in the tonic D major in m. 711, which is reached through an identical process of intervallic inversion and expansion. This preparatory passage for the chorale is shown in Ex. 4.3, in which the rising two-note figures are played fortissimo in the violins in mm. 693 and 695; when the progression continues pianissimo beginning in m. 697, this ascending sixth is heard in counterpoint with a falling tenth in the lower instruments. A few moments later, the gateway to the chorale is opened at last. Thus, despite the presence of touches of parody, this grand passage remains connected to the symphony in far-reaching ways. Perhaps the most suggestive of all these relations is bound up with the contrapuntal nature of the finale: the inversion and transformation of the Adagietto's expressive falling figure such that this energetic motive unlocks the chorale as a culminating affirmative gesture, one that now will not be negated, as it was in the second movement. In this context, the second chorale, not the first, is the definitive *Durchbruch* (breakthrough), triggered as it is by forces absent in the earlier part of the symphony.[58]

On the evidence of the Fifth Symphony, we need not accept as final Adorno's views that Mahler's "special tone" is "brokenness" or that the Adagietto verges on "shallow sentimentality."[59] The powerful contrasts and contradictory tendencies of this music are forged on many levels into a compelling integrated design.[60] In the end, the triumphant aura of the chorale seems less important than the transformation of musical material from the fourth to the final movement. At the recapitulation within the Adagietto, the striving energy of the arching melody turns inward as the reflective, passive beauty of harmonic diffusion and static contemplation assume primacy. This detachment from action is associated with artistic sublimation. Mahler reenacts here in unforgettable fashion that sinking into solitary meditation that was already historically foreshadowed in works such as the slow movement of Beethoven's Ninth Symphony and Sachs's melancholy introspection at the beginning of act 3 of *Die Meistersinger*.[61] True to those works but quite unlike the

Ex. 4.3. Mahler, Fifth Symphony, Rondo-Finale, mm. 690–98
(transition to the chorale).

Ex. 4.3. Continued.

Aschenbach of Mann and Visconti, Mahler refuses to remain within a hermetically insulated sphere. Instead, the finale of the Fifth confronts the world in a direct, playful, and aesthetically tangible sense, implying the ultimate insufficiency of solitary withdrawal and the indispensable need for a vigorous, if sometimes ironic, engagement with collective experience. These two perspectives are interlocked in the Fifth Symphony, with the Adagietto and Rondo-Finale interacting and enriching one another in a dialectical relationship, one that must have assumed special personal significance for Mahler beginning in 1901.

5

Folklore Transformed in
Bartók's *Dance Suite*

In his book *The World of Yesterday*, Stefan Zweig looked back at the land of his youth and early manhood, the Austro-Hungarian monarchy of the pre–World War I era, as a "world of security" in which "everything had its form, its appropriate measure and weight." Zweig observed further how

> In this vast realm, everything stood fixed and unmovable and in the highest posi-
> tion stood the aged Emperor; but should he die, one knew (or one expected) that
> another would come and that nothing would change in the well-designed frame-
> work. No one believed in wars, revolutions, or upheavals. Everything radical and
> violent seemed obsolete in an age of reason.
>
> This feeling of security was the cherished safeguard of millions, a common ideal
> of life. . . . Only he who could look without concern to the future enjoyed the pres-
> ent with wholehearted feeling. . . . With disdain one regarded earlier epochs, with
> their wars, famine, and revolts, as a time in which humanity was not yet mature
> and had not yet been sufficiently enlightened.[1]

With the historical distance of a century, we can recognize the multinational, poly-
glot Austro-Hungarian monarchy of that period as a precursor of the European
Union of today. Not just the security but something of the rich cultural interchange
of the region has since been restored, despite the irreparable, almost inconceivable
destruction wreaked through Hitler's dictatorship, when Austria was absorbed into
Germany while Hungary became allied to the Third Reich. For many decades,
from the aftermath of World War I until the collapse of the Iron Curtain in 1989

and beyond, the eastern parts of the former Habsburg monarchy have undergone tumultuous changes.

Stefan Zweig and Béla Bartók were exact contemporaries. Both were born in Austria-Hungary in 1881, and both died in exile from Fascist Germany and war-torn Europe: Zweig by his own hand in Brazil in 1942; Bartók of leukemia in New York City in 1945.[2] Other parallels extend into the musical sphere. Zweig was a prominent writer and occasional librettist whose operatic collaboration with Richard Strauss on *Die schweigsame Frau* (The silent woman) helped trigger his departure from Germany and whose outstanding collection of music manuscripts is now held in the British Museum. The composer Bartók did a different kind of collecting, gathering innumerable folk melodies from rural communities in Hungary, Romania, Slovakia, Moldavia, Wallachia, Bulgaria, and as far away as Algeria. He continued this research activity during the last years of his life in New York, working on a collection of Serbian and Croatian folk songs held at Columbia University. Through his fieldwork, Bartók was a pioneer ethnomusicologist, but fruits of this preoccupation were also absorbed into his creative work as composer.

The present chapter focuses on Bartók's *Dance Suite* from 1923, a sometimes underestimated piece that displays a provocative relation to the political circumstances of its composition. The work's unpretentious title has contributed to misunderstanding. In May 1925, after hearing the *Dance Suite* at the Prague Festival of the International Society for Modern Music, Theodor W. Adorno wrote about it as follows:

> The piece is called a suite not from modesty or coquetry; it is not at all a symphony and not inclined to appear as such in any of its parts. It owes its existence to particular circumstances and was composed for a concert commemorating the fiftieth anniversary of the unification of Ofen and Pest and is in this sense as well an occasional work. . . . A few transparent, recognizable character dances follow one another loosely; the ritornelli which connect them fill blank spaces rather than serve to organize the whole; and the finale, which makes reference thematically to the first movement, brings the familiar material together in a harmless way without striving for synthesis and without attempting very much in the way of contrapuntal combinations.[3]

Adorno acknowledges the work's "occasional" origins in commemoration of the fiftieth anniversary of the unification of Budapest as a single city, but he fails to consider the cultural circumstances of 1923 or the associations of the "recognizable character dances" linked by ritornelli.[4] Unlike Adorno, we have the benefit of hindsight and of the composer's own comments on his artistic goals and challenges as contained in letters and essays from later years. These sources as well as analysis of the work and its genesis support a different view, as we shall see, whereby the *Dance Suite* appears as an ambitious and original work, embodying what Bartók himself once described as an "Integritäts-Idee" (idea of integrity), a term alluding at once to a quality of unbroken wholeness and to a state of uprightness or unimpaired soundness.

The *Dance Suite* shows a political attitude different from what had earlier been characteristic of Bartók. Twenty years before, at the time he had composed his symphonic poem *Kossuth* in honor of Lajos Kossuth, the hero of the failed Hungarian revolution of 1848–49, Bartók displayed his nationalist passion through his traditional dress and patriotic emphasis on the Hungarian language. His parody of the Austrian national anthem in *Kossuth* provoked resistance to the work from Austrians while contributing to its success in Hungary. This phase in Bartók's artistic development preceded his intensive studies of folk music and the destructive events associated with the First World War and its aftermath. In the wake of the defeat of the Central Powers and the collapse of the Austro-Hungarian monarchy in 1918, a highly unstable period ensued. In October the first republic was declared, but in view of the chaotic situation and the need to severely compromise the territorial integrity of the country, the president of this first republic, Count Mihály Károlyi, yielded up power in March 1919 to the short-lived Communist regime, the Hungarian Soviet Republic under Béla Kun, which ruled only until summer. The Soviet Republic was swept away in August 1919 by the counterrevolution led by Miklós Horthy, whereby many violent actions against Socialists, Communists, and Jews ensued during the "White Terror" in 1919–20. According to the terms of the Treaty of Trianon in 1920, Hungary lost two-thirds of its prewar territory and one-third of its Magyar population. Many areas where Bartók had studied Hungarian folk music no longer remained in Hungary.[5]

Bartók was dismayed by the nationalistic conflicts besetting the new states carved out of the former Austro-Hungarian monarchy, a circumstance that largely put an end to his travels to gather folk songs. Furthermore, because he (along with Ernst von Dohnányi and Zoltán Kodály) had held cultural positions during the time of the revolution, he was badly positioned at the time of the counterrevolution. All these factors caused Bartók to consider leaving the country. He wrote about the situation in the early 1920s in a private document in which he stressed the lack of nationalistic fervor among the rural people of different languages and traditions: "And the poor people, the actual residents and workers in the contentious pieces of land? They wait with resignation, one could indeed say with indifference, for the end of conflict and the new beginning of a peaceful life such as has been missing for such a long time. For truly, the main body of the population, the rural people of different nationalities, lived during the time of Magyar hegemony in great harmony. Not a spark of chauvinistic hate could be felt among them."[6]

How, then, did Bartók regard his own role as a composer of art music who was deeply interested in rural music of diverse regions? For all his fascination with folk music, Bartók resisted identifying his own artistic work with those regional traditions that he valued. When in 1931 the Romanian author Octavian Beu described

Bartók in the draft of a lecture as a "compositorul român" (Romanian composer), Bartók wrote back urgently from Berlin, asking Beu to revise his draft:

> My position is as follows: I consider myself a Hungarian composer. On the basis of those original works, in which I employ melodies of my own, which are modeled or influenced by Romanian native music ("Volksmusik"), I can be as little characterized as a "compositorul român" as Brahms, Schubert and Debussy could be described as Hungarian or Spanish composers on the basis of original works in which they used material modeled on Hungarian or Spanish sources.... If your interpretation were correct, I would be justified just as well in being a "Slovakian composer"; I would be therefore a composer of threefold nationality![7]

Similarly, in an essay entitled "Racial Purity in Music" written in New York in 1942, Bartók opposes the kinds of ideas promoted by blinded ideologues such as Alfred Lorenz while looking back on his vast experience in exploring traditions of peasant music in diverse regions of the old Austrian monarchy and beyond.[8] For Bartók, the erection of artificial borders sealing off one people from another was damaging to such traditions, whereas contact with the unfamiliar stimulated a productive exchange of melodies and the development of new styles, enhancing individuality while also inhibiting any loss of character through incursion of a colorless international style.[9] As an example of the fruitful effects of cultural interpenetration and productive racial impurity, Bartók cited especially the folk music of Hungary, Romania, and Slovakia, which he knew so intimately.

Bartók's convictions about the challenge of successfully integrating folk music into new artistic compositions are most succinctly expressed in another letter from 1931, in which he claims that "folk music can only be a source of inspiration for the music of a country if the transplantation of its motivic material is the work of creative ingenuity."[10] This brings us to the unexpected opportunity that arose for Bartók in 1923 during a particularly difficult period of hyperinflation, political instability, and Fascist agitation. The composer himself alluded to the complexity of the situation in a letter to his publisher from April: "In addition, one new work each by Dohnányi and Kodály will be performed at the aforementioned festival concerts. The spicy thing about this business is that the now ultra–Christian National city government chose those same three Hungarian composers who formed the Music Cabinet during the Bolshevist regime."[11] The *Dance Suite* was Bartók's first commissioned work, commemorating fifty years of the unification of Buda and Pest. Yet Bartók's scope and ambition went beyond the purpose of this commission. His work targets the problem of how it was possible "to create coherent artwork in a world that [was] no longer whole," to borrow a formulation of Judit Frigyesi.[12] He seized this chance to raise a monument not just to the two joined cities but above all to the larger ideal of an undivided cultural context that he treasured but that no longer existed in reality.

The Genesis of the *Dance Suite* and
The Miraculous Mandarin

The major project whose genesis straddled that of the *Dance Suite* was *The Miraculous Mandarin*, a controversial one-act pantomime ballet to a text by Melchior Lengyel. Premiered in Cologne in 1926, *The Miraculous Mandarin* caused a scandal on account of its provocative sexual content; during Bartók's lifetime, the work was performed mainly as a concert suite, preserving about two-thirds of the music of the ballet. Bartók had made sketches for the *Mandarin* by 1917 and prepared an early version of the whole by July 1919.[13] He did not begin writing out the full score of the *Mandarin* until the spring of 1924, the year following the composition of the *Dance Suite*, which occupied Bartók between April and August 1923. Yet Bartók had completed a four-hand reduction of the *Mandarin* already by the spring of 1921, and he used this version while planning the orchestration. A sheet belonging with this draft and mainly filled with work on the *Mandarin* with notes for its orchestration also contains a pencil sketch (four staves from the bottom of the page) for the ritornello theme of the *Dance Suite* and ending with a rising octave on D (Fig. 5.1; transcription in Ex. 5.1).[14] The violin melody of the ritornello theme in the work as we know it begins with a sustained high G and falls through an octave, concluding on the lower G (Ex. 5.2).

The melodic similarity between this sketch and the ritornello theme in the finished work is too close to be accidental. Conspicuous parallels are the ascending fourth from G to C at the upbeat to m. 2 followed by slurred two-note figures as well as the turn figure on F, which drops a fourth to C in the penultimate measure. The lyrical violin theme of this ritornello suggests *verbunkos*, a type of characteristic Hungarian instrumental dance music with a long history. The name is derived from the German verb *werben*, which means, in particular, "to enlist in the army"; *verbunkos* was the characteristic accompaniment of a recruiting ceremony, such as is depicted in Fig. 5.2. In earlier times, when such melodies were played to help entice young men to join the service, the musicians were often gypsies. Features suggestive of that style here include not only the broad range of the violin melody but gestures such as the cadence pattern with a rapid turn figure dropping a fourth, as is present in both the sketch and the finished work (m. 131), suggesting perhaps a clicking of heels. The short-long rhythmic pattern at the end of the theme is also a trademark of *verbunkos* style.

The sketch contains some striking harmonic inflections that Bartók did not retain in the finished melody. The F major orientation of the melody is contradicted by the quarter note A♭ in m. 2. Subsequently, the upbeat to the following measure reestablishes the A before the melody then descends through an E major triad, with the second pitch now spelled as G♯. The ensuing turn figure on the F sounds

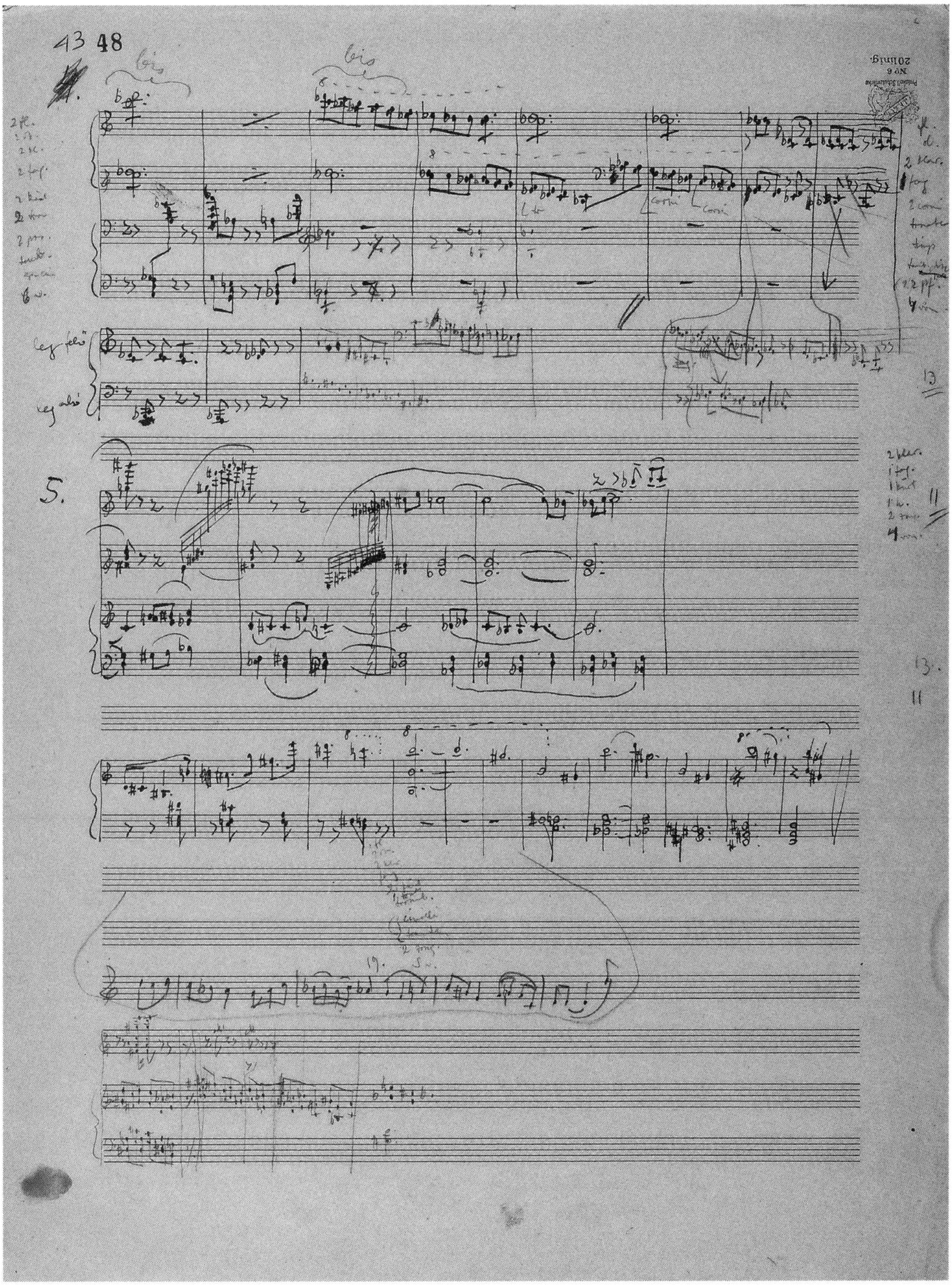

Figure 5.1. Draft for *The Miraculous Mandarin* containing the sketch for the ritornello of the *Dance Suite*, Sacher Foundation, Basel. Printed with permission.

Ex. 5.1. Transcription of the ritornello sketch.

Ex. 5.2. Ritornello in the finished work.

Figure 5.2. Military recruitment ceremony with
music in nineteenth-century Hungary.

G, preceding the final drop of a fourth and a rising octave that close the tune. This
version of the theme is full of such semitone conflicts.

The finished ritornello melody, on the other hand, adheres much more consistently to the opening rising interval of the fourth, first heard as F–B♭, while the
meter is shifted to $\frac{2}{4}$ in place of the $\frac{4}{4}$ of the sketch. It is revealing to compare this
later version of the melody to one of the Eight Hungarian Folksongs for high voice
and piano that Bartók collected in July 1907, more than fifteen years earlier. This

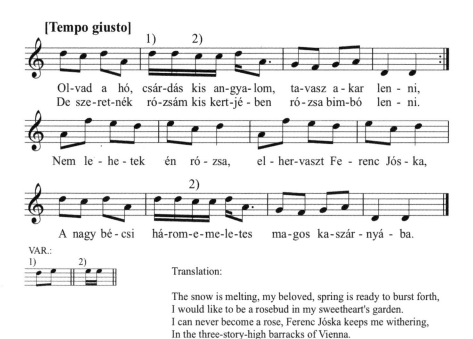

[Tempo giusto]

1) 2)

Ol-vad a hó, csár-dás kis an-gya-lom, ta-vasz a-kar len - ni,
De sze-ret-nék ró-zsám kis kert-jé-ben ró-zsa bim-bó len - ni.

Nem le - he-tek én ró-zsa, el - her-vaszt Fe - renc Jós-ka,

2)

A nagy bé-csi há-rom-e-me-le-tes ma-gos ka-szár-nyá - ba.

VAR.:
1) 2)

Translation:

The snow is melting, my beloved, spring is ready to burst forth,
I would like to be a rosebud in my sweetheart's garden.
I can never become a rose, Ferenc Jóska keeps me withering,
In the three-story-high barracks of Vienna.

Ex. 5.3. Hungarian soldier's song (from Vera Lampert, *Folk Music in
Bartók's Compositions: A Source Catalog*, 135–36).

is a Hungarian soldier's song whose text refers to the Austrian emperor, Franz Joseph, playfully in the diminutive as "Ferenc Jóska." The entire setting is recorded
in Bartók's field book as shown in Ex. 5.3.[15]

Like Bartók's sketch for the ritornello melody, this song spans the octave from
D to D and particularly emphasizes the falling fourth D–A. The first three notes,
furthermore, are D–C–D, as in the ritornello sketch. In other respects, however, this
song of a soldier's yearning for his beloved bears more similarity to the completed
ritornello melody of the *Dance Suite*. The meter is $\frac{2}{4}$, as in the completed ritornello,
and the interval of the fourth assumes more prominence. The first four measures
are based exclusively on the turn figure joined to a falling interval: first the fourth,
D–A, then the fifth, A–D. The second measure is an ornamented version of the
first measure, whereby the syncopated inflection emphasizes the falling fourth.
The form of the whole melody embraces sixteen measures in an A–A–B–A pattern,
whereby the initial four-measure phrase is initially repeated and then recurs after
the third phrase with its allusion to Franz Joseph. With its lowered sevenths, the
melody has a Dorian flavor, whereas the sixth scale step is not used.

Against this stylistic background, we can appreciate how sensitively Bartók has
shaped his ritornello theme, distancing it from its allusive models while enhancing
its expressive quality. Motivically, the theme is unified through its resourceful use

of the interval of the fourth. At its first appearance following the opening dance, the ritornello begins with a long sustained high G, and the music slows even further before falling to F and rising upward through a fourth to the B♭ at the outset of the Allegretto (m. 125). Several of the following measures are based on rhythmic diminution of the initial rising fourth, with the figure first heard as a quarter and two eighths now heard as an eighth and two sixteenths. The second, fourth, and sixth measures of the Allegro follow that pattern, sounding C–F, whereas in the fifth measure the motive of the rising fourth is shifted up a step, outlining D–G. At the same time, an overall pattern of three descending fourths spanning a tenth—from the high B♭ to F in m. 1, to C in m. 2, and from C to G in m. 7 of the Allegretto—provides a guiding framework for the melody. After the melodic statement up to m. 7 of the Allegretto, the entire phrase is repeated with varied orchestration, and Bartók then closes this first ritornello with a meditative six-measure Più lento coda.

The *Dance Suite* contains five dances followed by a finale that recalls and juxtaposes the themes heard in earlier sections. Within the overall formal design, the ritornello assumes a role somewhat comparable to the ritornello in Modest Mussorgsky's piano piece *Pictures at an Exhibition*. Bartók has inverted the function of the device, however, inasmuch as Mussorgsky's ritornello conveys the active movement of the observer from picture to picture. In Bartók's work, by contrast, most of the individual dances are highly dynamic, whereas the ritornello is infused with an atmosphere of dreamlike reflection and reminiscence. Bartók omits the ritornello prior to the slow Arabic dance (no. 4), surely because the expressive character of the ritornello would here have diminished the impact of the following Molto tranquillo.[16] That the fifth dance proceeds without a break into the finale makes sense, since the ritornello is also recalled within this closing section, whose recapitulatory character lends a sense of formal integration to the whole.

Bartók's *Dance Suite* displays intriguing parallels to *The Miraculous Mandarin*, despite the highly contrasting character of the two works. Whereas the *Dance Suite* tends to idealize the cultures of rural life, the *Mandarin* begins with a frightening depiction of depraved urban life, as a trio of hoodlums exploit a young woman for financial gain, using her to lure victims to be robbed. The action turns on the third victim, the uncanny, lonely figure of the rich Chinese, whose strength seems to emerge from another sphere of being and whose love awakens the suppressed humanity of the girl before he succumbs at last to the brutality of the hoodlums.[17] Musically, connections to the *Mandarin* exist in the first two dances of the *Suite*. As György Kroó has observed, the opening bassoon theme of the first dance gradually develops into a lively trumpeting "mandarin" character before returning to the quiet atmosphere of the beginning, whereas the powerful second dance invites comparison with the chase scene in the middle of the pantomime, when the mandarin pursues the girl.[18] As we have seen, Bartók was orchestrating the *Mandarin* in the same period he was composing the *Dance Suite*. His goal in composing the latter work was not merely to group together a series of folkloric dances but to seek new artistic solutions through a resourceful "transplantation of motivic material," as he put it in 1931.

The links connecting the *Dance Suite* to the expressionistic idiom of the *Mandarin* lend surprising dramatic weight to the opening dances. Like Stravinsky's *Rite of Spring* ballet from a decade earlier, Bartók's *Dance Suite* begins with a bassoon theme, a subject played here by a pair of bassoons. Bartók drew attention to an Arabic character in this opening Moderato, a character that is conveyed in part through the narrow range of the melody.[19] The rhythmic shaping of the theme displays a general kinship to the type of Transylvanian-Hungarian folk songs known as *kanásztánc* (swineherd) melodies, in which a succession of even impulses can lead to a pair of longer notes; that pattern is reflected here in the twelve eighth notes in mm. 2–4 leading to the two As articulating each beat in m. 5. The theme displays a quality of deceptive simplicity. Each of its first seven measures begins on A, whereupon the line drops emphatically to a sustained G played *forte*, with motives in multiple voices played *forte* and *martellato* in the strings and piano (Ex. 5.4). Bartók's nuanced slurring in the bassoon theme prevents monotony, bringing out different intervals in different rhythmic positions. In m. 2 the third note, A♭, is slurred to C♭; in m. 3 the slur is shifted back to B♭–A♭; in m. 4 the slur falls on A–B♭. Bartók moves the successive slurs closer together, producing an effect of intensification. Benjamin Suchoff describes this arrangement of slurs as "an ingenious adaptation of Romanian 'shifted' rhythm," resulting in an emphatic rendition of these changing intervals.[20] The opening subject of the *Dance Suite* involves a resourceful transformation and synthesis of elements drawn from diverse sources.

Starting in m. 15, the opening theme is repeated in varied form, with the bassoons now playing in octaves, while the answering martellato phrases lead into new, more developmental continuations. More tranquil passages alternate with more energetic ones, until the climax of the movement is reached in the Vivo section, with the reinforcement of the horns and trumpets. In this passage, the sense of a restricted range or style is overcome, and an affinity to the agitated sound-world of the *Mandarin* can be felt. The culminating fortissimo sonority in m. 101 contains a prominent A doubled in several octaves, supported by adjacent pitches, including G♯ and B. Regarded enharmonically, these tones are equivalent to A♭ and C♭, which belong to the four-note cell that dominates the opening bassoon melody (Ex. 5.5). Bartók's dramatic development of his material, which goes far beyond any folkloric style, concentrates the bundle of pitches unfolded horizontally in the bassoons at the outset.[21] The Vivo passage brings a dramatic transformation, which is nevertheless closely linked to the original Arabic dance. In the ensuing closing passage of this Moderato movement, the tranquil opening theme is recapitulated, yet it undergoes a striking change in timbre, beginning pianissimo in the tuba, with imitative entries in the trombones leading back to the bassoon.

Ex. 5.4. Bartók, *Dance Suite*, opening theme of the first movement. *Dance Suite*, SZ77, by Bela Bartók. © Copyright 1924 Boosey & Hawkes, Inc. for the USA. Copyright Renewed. Reprinted by permission.

The last note of the bassoon is an accented, protracted G, initially reinforced by the deep resonance of the tuba.

Here a remarkable upward registral shift introduces the ritornello theme. The low G from the bassoon is transferred upward three octaves to the violins; a harp glissando reaches up yet another octave with the first beat of the Allegretto and highest note of the melody (m. 125). Although the genesis of this theme is connected to a Hungarian *verbunkos* character, as we have seen, its sonorous realization is refined and idealized, distancing the music from its roots.

The second dance, the Allegro molto, with its agitated driving rhythms, low register, and dark harmonic coloring, makes an even stronger contrast to the ethereal ritornello subject. The key interval here of the motivic cell is the minor third D♭–B♭, which dominates the opening measures (Ex. 5.6). The downward direc-

Ex. 5.4. Continued.

tion of the third interval is emphasized, and the culmination of the phrase comes as the minor third interval is reproduced downward as B♭–G–B♭ in mm. 7–8. The trombone slide gives this intervallic relation a vivid, forceful extravagance.[22] Three times subsequently, these flamboyant trombone slides recur. At the repetition of the opening subject, Bartók emphasizes the subject through an upward motivic shift to E♭ and temporary change in meter from $\frac{2}{4}$ to $\frac{3}{4}$, as well as a ritardando and intensification to fortissimo in the measure preceding three measures of slides. In the next parallel passage, the intensity of the music destabilizes the revolving cam between pitches a minor third apart, absorbing meter changes comparable to Stravinsky's *Rite of Spring*, with shifts from $\frac{2}{4}$ to $\frac{3}{4}$, $\frac{5}{8}$, and $\frac{3}{8}$ time within seven measures. The onset of fortissimo comes here on F♭, with the ensuing trombone slides extended through four measures. Finally, in the Più mosso passage, the violins and winds escape the registral confinement of the rhythmic ostinato once and for all, driving into the lofty highest register at the $\frac{5}{8}$ measure preceding the trombone slides, which now occupy five measures.

The driving force of such repetitive motivic figures, often emphasizing the interval of a minor third, in conjunction with frequent changes of meter are also characteristic of the powerful chase scene at the center of *The Miraculous Mandarin*, when the mandarin pursues the terrified girl. At a climactic juncture, the stage directions read that "the Mandarin stumbles but rises again like lightning

Ex. 5.5. Bartók, *Dance Suite*, Vivo section of the first movement, mm. 97–102.
Dance Suite, SZ77, by Bela Bartók. © Copyright 1924 Boosey & Hawkes, Inc.
for the USA. Copyright Renewed. Reprinted by permission.

Ex. 5.6. Bartók, *Dance Suite*, opening theme of second movement. *Dance Suite*, SZ77, by Bela Bartók. © Copyright 1924 Boosey & Hawkes, Inc. for the USA. Copyright Renewed. Reprinted by permission.

and continues the chase more passionately than before." As the tempo shifts to *sempre vivace*, Bartók employs a series of trombone slides through the interval of a minor third. These descending glissando slides for the trombones are pitted against brilliant rising gestures in the strings and winds, reminding us of the last climax in the Allegro molto of the *Dance Suite*. The use of the trombones and their glissando motive through a minor third has far-reaching significance in Bartók's pantomime, and the affinity of the passages in the *Dance Suite* to the *Mandarin* is suggestive.[23] We are dealing here not simply with "transparent, recognizable character dances" but with a meaningful interpenetration of styles in a work of considerable depth and complexity.

The Aesthetics of Folk Song Imitation

In a canceled passage of a lecture Bartók held in Budapest in 1931, he specified for the first time some distinct aspects of his compositional assimilation of folk music:

> Another example of folk song imitation is provided by my orchestral work the "Dance Suite." This consists of 6 smaller dance-like movements, of which one, the ritornello, as its name implies, returns repeatedly as a leading-motive [*leitmotiv*]. All of the movements utilize imitations of rural music as their thematic material. For the entire work has this goal: to realize a sort of idealized folk music, or I could say a kind of arrangement of poetic rural music such that the individual movements of the work display certain specific musical types.—The models employed stem from folk music of various nationalities: Hungarian, Wallachian, Slovakian, even Arabian; beyond this, here and there is a mixture of these types.[24]

What is clear from this description and from analysis of the *Dance Suite* is that Bartók's musical world is by no means identical with folk music but involves an idealizing imitation of folk song idioms. In his aforementioned letter from 1931 to Octavian Beu, Bartók described his artistic goal as "the brotherhood of peoples, a brotherhood despite all war and strife," a conviction he held in resistance to attacks against him by "chauvinists" a decade earlier, during the period of the counterrevolution.[25]

Bartók built on an older tradition of assimilating folk idioms. In his letter to Beu, he named Brahms, Schubert, and Debussy in this regard. In the Austrian context, one also thinks of the heritage of "popular" style stemming from some of Haydn's symphonic finales or Mozart's *Magic Flute*. Beethoven's extensive experience with folk song also springs to mind. His use of folk song is familiar, for instance, from the Russian themes incorporated into the "Razumovsky" Quartets, including the famous "Slava!" subject used in the Maggiore section of the third movement of op. 59, no. 2. Beethoven also made many arrangements of songs from various nations and composed variations on folk melodies.[26] This extensive experience with folk song left its mark on some of the celebrated works of his last decade, such as the Ninth Symphony and the Piano Sonata in A♭ Major, op. 110. The "Freude" theme of the Ninth, with its conjunct vocal motion and circular intervallic pattern outlining thirds, belongs in this context, all the more because of the association of the theme with brotherhood in the text by Friedrich Schiller: "Alle Menschen werden Brüder" (All human beings become siblings). Beethoven's painstaking labors on the "Freude" theme were directed toward a kind of imitation and idealization of folk song. Like Beethoven, Bartók embraced the idea of an open work of art, and the integration of folk idioms played a significant role in this connection.[27]

In Bartók's *Dance Suite*, the "creative ingenuity" of transplanting motivic material reflecting folk idioms assumes a highly distinctive form. He sought to integrate his chain of dances not just through use of the ritornello but through a structural logic according to which successive dances after the first piece build on the intervallic foundation of the preceding music. As we have seen, the opening Moderato with its partly Arabic character stresses a narrow range of intervals and in particular the interval of the major second. It is possible to regard the bassoon theme at the outset as based primarily on a configuration of a pair of major seconds a semitone apart. Thus after the opening glissando gesture in the piano and the downbeat on A in the bassoons, the following measures rely melodically on a series of repeated falling seconds from B♭ to A♭ alternating with falling seconds from C♭ to A (whereby C♭ is enharmonically equivalent to B). This configuration is stressed in the analysis of Ernő Lendvai, who comments on the parallel motivic structure in the second movement, the Allegro molto, in which the dominating interval is the descending minor third, D♭–B♭. As we have seen, this obsessive emphasis on the minor third is extended in the striking trombone slide outlining the next falling minor third, B♭–G, as is heard already in m. 7 of the movement.

Lendvai observes that the theme of Bartók's third movement, the lively Allegro vivace, combines primary intervallic elements of the first two dances. A structural outline of the first three movements is shown in Ex. 5.7.[28] Lendvai's approach has the merit of helping elucidate how the intervallic framework devised by Bartók evolves organically from piece to piece. Bartók's registral ascent, with the second and third movements beginning about an octave higher than the preceding movements, contributes to this effect, as does the increasingly differentiated treatment of rhythm. The sum of semitones from the major second (2) and minor third (3) equals the perfect fourth (5), which becomes the prominent opening descending interval of the third dance. The second measure of the melody of the Allegro vivace consists of the descending minor third E–C♯ and major second C♯–B, which together span the interval of the descending fourth E–B. This pattern is often articulated rhythmically through groups of sixteenth notes. It is striking how consistently this intervallic complex makes up the pitch content of Bartók's theme. Furthermore, a vertical arrangement of fourths in chords is also prominent.

First movement

Second movement

Third movement

Ex. 5.7. Bartók, *Dance Suite*, intervallic structure of movements 1–3. *Dance Suite*, SZ77, by Bela Bartók. © Copyright 1924 Boosey & Hawkes, Inc. for the USA. Copyright Renewed. Reprinted by permission.

Lendvai's analyses of Bartók's music according to the principle of the golden section are not always convincing,[29] but that general approach has merit in this instance. The primary intervals in the opening dances yield a division of the controlling interval of the fourth in the third dance; thus the numerical proportions 2:3 as reflected in the first and second dances recur as intervallic components of the perfect fourth in the third dance: 5 = 3 + 2. As this analysis reminds us, Bartók strove in his music for structural integrity both within and between the separate pieces and in the form of the whole. The grouping of dances evoking diverse regions and held together by the *verbunkos* ritornello is only one aspect of the composition, which should indeed be heard not as merely a suite but as a "continuous, uninterrupted work," as Halsey Stevens puts it.[30] This brings us to another aspect of the genesis of the *Dance Suite* that pertains to the balance between its incorporation of diverse national dances, on the one hand, and its structural integrity as an integrated artwork, on the other.

The manuscripts for the *Dance Suite* held in the Paul Sacher Stiftung in Basel include a short score for the work containing a movement not included in the finished piece. This manuscript was formerly in the possession of Peter Bartók. In the canceled passage from his 1931 lecture cited above, Bartók referred to the presence of a Slovakian dance in the *Dance Suite*. No such piece exists in the orchestrated final version of the work, yet this Slovakian dance is found in the short score, together with an additional statement of the ritornello. Plates 4 and 5 show these pages of the short score. The discarded movement originally fit between

Ex. 5.8. Transcription of beginning of Slovakian dance.

movements two and three and included sixty-six measures with an additional ten
measures in the following ritornello. A transcription of the opening section of the
Slovakian dance as it appears in the draft is provided in Ex. 5.8.

Why was the Slovakian dance excluded from the finished composition? Entirely
apart from his stated idea of including "specific types" from a range of regions,
including Slovakia, Bartók could well have had personal reasons for wishing to
include a Slovakian dance movement. After all, the cultural regions he singled out
are precisely those in which he did extensive fieldwork, including Arabic areas of
North Africa. Bartók's choice of dance types has an autobiographical resonance.
In this context, the removal of the Slovakian dance represents a real loss.

When we regard the Slovakian dance in the context of the pieces we have discussed, Bartók's probable motivation for the excision nevertheless seems apparent.
The melody is placed in the major mode and is doubled in thirds, unfolding over
a tonic pedal point in the bass. The main subject occupies eight measures in two
four-measure phrases. In each of these phrases, the opening measure is followed by
two measures of rhythmic decoration of this pattern in sixteenth notes, leading to
a resting point on the quarter note F, the tonic. Although the repeated dissonance
of B♭ in the upper voice against B two octaves lower is striking and characteristic,
and the continuation contains colorful harmonic shifts and brief changes of meter,
Bartók remains close to this thematic model in his draft. This dance is simpler

than those that precede and follow it, and in its position as the third piece, following the Allegro molto and preceding the Allegro vivace, it would have disrupted the logical sequence we have described. At this point in the genesis of the *Dance Suite*, a conflict evidently arose between two different dimensions of the work: the array of dances alluding to the various rural dance types, on the one hand, and the musical-dramatic design embracing their succession, on the other. The evident priority of the musical-dramatic design accounts best for the disappearance of the Slovakian dance.[31]

The Allegro vivace, by contrast, is admirably placed in the context of the work as a whole. The distinctive character of the opening giocoso melody, with its Hungarian associations, is bound up with the missing third and sixth degrees of the scale. The B mode lacks a D or D♯ as well as a G or G♯. Hence the very quality that stems from its folkloric roots allows it to function especially well structurally as the third link in the chain of successive dances. Its intervallic framework of fourths divided into minor thirds plus major seconds (E descending to B in m. 2, with C♯ as the connecting tone) brings the defining intervals from the preceding dances into a new configuration whose regional color is intimately bound up with its structural limitations. Another conspicuous aspect of the movement is the presence of thematic dualism, since Bartók pairs the Hungarian tune with a colorful, exuberant second dance featuring a violin melody with Romanian associations. The stamping rhythm of the Romanian dance involves shifts of meter between $\frac{3}{4}$, $\frac{2}{4}$, and $\frac{5}{8}$ time. This quality of dualistic thematic contrast prefigures the finale of the *Dance Suite*, in which Bartók draws together a variety of subjects drawn from the earlier movements.

The Allegro vivace also contains hints of what lies beyond its boundaries. In the passage preceding the final Vivacissimo, quiet, pulsating sonorities juxtapose two adjacent fourth chords, which together contain six different pitches. This passage leads through a ritardando to a moment of inwardness at the Lento, played pianissississimo, in which two solo violins reach up to the high G♯ (the previously missing sixth degree of the B scale) and then quietly sound the seminal falling fourth B–F♯ that had launched the dance. The serene expressivity and richness of sonority of this passage foreshadows the following slow movement, the Molto tranquillo. Bartók then brings this movement to a rousing close in the Vivacissimo: the falling fourth B–F♯ is affirmed fortissimo in the full orchestra, in the fastest tempo yet, while the final gesture is capped by that high G♯ earlier missing from the theme.

Bartók associated the fourth dance with an urban type of Arabic music. In this mysterious, nocturnal piece, the vertical dimension is contrasted with the horizontal: soft, ethereal chords resonating in the strings, harp, piano, horns, and winds are juxtaposed with profiled melodic phrases sounding in lower registers in the English horn and bass clarinet. In the second of these lyrical phrases, the melody descends stepwise through a perfect fourth, D♭–A♭, before dropping a minor third,

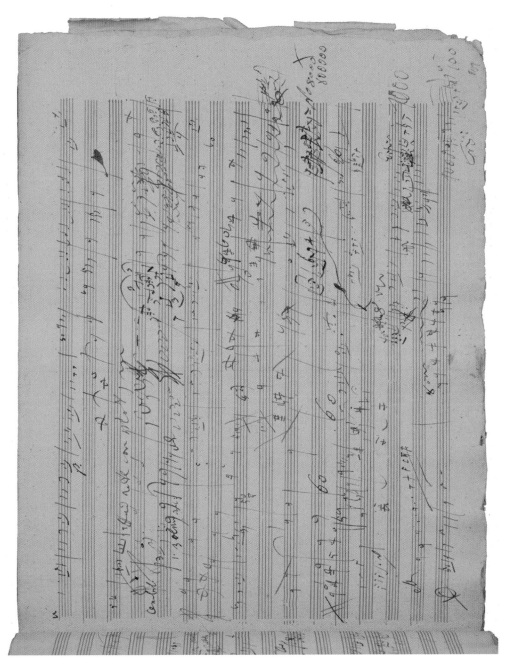

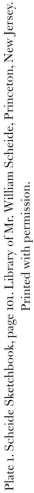

Plate 1. Scheide Sketchbook, page 101. Library of Mr. William Scheide, Princeton, New Jersey. Printed with permission.

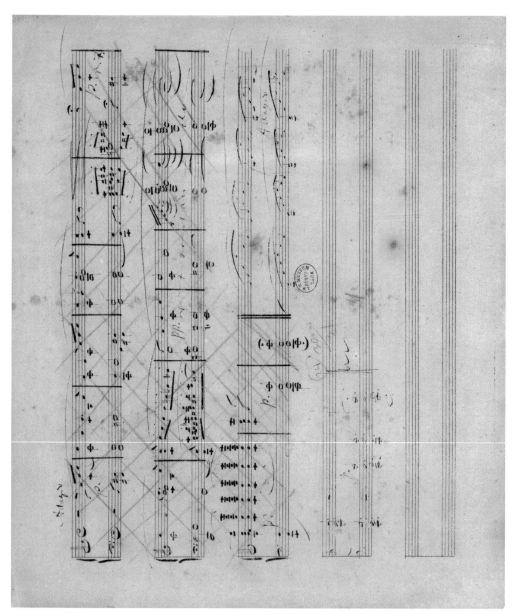

Plate 2. Corrected copy of Schumann's Fantasie op. 17, National Széchényi Library, Budapest (MS Mus. 37), final page.

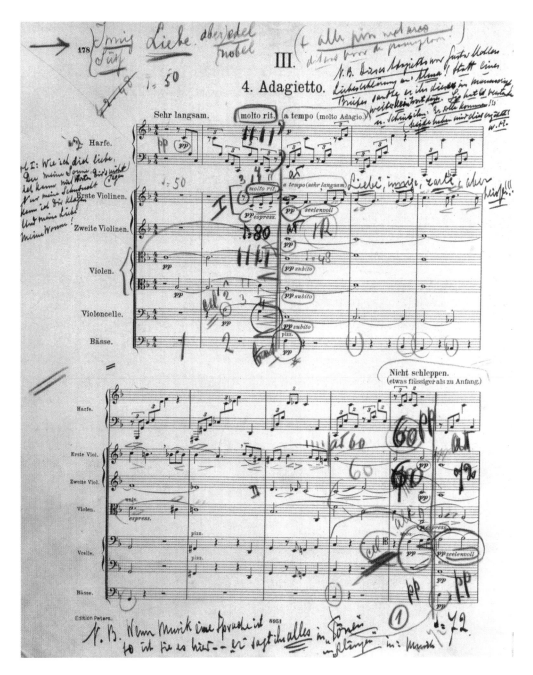

Plate 3. Mengelberg's conducting score of the Adagietto, page 1.
Willem Mengelberg Foundation, Nederlands Muziek Instituut, Den Haag.
Used by permission.

Plates 4–5. Draft of *Dance Suite* showing Slovakian dance,
Sacher Foundation, Basel. Printed with permission.

53 PS 1

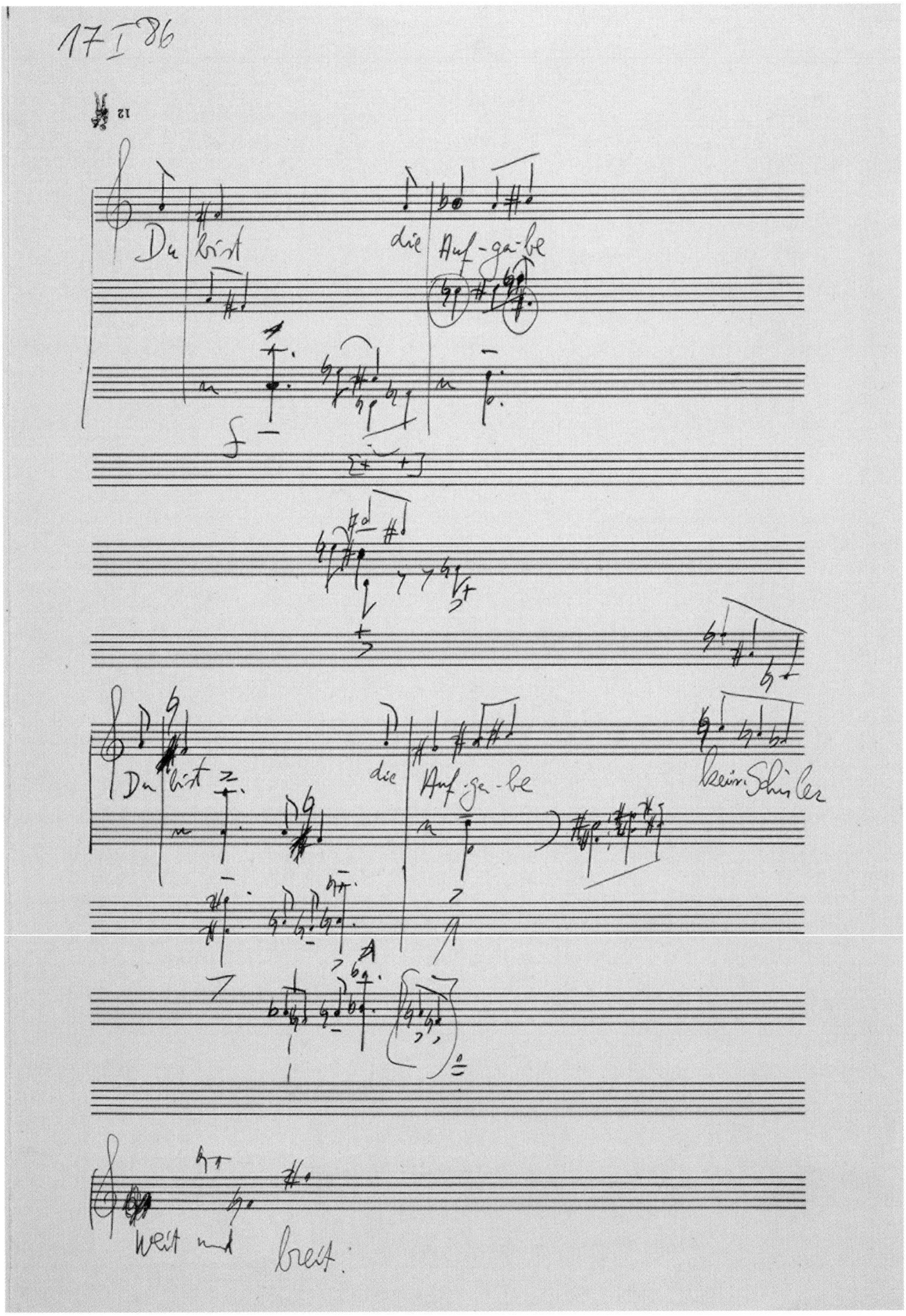

Plates 6–7. Drafts of unpublished setting of "Du bist die Aufgabe,"
Sacher Foundation, Basel. Printed with permission.

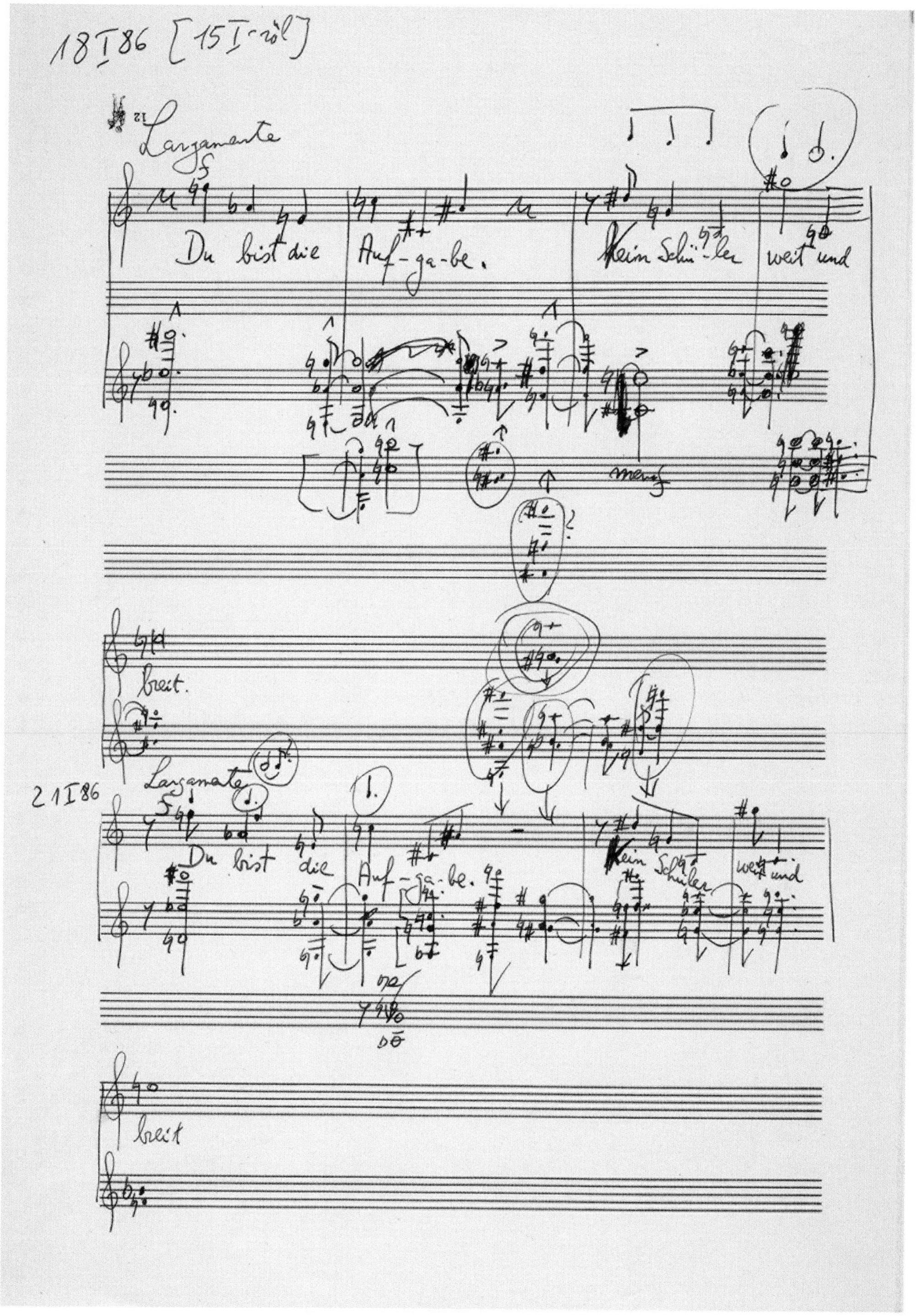
18 I 86
Du bist die Auf-ga-be.
Kein Schü-ler weit und
breit.
21 I 86
Du bist die Auf-ga-be.
Kein Schüler weit und
breit

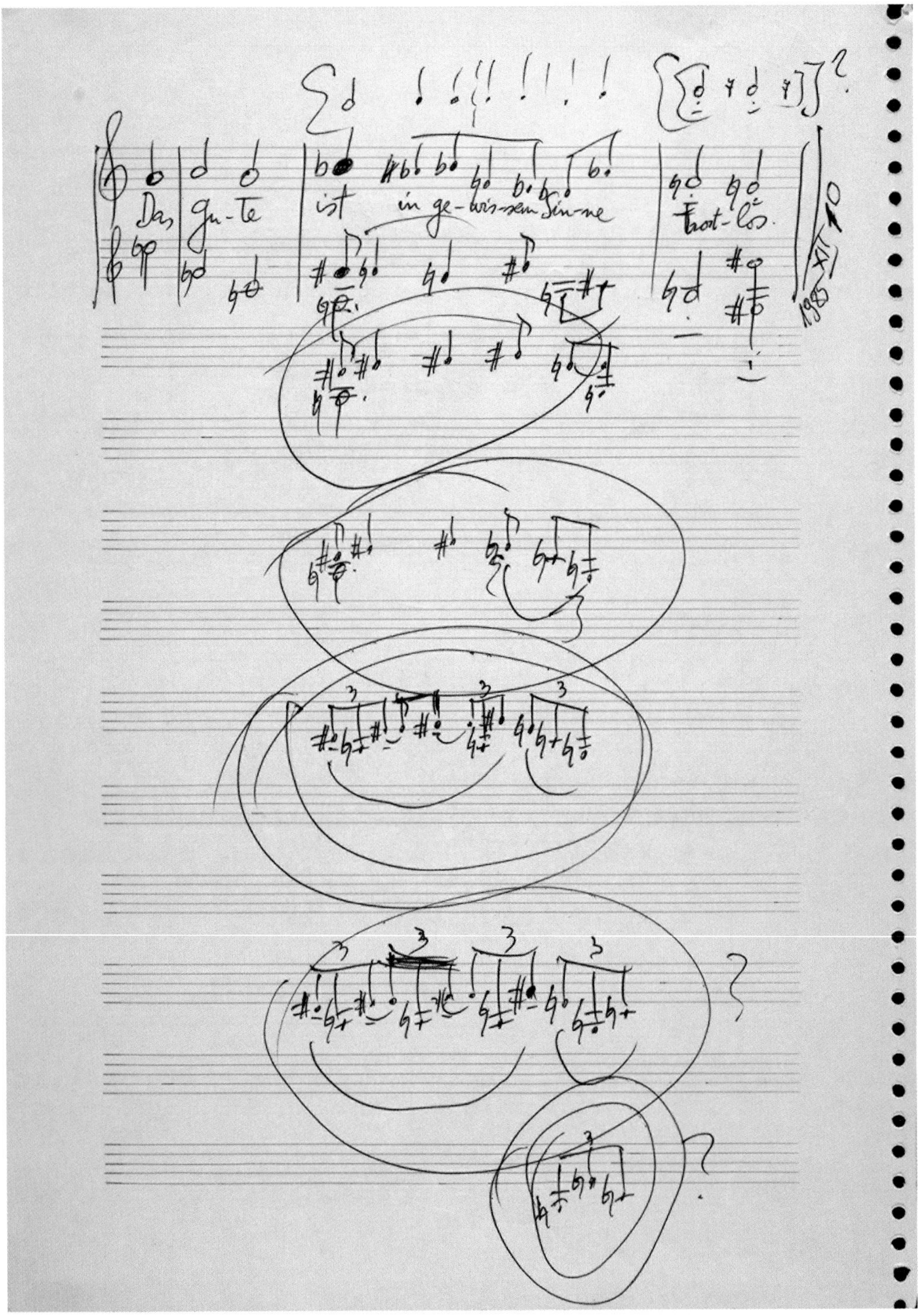

Plate 8. Sketches for a setting of "Das Gute ist im gewissen Sinne trostlos,"
Sacher Foundation, Basel. Printed with permission.

to F. This progression may be heard as a melodic elaboration of the seminal falling fourth from the previous movement, the Allegro vivace, joined to the insistent minor third interval from the second movement, the Allegro molto. In structural terms, the components are now 8 = 5 + 3, with the minor sixth embodying eight semitones, two-thirds of the span of an octave.[32] The principle of gradual intervallic expansion thus remains audible in this remarkable slow movement, the meditative center of the work. The ritornello receives an abbreviated, delicately muted expression: its final phrase corresponds to the oboe from the end of the second movement, but the final interval now drops a fourth, from A♭ to E♭, echoing the prominent falling fourths of the Arabic melody.

"Brotherhood despite All War and Strife": The Finale of the *Dance Suite*

In his aforementioned letter to Octavian Beu, Bartók described the fifth dance, marked *Comodo*, as "so primitive that one can only speak of a primitive peasant character here, and any classification according to nationality must be abandoned."[33] Its lack of formal autonomy is confirmed by its direct continuity into the finale. The music is reduced in the Comodo to a rhythmic pattern of repeated impulses with a semitone vacillation involving a turn figure. The soft dynamic level of pianissimo and long-held pedal point on E contribute to its elemental character. As we have seen, Bartók built up the sequence of preceding movements on the basis of an intervallic progression, whereby the first piece emphasizes the interval of the major second. In this context, the Comodo exploits an even more fundamental configuration through its stress on the half step E–F in its hushed opening section. A dynamic element is nonetheless present, as is reflected in the way the motivic shift from E to F in m. 1 is already intensified in m. 2 by a pair of turn figures emphasizing the half step F–E. In the ensuing fortissimo section, Bartók reverses the direction of the semitone relation, now emphasizing E♭, a half step lower than E. As the dynamic level of the music softens to pianissimo in the measure before the shift in tempo to allegro at the outset of the finale, he restores the F–E half step with which the dance had begun.

Like the Comodo, the finale begins pianissimo and with the same rhythmic pattern over a pedal point, here placed on C. All of the instruments enter in turn with this motivic material, echoing the repeated notes and semitones familiar from the Comodo. Strictly speaking, the finale begins without fresh and distinctive content. Instead, what strikes a new note is the emergence of marcato accents in the trombones and then in the trumpets (mm. 5–17). This material, however, is not actually new: Bartók draws the theme in mm. 9–12 from mm. 77–83 of the opening Moderato movement, the passage leading to the climactic Vivo section. Despite changes in meter and in orchestration, the thematic recall is direct and unmistakably emphatic: the theme that had been played by woodwinds in the first movement is performed here by trombones with trumpets (Ex. 5.9).

It will be seen that the motive in mm. 9–10 is a rhythmically profiled version of the bassoon line from the very beginning of the work, whereby a pair of falling second intervals follows the initial pitch. Whereas the opening notes of the Moderato were A–B♭–A♭–C♭–A, with falling whole steps between B♭ and A♭ and C♭ (enharmonically equivalent to B) and A, that pattern reappears here as D–E♭–C♯–E–D, with falling whole steps between E♭ and C♯ (enharmonically equivalent to D♭) and between E and D. Bartók reinforces and intensifies this motive of two descending whole steps a half step apart through the continuation, as the four-note motive E♭–C♯–E–D is reiterated in rhythmic diminution, expressed as three eighth notes leading to an accented quarter note. He therefore launches his finale by recalling a developmental passage from the opening movement, signaling the role of the finale as a culminating synthesis in the formal design of the whole. From this perspective, we can appreciate the logic of Bartók's elemental fifth movement with its stress on motivic half steps. Structurally, the Comodo movement withdraws to a more fundamental level than any of the earlier movements. From this basic platform, Bartók constructs a new synthesis in his finale, drawing on the music of earlier movements while exploring their interrelationship in a single continuity.

At the beginning of the Più allegro in mm. 18–19, Bartók emphasizes the interval of the minor third in the trombones, trumpets, and tuba. He returns to his obsession with minor thirds with a vengeance at the end of this section, in which the trumpets and horns pounce on this interval, reaching a penetrating triple *forte* climax in m. 35. The motivic concentration on minor thirds inevitably recalls the second movement of the work, though not yet as a direct recapitulation of thematic material. From the music of the Comodo through the first thirty-five measures of the finale, Bartók recaptures the progression of broadening intervallic concentration in a new way, moving from half steps to whole steps and then minor thirds.

The main body of the finale is anchored in its form by passages recalling the first three movements and the ritornello. Bartók bypasses the slow movement in this framework, but he incorporates several recapitulatory passages within the larger continuity in $\frac{2}{4}$ meter. The Meno vivo (mm. 36–54) provides an apotheosis of the bassoon theme of the first dance, which now sounds in the full orchestra, triple *forte*. The theme is extended here, and the main weight of the melodic climax (mm. 52–54) falls on A, with spinning figuration in the winds emphasizing this pitch, which also resonates in the trumpets. This gesture might perhaps be regarded as a kind of transformation of the climactic passage emphasizing A in m. 101 of the first movement. The continuation recalls the third movement in a more relaxed, allegretto tempo. In this section, more than ever before, we can note a motivic family resemblance between the individual pieces Bartók has assembled in his *Dance Suite*. A rhythmic motive of steady pitch repetitions, for instance, is prominent in

Ex. 5.9. Bartók, *Dance Suite*, finale, mm. 9–12. *Dance Suite*, SZ77, by Bela Bartók.
© Copyright 1924 Boosey & Hawkes, Inc. for the USA. Copyright Renewed.
Reprinted by permission.

the accompaniment to the Allegretto, as well as in the continuation at the *a tempo* marking in m. 65, where the oboe takes up the repeated pitches as well as the turn figure a half step higher, thereby recalling the Comodo. The opening bassoon subject and its apotheosis in the Meno vivo also involve such rhythmic pitch repetitions, inasmuch as each of the first several measures begins with the same note, A, for example. The configuration of repeated pitches is contained within the Meno vivo subject, and Bartók emphasizes some of these patterns through colorful details of orchestration, such as giving the flutes and piccolo the high B in each of the first three measures as the falling second is enlarged to a major ninth. In subsequent passages, such as the climax emphasizing A in mm. 52–54, the motive of repeated impulses appears as accented chords in the brass, while trills sustain G♯ and A in the strings. Such passages display an affinity to the third movement, and particularly to the exuberant Romanian dance.

Adorno's judgment that "the finale, which makes reference thematically to the first movement, brings the familiar material together in a harmless way without striving for synthesis" misses the point in that the finale "makes reference" not simply to the first movement but to *all* of the preceding movements except for the nocturnal Molto tranquillo. The finale lacks much independent thematic material; it lives by developing motivic and rhythmic elements drawn from the preceding movements. The form of the *Dance Suite* as a whole has three parts: the first three movements in faster tempi; the contrasting slow movement; and then the Comodo and the finale, which does indeed "strive for synthesis" while avoiding literal repetition of the musical content of the earlier dances.

That the finale is not so harmless as Adorno thought is shown by the close juxtaposition of the Presto and Molto tranquillo sections (mm. 94–119). The theme in minor thirds from the Allegro molto receives an intense, almost threatening expression here, with the full orchestra playing fortissimo to triple *forte* in the fastest tempo yet heard. Following this ominous outburst, Bartók offers a balancing resolution through the final appearance of the dolce ritornello theme in the solo violins, whose gentle melody emerges out of the magical ascent of the harp glissando. This represents a precarious balance of opposites: dark, uncanny forces lurking in the Presto are held at bay by the idealized vision of the ritornello theme. In the ensuing final passages of the finale, from mm. 149 to 163, disruptive music is again heard, spearheaded by the brass instruments. Their intrusive marcato accents are reminiscent of the agitated passages in the first movement, which show in turn an affinity to the world of *The Miraculous Mandarin*, as we have seen. Only in the final thirty-odd measures, beginning in the Allegretto with the recall of the theme from the third movement and leading into the impetuous music of the closing Allegro molto, with its rather abrupt ending, are all shadows purged.[34]

The case of the *Dance Suite* allows us to reassess a central topic in discussions of Bartók's music since the 1920s: the role of a stylistic synthesis embracing models ranging from Bach and Beethoven to Liszt and Richard Strauss, not to mention the diverse traditions of folk song we have mentioned. In a recent study, Balázs Mikusi has summarized the debates over the "Bartókian synthesis" that unfolded during the twentieth century.[35] Whereas Lendvai advanced overstated arguments for the *történeti szükségszerüség*, or "historical necessity," of the "axis system" he claimed to discover in Bartók's music, Bence Szaboleci drew attention to the composer's capacity "to melt into his own musical language the elements of different folk musics, and to appropriate the innovations of new European music."[36] By the 1970s, János Kárpáti had identified a "striving towards synthesis . . . [as] the most important and most firmly fixed feature of Bartók's creative activity."[37] Counterarguments have been advanced especially by some English-speaking critics such as David Cooper and Arnold Whittall; the latter has characterized Bartók's music as "an unstable music with complex and fragmentary boundaries," suggesting that Adorno's critique may hold validity.[38]

As we have seen, Adorno's critique of the *Dance Suite* does not withstand scrutiny. On the other hand, we can endorse Mikusi's assessment that Bartók typically juxtaposes elements without effacing their distinctive character.[39] At the same time, in the *Dance Suite* the successive movements build upon one another to explore fundamental aspects of the tonal system, exhibiting qualities of complementarity while conveying a tangible sense of integration or synthesis that coexists with the vivid dramatic contrasts of the music. This point could be explored beyond the examples we have considered. In the closing Allegro molto of the finale, for example, the emphasis on the motive of a slurred whole step D–C dropping a minor third to A corresponds audibly to the basic intervallic structure of the opening dances (with their pervasive stress on these descending intervals) while also echoing the opening peak phrase of the ritornello. In his closing fortissimo gesture, Bartók sets off this impetuous motive by a fermata before resolving it forcefully into the final G major sonority.

This impressive composition embodies Bartók's resilient artistic response to the depressing developments and irreconcilable conflicts of the early 1920s. His years of traveling to collect folk songs lay behind him, and the very idea of the commission—celebration of Budapest's first half-century as a unified city—raised deeply uncomfortable issues in view of the political fragmentation and nationalistic turmoil that beset his native Hungary, a land that less than a decade earlier had seemed deceptively stable and secure. From Bartók's perspective, the peasants whose music he treasured were primary victims of this changed situation; the rich interpenetration of cultures he cherished was to suffer appallingly in the following decades up to the composer's death in 1945.

The *Dance Suite* is delicately balanced between cultural plurality and integration, whereby the presence of Arabic influences expands its range of contexts beyond Christian Europe. At the same time, as the composer stressed, this work relies on imitations of folk music styles rather than on direct quotation. For Bartók, the integrity of the artwork assumed priority over a political or symbolic program. It is telling that in the draft version of the finale of Bartók's *Dance Suite*, the Slovakian dance nowhere appears, although each of the other faster dances is employed in the finale. A likely reason for the deletion of the Slovakian dance was its lack of organic connection either to the sequence of opening pieces or to the finale, which otherwise absorbs so much thematic material from earlier dances into a new continuity.

We shall conclude by reconsidering what David E. Schneider has described as Bartók's "peculiar blend of national pride and openness to many cultures at a time and place in which political conflicts encouraged a crudely reductive discourse about nationality and culture."[40] A generation earlier, at the time of his symphonic poem *Kossuth*, Bartók himself had assumed a more aggressive Hungarian nationalist stance, as we have seen. He later disavowed this position in favor of a more international or cosmopolitan perspective and eventually embraced the vision of a multiethnic state or "brotherhood of peoples," a richly ambiguous notion.[41] In the *Dance Suite*, the Hungarian leadership of this multicultural union seems embodied in the recurrent ritornello theme with its allusion to *verbunkos* style, yet the "recruitment" association points in turn to the historical dominance of the Austrian Habsburg monarchy. After the collapse of the monarchy in 1918, the virtues of that lost "world of security" became more apparent; the earlier critic of the monarchy became its belated defender. On the other hand, Bartók's insistence, as in his remarks to Beu, on the "purity" of sources has nothing to do with ethnicity but is bound up with his distaste for "vulgar" popular music and especially his dislike of the influence of urban popular music on rural peasant music.[42] While remaining somewhat reticent about the character of his own art, Bartók held fast to the idea of folk music as embodying an authentic communal expression, aspects of which could be productively assimilated in turn into art music.

In his typically direct manner, Bartók gave clearest expression to his aesthetic attitudes and goals in his important letter to Beu. So we shall grant him the last word:

> My actual idea . . . of which I am entirely conscious—ever since I found myself as a composer—is that of the brotherhood of peoples, a brotherhood despite all war and strife. I try to serve this idea in my music—inasmuch as my abilities enable me; for that reason I do not distance myself from any influence, whether it be Slovakian, Romanian, Arabian or some other source. But the source must be pure, fresh, and healthy! On account of my—let us say, geographical—position, the Hungarian source is closest to me, hence the Hungarian influence is strongest. Whether my style—regardless of its different sources—has a Hungarian character (and that is the point) is for others to judge, not me. For my own part, I do feel that it has. For character and milieu must somehow stand in relationship to one another.[43]

6

Kurtág's *Kafka Fragments* and *Hommage à R. Sch.*

Like Franz Schubert's *Winterreise* cycle, György Kurtág's *Kafka Fragments*, op. 24 (1985–86), centers on the archetypal theme of wandering, the seeking of a path that remains profoundly elusive. Certain of the trenchant texts extracted by Kurtág from Kafka's diaries and letters call into question or even deny the very existence of such a path, or *Weg*.[1] Yet for Kurtág as for Schubert, the need to keep searching for the elusive goal is inescapable, an existential necessity. So central is this theme that it dominates the entire second part of the four-part structure of the *Kafka Fragments* as well as numerous other songs.

In its overall length, taking approximately an hour in performance time, the *Kafka Fragments* is comparable to Schubert's masterpiece, despite the intense compression of Kurtág's style, which is often reminiscent of Webern.[2] Like many earlier song composers, Kurtág employs a single instrument to accompany the soprano on her journey, replacing the piano in this role by the violin. One trigger for his choice of the violin was the last song in part III, the "Szene in der Elektrischen" (Scene in the electric streetcar), whose text is among the first entries in Kafka's diary. In Kurtág's setting of the text of this suggestive, almost operatic dream-vision, the dancer Eduardowa is accompanied by *two different* violinists, who are distinguished in performance by a change in instrument and tuning, with the single violinist changing position on the stage to signal the switch in role. The musical setting of the opening sentence has a floating, improvisatory quality, punctuated by a single bar line—the one placed after the words "a lover of music" and preceding "travels everywhere." In what follows, two contrasting styles of music are offered by the violinist: a waltz of somewhat popular, sentimental character (as is especially noticeable at "E-lek-tri-schen") and then a lively, fiery idiom strongly suggestive of a Romanian dance. The Romanian dance is appropriately brash, fittingly unfitting (*unpassend*). These two styles are associated in turn with Eusebius and Florestan, respectively, the contrasting personality types used by Schumann, a composer whose legacy is especially important to Kurtág.

The challenge of Kurtág's style has much to do with his openness to the artistic legacy of the past.[3] He does not profess to negate the past in achieving an artwork in the present; in Bartók's terms, this music represents an evolution, not a revolution. Yet Kurtág is keenly sensitive to the pitfalls of composition in an age often beset by trends and oversimplification under the banner of slogans such as "modernism" and "postmodernism." A distinguished performer and teacher, he is urgently concerned that his works be adequately conveyed in concerts and recordings. In approaching the *Kafka Fragments*, we do well to recognize the indispensable tensional balance between sharply contrasting yet complementary aesthetic attitudes such as freedom and determination, imaginative fantasy and structural necessity. The oasis of the self; despair over human fallibility and vulnerability; skepticism about goals; the discernment of meaning in the apparently trivial; the wasting away of time; the unexpected presence of the uncanny: all of these soul-states surface in different ways in the pithy aphorisms from Kafka as set by Kurtág.

In the architecture of the whole cycle, the prominent ideas of the path and its negation, on the one hand, and of a pair of wandering protagonists, on the other, are emphasized. An outline of the forty pieces is provided in Fig. 6.1. The processional ostinato of I/1, "Die Guten gehn im gleichen Schritt" (The good march in even steps), with its straightforward, rigid alternation of C and D in the violin representing the overconfident steps of the "Good," provides a point of reference for the playful, capricious movements of the "others" performing "dances of time," as conveyed in the vocal part.[4] The steady steps of "Die Guten gehn" also serve as springboard for the covering up of the "path" with autumn leaves in I/2, whereas the extended setting of "Der wahre Weg" (The true path), which forms the entirety of part II, submits the overextended notion of the "true path" to decisive critique. As we have seen, the last piece in part III, "Szene in der Elektrischen," employs the pair of violinists associated with Eusebius and Florestan, whereas the final piece of part IV and of the entire cycle, "Es blendete uns die Mondnacht" (The moonlit night dazzled us), culminates with the image of a pair of snakes creeping through the dust, an ironic image with autobiographical resonance for Kurtág and his pianist wife, Márta Kurtág (although in no way limited to this personal association). The slithering of the snakes once more evokes the notion of a quest for an elusive path, while the scene is illuminated from an unearthly remove through moonlight.

Kurtág's Jewish cultural background (which he shares with Kafka) surfaces in pieces like the "Hasidic Dance" "Einmal brach ich mir das Bein" (Once I broke

Teil I	Part I
Die Guten gehn im gleichen Schritt…	The good march in step…
Wie ein Weg im Herbst	Like a pathway in autumn
Verstecke	Hiding-places
Ruhelos	Restless
Berceuse I	Berceuse I
Nimmermehr (Excommunicatio)	Nevermore (Excommunicatio)
"Wenn er mich immer frägt"	"But he just won't stop asking me"
Es zupfte mich jemand am Kleid	Someone tugged at my clothes
Die Weißnäherinnen	The seamstresses
Szene am Bahnhof	Scene at the station
Sonntag, den 19. Juli 1910 (Berceuse II)	Sunday, 19 July 1910 (Berceuse II)
Meine Ohrmuschel…	My ear…
Einmal brach ich mir das Bein	Once I broke my leg
Umpanzert	Enarmoured
Zwei Spazierstöcke	Two walking-sticks
Keine Rückkehr	No going back
Stolz (1910/15. November, zehn Uhr)	Pride (15 Nov. 1910, 10:00)
Träumend hing die Blume	The flower hung dreamily
Nichts dergleichen	Nothing of the kind

Teil II	Part II
Der wahre Weg	The true path

Teil III	Part III
Haben? Sein?	To have? To be?
Der Coitus als Bestrafung	Coitus as punishment
Meine Festung	My fortress
Schmutzig bin ich, Milena…	I am dirty, Milena…
Elendes Leben (Double)	Miserable life (Double)
Der begrenzte Kreis	The closed circle
Ziel, Weg, Zögern	Destination, path, hesitation
So fest	As tightly
Penetrant jüdisch	Offensively Jewish
Verstecke (Double)	Hiding-places (Double)
Staunend sahen wir das große Pferd	Amazed, we saw the great horse
Szene in der Elektrischen	Scene on a tram

Teil IV	Part IV
Zu spät (22. Oktober 1913)	Too late (22 October 1913)
Eine lange Geschichte	A long story
In memoriam Robert Klein	In memoriam Robert Klein
Aus einem alten Notizbuch	From an old notebook
Leoparden	Leopards
In memoriam Joannis Pilinszky	In memoriam Joannis Pilinszky
Wiederum, wiederum	Again, again
Es blendete uns die Mondnacht…	The moonlit night dazzled us…

Figure 6.1. Kurtág's *Kafka Fragments*, op. 24.

my leg) (I/13) and "Penetrant Jüdisch" (Insistently Jewish) (III/10). Kafka's diaries only survived because his friend and literary executor, Max Brod, refused to destroy them as specified in Kafka's will. Instead he published them after having fled from Prague to Israel in 1939, after the annexation of Czechoslovakia by Nazi Germany. In Kurtág these precious fragments found a reader who knew what it meant to live a clandestine, partial existence in the shadows.

Our approach to the *Kafka Fragments* will be indirect. We shall first consider the compositional genesis of the cycle and chart the deliberations over what pieces to include in the work and in what order. The sketches and drafts for "Du bist die Aufgabe" illustrate characteristic features of Kurtág's working procedure. This leads in turn to a consideration of the important links connecting the *Kafka Fragments* to another of Kurtág's major compositions, the *Hommage à R. Sch.* In the last two sections of this chapter, we shall examine selected songs of the cycle in detail, giving special attention to "Der wahre Weg," which forms the whole of part II.

Kurtág's original engagement with the Kafka texts reaches back to the 1950s: "I received the writings of Kafka . . . for the first time from Ligeti. [I could at first] not do much with them. *The Trial* remained foreign to me, but it was in Paris [in] 1957/58, I believe, through *The Metamorphosis*, that I found access. Gradually Kafka became more and more important for me. Over a long period I simply wrote out and collected fragments from diaries or letters, which seemed to me suitable for composition on account of their poetic qualities or complex content."[5] Sustained composition of the cycle began in the summer of 1985. Kurtág was then occupied with the writing of a piano concerto, a work for which he made sixty pages of sketches and assigned the opus number 21, although the concerto has remained unfinished to the present day.[6] Displacing his labors on the concerto, the Kafka project assumed priority, and Kurtág recalled how "almost by accident I began to sketch the music to a few of the selected texts, like a little boy relishing a forbidden treat."[7]

A trace of the unrealized piano concerto is preserved in Kurtág's inscription under the title of I/17 of the *Kafka Fragments*, "Stolz" (Pride): "Promise to Zoltán Kocsis: there will be a piano concerto." During that summer of 1985 Kurtág interrupted his work on the concerto for Kocsis while he was engaged with courses and performances at the Bartók seminar held at the ancient town of Szombathely in western Hungary; it was there that the Kafka texts exerted their hold over him and that some of the songs were conceived in rapid succession.[8] Kurtág's compositions often harbor allusions as well as messages and homages, which absorb moments of the biographical context drawn from real life into a rich and subtle artistic world. At Szombathely that summer were two musicians who played key roles in the genesis of the *Kafka Fragments*: Adrienne Csengery, the soprano who first performed and recorded the cycle, and András Keller, the violinist who joined Csengery in those performances and in the initial recording of the *Kafka Fragments*. Csengery's wide vocal range accommodated the challenging low register of parts of the *Kafka Fragments*, such as "Der wahre Weg," while her operatic experience and dramatic verve prepared her for the vivid contrasts and dark humor of other songs. Keller assisted the composer with the elaborate violin part, which tests the limits of artistic realization. As Kurtág himself put it, referring to the violinist in a published interview: "I sometimes think: Keller has proven to me that *Kafka* [the *Kafka Fragments*] is a work of genius."[9]

In "Stolz," the song whose inscription alludes to the pianist Zoltán Kocsis, the opening sentence "Ich werde mich nicht müde werden lassen" (I will not let myself become tired) suggests a display of proud defiance from a weary wanderer, reminding us distantly perhaps of Schubert's "Muth" setting toward the end of *Winterreise*. The Kafka diary entry used for "Stolz" continues with an expression of firm resolution: "I will dive into my story even if that should lacerate my face." In a similar vein, Kurtág's I/16, "Keine Rückkehr" (No return), might invite comparison with Schubert's "Der Wegweiser" (The signpost). Kafka's "From a certain point on there is no turning back" aligns with Wilhelm Müller's closing lines: "I must follow a path from which no one has ever returned." Nonetheless, such parallels should not be overstressed, and only within the internal context of the *Kafka Fragments* can we begin to do justice to the work as a whole.

Kurtág has acknowledged the assistance of the Hungarian music scholar and performer András Wilheim in helping to order the forty individual pieces that make up the *Kafka Fragments*, and Wilheim's role was indeed important.[10] Once he had composed the individual settings, Kurtág knew that "Die Guten gehn im gleichen Schritt" belonged at the beginning, "Der wahre Weg" near the middle, and "Es blendete uns die Mondnacht" at the end of the cycle. However, the precise ordering of the many other songs remained unclear. An undated overview of the evolving order of the cycle in Wilheim's hand is preserved on three sheets now held in the Sacher Archive in Basel (Figs. 6.2–6.4). This tentative outline of the cycle is in three parts rather than four, since "Der wahre Weg" is not yet designated as a separate part, though its position at the bottom of the first sheet corresponds to its final placement in the finished work. The spatial allocation of the songs on sheet 1 reflects to some extent their role in the overall narrative structure. For example, the opening two songs, with their emphasis on the path, or *Weg*—whether followed in marchlike conformity (no. 1) or obscured through the fall of leaves (no. 2)—are placed together at the top left. On the other hand, the contrasting trio of songs at the end of part I—"Stolz," the "Hommage à Schumann," and the passionate negation of "Nichts dergleichen" (Nothing of the kind)—are notated at the bottom left of this sheet. Another pairing of songs is seen at the top right, with "Berceuse I" followed by "Nimmermehr." These two songs became nos. 5 and 6 of part I, whereas "Haben? Sein?" (To have? to be?), which was written below them and then crossed out, was eventually deployed not in part I but later in the cycle, at the beginning of part III.

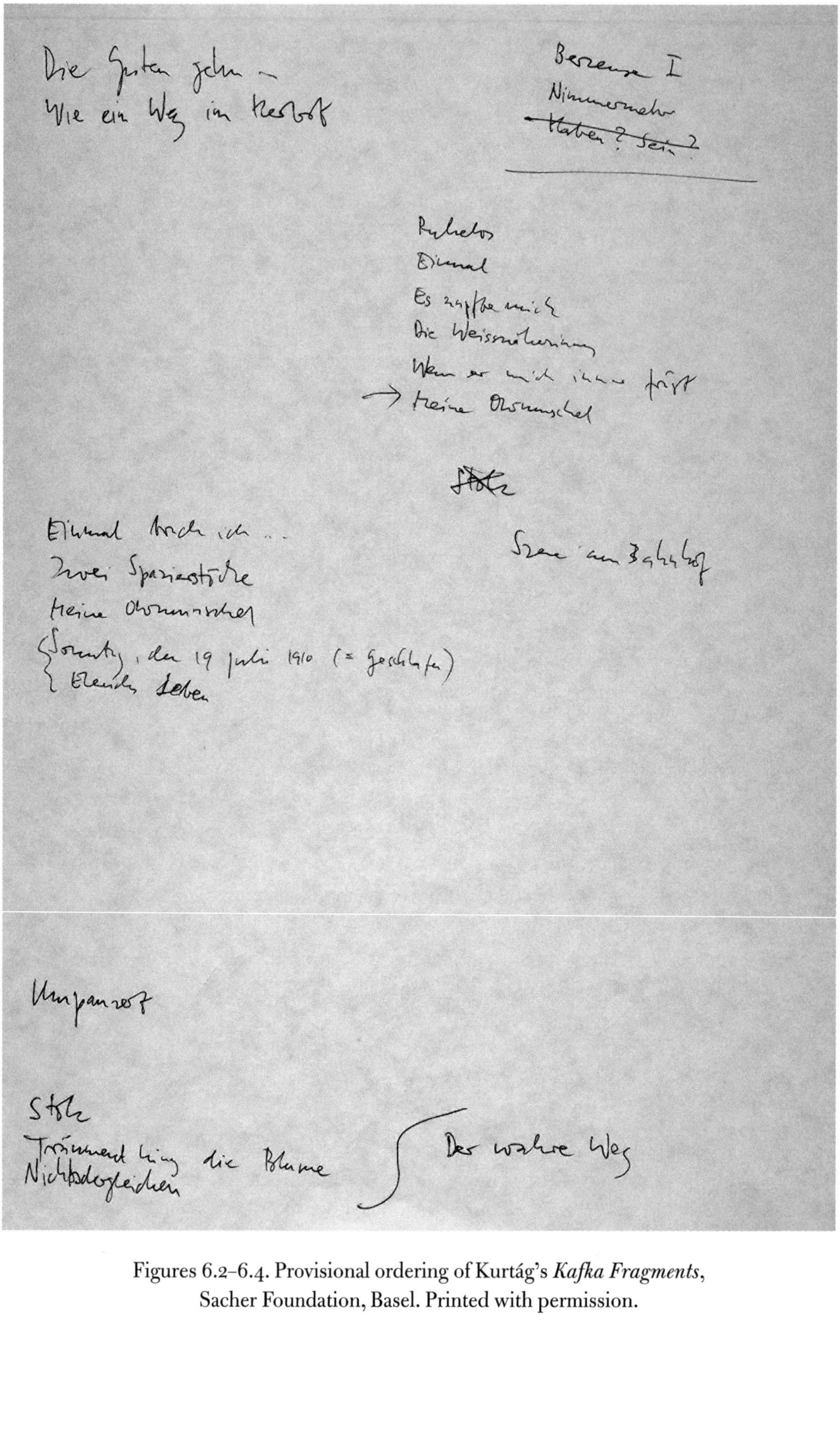

Die Guten gehn —
Wie ein Weg im Herbst

Berceuse I
Nimmermehr
Haben? Sein?

Ruhelos
Einmal
Es zupfte mich
Die Weissnäherinnen
Wenn er mich immer fragt
→ Keine Ohrwunschel

Stolz

Szene am Bahnhof

Einmal brach ich ...
Zwei Spazierstöcke
Keine Ohrwunschel
{ Sonntag, den 19 juli 1910 (= Geschäfte)
{ Elendes Leben

Umpanzert

Stolz
Träumend hing die Blume
Nichtsdergleichen

{ Der wahre Weg

Figures 6.2–6.4. Provisional ordering of Kurtág's *Kafka Fragments*,
Sacher Foundation, Basel. Printed with permission.

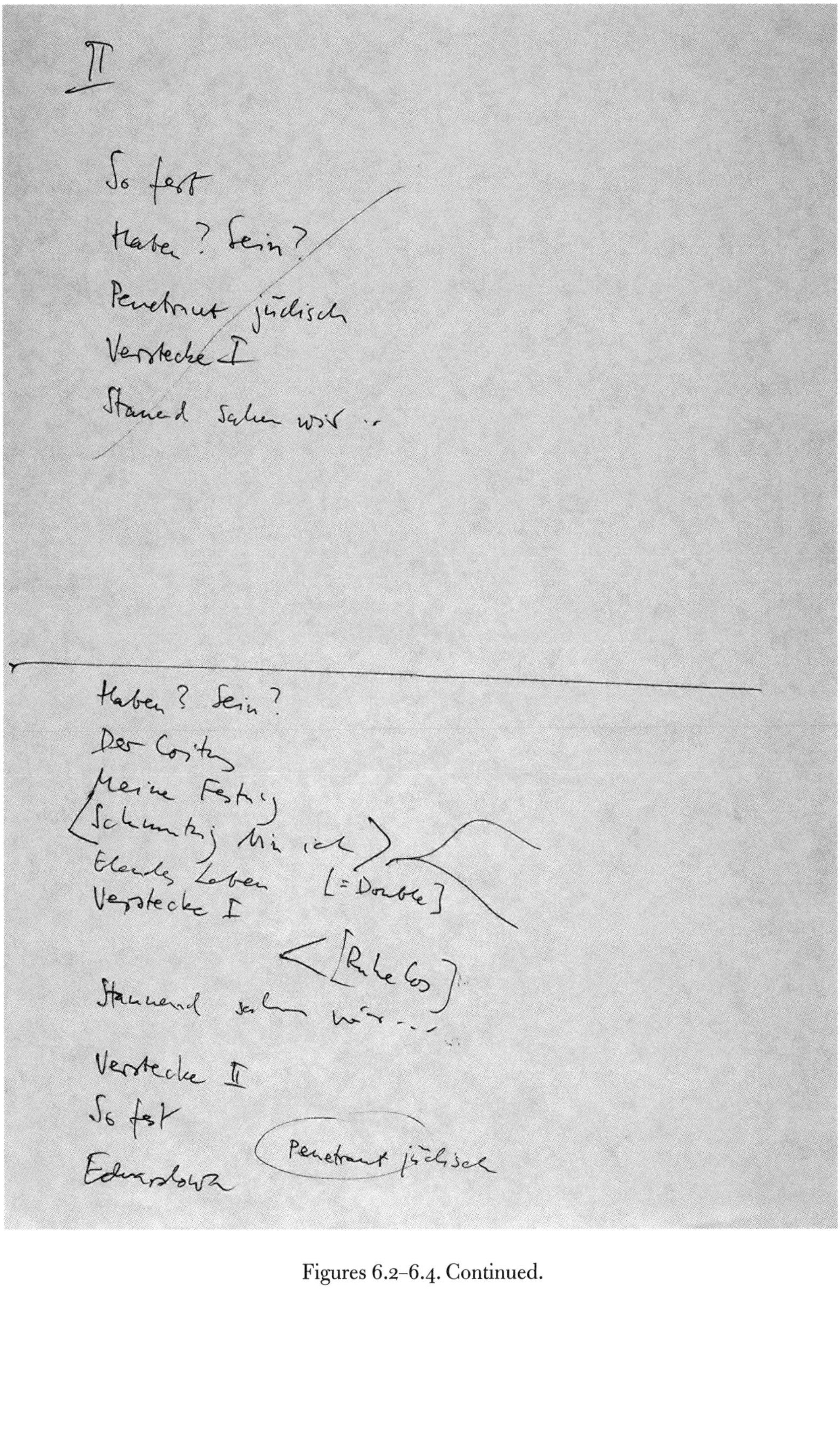

II

So fest
Haben ? Sein ?
Penetrant jüdisch
Verstecke I
Staunend sehen wir ..

Haben ? Sein ?
Der Cosntz
Meine Festig
[Schäumtig Mir ich]
Elendes Leben   [= Double]
Verstecke I

        < [Rule 6o)]

Staunend sehen wir ...

Verstecke II
So fest
Edensbush   (Penetrant jüdisch)

Figures 6.2–6.4. Continued.

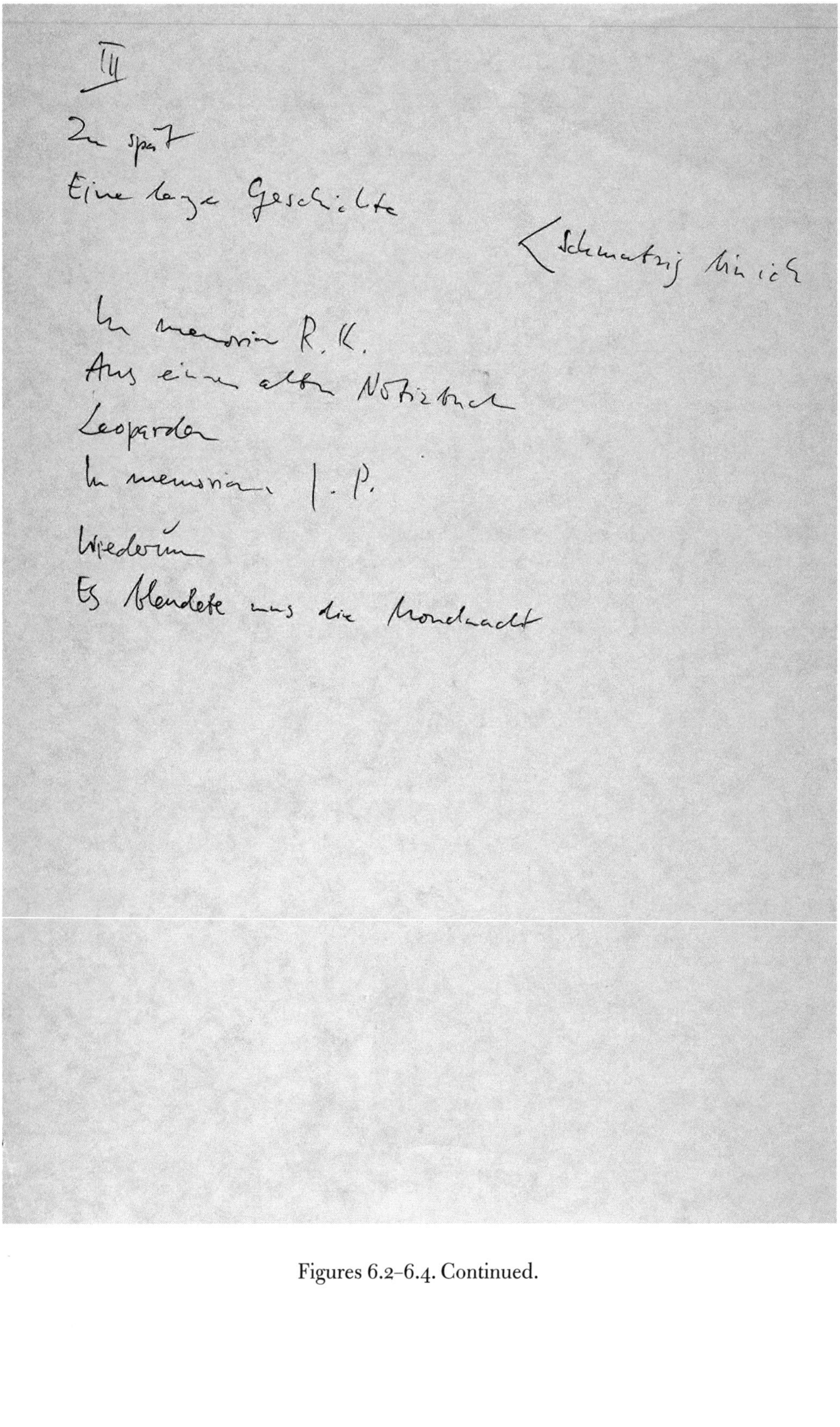

III

Zu spät

Eine lange Geschichte

< Schematzig bin ich

In memoriam R. K.
Aus einem alten Notizbuch
Leoparden
In memoriam J. P.

Wiederum
Es blendete uns die Mondnacht

Figures 6.2–6.4. Continued.

When András Wilheim wrote out this overview, the arrangement of the many short pieces in part I remained uncertain. The grouping in the upper-right center of the sheet largely diverges from the final order. "Verstecke" (Hiding places) (no. 3) is missing here and was eventually transferred to part I from what was then part II. "Ruhelos" (Restless) is close to its final position (no. 4), yet the four following songs on the sheet were allocated as nos. 13, 8, 9, and 7 in the finished work; only the pairing of "Es zupfte mich jemand am Kleid" (Someone tugged at my clothes) and "Die Weissnäherinnen" (The seamstresses) was retained, with their common thread of apparel, at first pulled at and then drenched. "Stolz" was considered for inclusion in this section and then crossed out. The position of "Umpanzert" (Fortified) was clearly unsettled until this song finally took its place in the order between "Einmal brach ich mir das Bein" (Once I broke my leg) and "Zwei Spazierstöcke" (Two walking sticks).

The second sheet shows two radically different sequences for pieces in part III (here still designated as part II), neither of which yet contains all of the songs included in the finished cycle. Whereas the first listing bears little resemblance to the completed work, the second already reflects many of its essential features. Here the beginning and end of the sequence—"Haben? Sein?" and the "Eduardowa" setting with the two violinists—are present, but the middle of the sequence diverges substantially from the completed work. Two songs notated here—"Verstecke I" and "Ruhelos"—were shifted back to part I, whereas three others are absent: "Der begrenzte Kreis ist rein" (The closed circle is pure), "Ziel, Weg, Zögern" (Destination, path, hesitation), and "So Fest" (So tightly). The final sheet of the overview, on the other hand, sets out all eight songs from part IV in their final order while revealing that Kurtág contemplated placing "Schmutzig bin ich, Milena" (I am dirty, Milena) as the third song in this part before he incorporated that piece into part III as the third song, following "Meine Festung" (My fortress). The title of this latter song—"Meine Gefängniszelle—meine Festung" (My prison cell—my fortress)—appears as a title on the cover sheets to each part of the cycle in the autograph score held in Basel, but Kurtág removed these titles when the work was published in 1992.

Other pieces are emphasized through a process of doubling, as two settings of the same text are employed. In the finished work, "Verstecke" is doubled as I/3 and III/9 and "Geschlafen, aufgewacht" (Slept, woke) as I/11 and III/5. Kurtág furthermore entitles the first of these latter songs not according to the text but according to Kafka's dated diary entry "Sunday, 19 July 1910," and he supplies a further designation in parentheses: "Berceuse II." By this means, he stresses its affinity with I/5, which is labeled "Berceuse I" and shares the association with sleep: "Wrap your overcoat, O lofty dream, around the child." This strategy amounts to a doubled process of doubling and points to the far-reaching network of poetic associations that connect the *Kafka Fragments* to one another.

Kurtág's Kafka Fragments *and* Hommage à R. Sch.   171

In this context, it is not surprising to discover through the numerous sketches in the Sacher Foundation that Kurtág (with the assistance of András Wilheim) contemplated but ultimately rejected even more doubled pieces and additional Kafka settings. Like Beethoven, Kurtág makes extensive use of bound sketchbooks alongside sketches and drafts written on loose papers.[11] This vast body of material sheds light on what lay beyond the boundaries of the work as we know it. We shall now consider some of the pieces that found no home in the finished *Kafka Fragments* as well as some far-reaching links between Kurtág's Kafka project and his other compositions.

Beyond the Margins: Other Kafka Settings and the *Hommage à R. Sch.*

Kurtág composed five additional Kafka settings, including four texts set in 1985: "Es wird ein Ruf laut aus dem Fluss" (A cry sounds from the river), "Das Gute ist im gewissen Sinne trostlos" (The good is in a certain sense bleak), "Ich habe niemals die Regel erfahren" (I have never learned the rules), and "Wie fern sind mir zum Beispiel die Armmuskeln" (How distant from me are my arm muscles, for example). Perhaps the most intriguing of all the unused songs is the setting of "Du bist die Aufgabe, kein Schüler weit und breit" (You are the assignment, no student far and wide), which is preserved on four drafts held on two pages dated 17–21 January 1986 (Plates 6–7). These pages illustrate distinctive aspects of Kurtág's working method in conceiving and revising the text setting and violin part.

We witness in these successive sketches a process of exploring possible motivic connections and echoes whereby the music reflects and amplifies Kafka's pithy formulation. Kurtág's attempt at the top of the sheet dated "17 I 86" includes just the first phrase: "Du bist die Aufgabe." The points of natural accentuation are placed on "bist" and "Auf-," which are set on downbeats of the duple meter. Kurtág mimics the A–F♯ motive in the violin at the beginning of the first full measure and then immediately emphasizes the A through an octave played *forte* and reaching a higher register. This artistic strategy embodies the presence of the subject "Du" (you) in the manner of a *Ding-Gedicht* (thing-poem); "you" is thereby reflected in the sustained sounding of the A, as transferred from the voice to the violin. The second attempt at the bottom of the first page provides a setting of the entire text. Here we see Kurtág continuing to employ imitations in the violin of the initial falling motive A–F♯ or A–F at "Du bist." On the other hand, the setting of the final words "weit und breit" (far and wide) utilizes the high register in the voice while setting off these lofty pitches through the steep drop of more than an octave at the connective word "und" (and).

The following day, when he returned to "Du bist die Aufgabe," Kurtág focused his attention on a fuller sonorous realization of the violin part but also made rhythmic and metrical changes in the text setting. "Du" is now no longer set as the upbeat, and it *follows* the initial sonority D–E♭–F♯ in the violin. The first vocal phrase "Du bist die Aufgabe" is now given a unified setting without any pause for the violin's response. Indeed, the position of the descending vocal line starting on a high F marked *forte* suggests that Kurtág has here shifted his basic idea for the violin line to the vocal part.

On the other hand, the initial sonority now stems not from the singer but from the violinist, and there is clearly a relationship between the opening accented chord on the downbeat and the later syncopated sonorities, which contain some of the same intervals, such as the minor ninth. Kurtág experiments with various alternative versions of these violin sonorities, whereas his setting of "Kein Schüler weit und breit" remains rather close to the original conception. Yet further refinements were made in the last preserved version of "Du bist die Aufgabe," dated from 15–21 January 1986, a span of days that evidently reflects the whole period of preoccupation with this setting (Fig. 6.5). This is a polished clean copy containing various improvements, including a soft echo of the words "kein Schüler" without accompaniment, a vocal slide through the interval of a minor ninth at "weit," and a series of subtle gestures in the violin at the close.

If this setting of "Du bist die Aufgabe" had been used in the *Kafka Fragments*, it likely would have fit in part III, perhaps after "Ziel, Weg, Zögern."[12] Other unused settings would also have related, sometimes closely, to songs in the finished work. For instance, Kurtág's contemplated use of "Das Gute ist im gewissen Sinne trostlos" (The good is in a certain sense bleak) would immediately have called up associations with the very first song, "Die Guten gehn im gleichen Schritt." The decision of whether and how to incorporate individual pieces would not have been a simple process. On 10 December 1985, about four months after composing "Die Guten gehn im gleichen Schritt," Kurtág made sketches and drafts for the setting of "Das Gute ist im gewissen Sinne trostlos." These entries are found in Sketchbook 63 in the Sacher Foundation, spread across three pages of this spiral notebook. The second of these pages is seen in Plate 8. On the preceding page, Kurtág set the opening words "Das Gute" to quarter notes on G–A–G, paralleling the beginning of the voice part in "Die Guten gehn im gleichen Schritt," the first song of the cycle. Kurtág submitted many features of these initial sketches to critical scrutiny, writing circled alterations for both the vocal part and the violin part.

On Kurtág's second page of work on "Das Gute ist in gewissen Sinne trostlos," as shown in Plate 8, one still readily notes the close connection to the preexisting setting of "Die Guten gehn." The alternation of G and A in uniform note values in the vocal part at "Das Gute ist" recalls the setting of "Die Guten gehn" in the opening song, and the downward extension later to half notes on F and E for the two syllables of "trostlos" (bleak) provocatively associates "good" with "bleak." As we see from the sketch leaf, Kurtág tried out several different versions of the

Figure 6.5. Fair copy of setting of "Du bist die Aufgabe,"
Sacher Foundation, Basel. Printed with permission.

violin part in the penultimate measure and also submitted the rhythm of the vocal setting to close scrutiny. A pair of drafts for the setting completed two days
later put more distance between this song and "Die Guten gehn." Were Kurtág to
have used this setting, one imagines that it would need to have been placed at a
certain remove from the original setting, since this return to the "Good" involves
a recapitulatory character.

In one instance, "Der Coitus als Bestrafung" (Coitus as punishment), Kurtág
seems to have considered doubling the setting but did not use the first of the
two songs to this text. The unused version employed a prominent double-dotted
rhythm throughout the violin part and in the voice as well up to the word "Glückes"
(happiness), where longer notes appear for the first time. This rhythmic idiom
suggests French overture style; one of the drafts of the song dated 4 October 1985
includes the designation "all' Overtura francaise." In the finished work (III/2),
on the other hand, the word "Glückes" is sustained through an entire measure,
bringing a more pronounced softening of character and dynamics.

While a small collection of settings was removed in the compositional process, a
striking *insertion* took place with the late incorporation of "Der begrenzte Kreis ist
rein" (The closed circle is pure) as no. 6 of part III. Along with the following setting
of "Ziel, Weg, Zögern" (III/7), this is the only song from part III that is missing from
the overview (Figs. 6.2–6.4). "Der begrenzte Kreis" receives a certain emphasis
through its placement following the double of "Elendes Leben." Moreover, "Der
begrenzte Kreis" itself represents an especially fascinating example of doubling,
since this setting is reused not within the *Kafka Fragments* but in an independent
composition, the *Hommage à R. Sch.*, op. 15/d, for clarinet (also bass drum), viola,
and piano. The *Hommage à R. Sch.* was begun before the *Kafka Fragments*, as its
opus number implies, and material for its first and last movements was conceived
already by the 1970s.[13] On the other hand, the *Hommage à R. Sch.* was completed
only several years after the *Kafka Fragments*, in 1990.[14]

One stimulus for the *Hommage à R. Sch.* was Kurtág's acquaintance with
Schumann's *Märchenerzählungen*, op. 132, for clarinet, viola, and piano, the same
distinctive instrumental combination employed in the *Hommage*. The six movements of the *Hommage* are full of references to Schumann. Here, as in the "Eduardowa" movement of the *Kafka Fragments*, Kurtág plays with the Schumannesque
idea of associating contrasting types of music with Eusebius and Florestan. At
the head of the first movement is the inscription "merkwürdige Pirouetten des
Kapellmeisters Johannes Kreisler" (strange pirouettes of the Kapellmeister Johannes Kreisler), an allusion to Schumann through his favorite author, E. T. A.
Hoffmann, the creator of the brilliant but deranged artist-figure Kreisler.[15] (This
context of allusions also conjures up thoughts of the young Johannes Brahms, who
regarded himself as the "young Kreisler.") Kurtág's inscription to the last piece of
his *Hommage*, "Meister Raro discovers Guillaume de Machaut," makes reference

to Schumann's intermediary figure Raro, a kind of musicological superego who negotiates between the divergent spheres of Eusebius and Florestan. Those split worlds are represented in the *Hommage* in piece no. 2, entitled "der begrenzte Kreis" (the closed circle), and in no. 3, ". . . und wieder zuckt es schmerzlich F. um die Lippen . . ." (. . . and again it quivers painfully on Florestan's lips . . .), which is marked *Feroce, agitato*.

"Der begrenzte Kreis" was conceived for the *Kafka Fragments* on the basis of a Kafka text. The larger context of the passage from Kafka's diary includes the following passage: "Wo finde ich Rettung? . . . In mir selbst gibt es ohne menschliche Beziehung keine sichtbaren Lügen. Der begrenzte Kreis ist rein." (Where do I find rescue? . . . In myself there are no visible lies apart from human relationships. The closed circle is pure.)[16] Apart from any resonance with "Kreisler" that may have encouraged its incorporation into the *Hommage à R. Sch.*, "Der begrenzte Kreis" thus stands above all for the inner sanctuary of the self as a spiritual refuge and source of consolation. In the *Kafka Fragments*, Kurtág's setting of the "closed circle" employs an acoustical purity involving perfect fifth intervals in the violin as well as a very sustained vocal setting of the word "rein" (pure) in the voice. It makes sense for Kurtág to have attributed the "closed circle" piece to Eusebius in the *Hommage à R. Sch.*, and Kafka's words appear silently in this score. Eusebius is of course introspective, like Franz Kafka. Through his doubling of "Der begrenzte Kreis," Kurtág creates a point of intersection between these two compositions, enriching the aesthetic context of both works.

Kurtág's setting of "Der begrenzte Kreis" as III/6 of the *Kafka Fragments* has two parts: a close canon at the unison between voice and violin for "Der begrenzte Kreis," followed by a silence and then a setting of the last two words (Ex. 6.1). The final word, "rein," is sustained on an E in the soprano, converging with the violin on this same note at the beginning of the last measure. The purity of the perfect fifth C–G in the violin at "rein," which encircles the sustained E in the voice, is sensitively reaffirmed and heightened through the following unison on E. The canon at "Der begrenzte Kreis" represents the two complementary halves of a complete entity, while the two notes of an added voice in the violin—the rising second G♯–A♯—are inverted in the following measure, linking the two parts of this thoughtful musical aphorism. The tensional dissonance elsewhere in the cycle makes Kurtág's setting of "Der begrenzte Kreis" stand out all the more, conveying an extraordinary serenity through straightforward means. Thomas Bösche has referred to the way in which an "unfulfilled yearning for a wondrous beautiful sound invests [Kurtág's] works like a forbidden fruit; from time to time it can be tasted, but then almost secretly."[17]

Isorhythmic technique, whereby a fixed sequence of pitches appears with a repeating rhythmic pattern, is particularly associated with the medieval composer

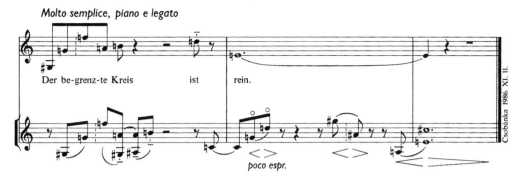

Molto semplice, piano e legato

Der be-grenz-te Kreis   ist   rein.

poco espr.

Csobánka 1986. XI. 11.

Ex. 6.1. Kurtág, *Kafka Fragments*, "Der begrenzte Kreis." Editio Musica Budapest.
Printed with permission.

Guillaume de Machaut, and the concluding piece of the *Hommage*, entitled "Ab-schied" (Farewell), develops this thread. What is readily audible is how the five-note motive beginning with a two-note slur spanning a major seventh from Eusebius's "closed circle" is developed as a six-note ostinato to serve as the basis for the passacaglia-like structure of "Abschied," by far the longest of the six pieces of the *Hommage à R. Sch.* The five-note motive stems from the five syllables of Kafka's text: "der be-grenz-te Kreis." Yet already overlapping with this version of the motive is a six-note version played in the viola con sordino and pianissimo. In "Abschied" this idea connects to the many repetitions of the six-note figure played in the lowest possible register of the piano, played una corda, misterioso, and triple pianissimo. On a larger formal level, the music unfolds in two-measure units, beginning with the piano alone, with the clarinet and viola entering in the third measure.

It is not accidental that Kurtág's "Abschied" begins and ends with the major seventh interval C–B in the deepest register of the piano. In German musical notation, these pitches are C–H, which corresponds to the last letters in the title of Kurtág's work: *Hommage à R. Sch.* These notes already provide the first pitches of the Kapellmeister Kreisler's opening pirouette in the first piece—a salute to Schumann. In the first measure of "Abschied," the pianist first sounds the notes C and B together in the lowest registers before these two pitches are played succes-sively as a slurred C–B figure in the upper-middle register (Ex. 6.2). The sound of C–B resonates to the end of the long measure, sustained by the slur to the chord in half notes, which superimposes these notes as minor seconds. In the middle of the measure, the crucial six-note figure unfolds as a threefold grouping of these note pairs, beginning with B–C. Thereafter this motivic pattern is repeated in all but the last four measures. Variations in pitch level appear, but the music does not stray far from the original position on C–H, and it returns to this sound at the end. The closing punctuation to the hypnotically constant and seemingly endless succession

Ex. 6.2. Kurtág, *Hommage à R. Sch.*, "Abschied," beginning.
Editio Musica Budapest. Printed with permission.

of motivic repetitions in "Abschied" is marked by the sonorous transformation in the very last measure of the movement, when the clarinetist lays down his or her instrument to supply a single soft but heavy stroke on the bass drum.

The haunting repetitions in this mysterious litany harbor a Bachian reference. Allowing for the pitch repetitions in the six-note pattern B–C–B–B♭–A–B♭, four different pitches are sounded. The downward extension of the C–B dyad to B♭–A exposes these four pitches as the focus of the six-note ostinato figure. According to German musical terminology, B♭ is expressed as B, and B is expressed as H. The notes highlighted in the ostinato bring to sound a version of the famous symbolic motive BACH, the chromatic motive that Johann Sebastian Bach incorporated as a kind of musical signature into the unfinished quadruple fugue of his *Kunst der Fuge* shortly before his death in 1750. Kurtág's handling of this motive displays polyphonic aspects, as when the clarinet plays a rhythmically compressed version of the six-note figure in sixteenth notes against the ostinato in eighth notes heard in the lowest register of the piano.

The compositional origins of "Abschied" reach back to 1976, yet the incorporation of the Eusebius version of the "closed circle" dates from a decade later, in late 1986, representing as it does a spillover from Kurtág's preoccupation with the *Kafka Fragments*. The first performance of the Schumann *Hommage* took place in 1990, several years after completion of the *Kafka Fragments*. Thus the genesis of the *Hommage à R. Sch.* both frames and intersects with the compositional evolution of the *Kafka* project, Kurtág's magnum opus of the 1980s.

Yet the association with Schumann in the *Kafka Fragments* goes further. Kurtág's cycle contains its own *Hommage à Schumann* in I/18, the setting of "Träumend hing die Blume" (The flower hung dreamily). The poetic image of the flower in relation to Schumann is richly allusive, calling to mind some of the consoling songs in the *Dichterliebe*.[18] Kurtág's use in the piano of the high, floating, dolcissimo sonority of the minor ninth G♭–F in "Träumend hing die Blume" begins and ends the song (Ex. 6.3). Marked *Äusserst ruhig und zart* (Extremely quiet and tender),

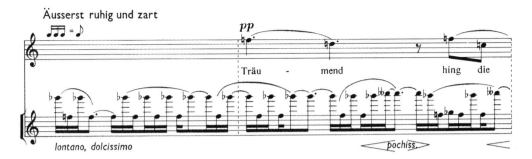

Ex. 6.3. Kurtág, *Kafka Fragments*, "Träumend hing die Blume," beginning.
Editio Musica Budapest. Printed with permission.

this suspended sound unfolds in triplet sixteenths, creating an ethereal texture somewhat reminiscent of late Beethoven, as in passages of the Arietta movement of his final Piano Sonata, op. 111.[19] The gently yearning character evoked here might also be compared with the very beginning of Schumann's *Dichterliebe*, in which the expressive dissonance of the first two notes—C♯ against D—already prefigures a whole world of feeling.[20] The admirable recording of "Träumend hing die Blume" sung by Juliane Banse with violinist András Keller conveys the dreamlike state with exquisite sensitivity.[21]

Here as elsewhere, it is important to perceive what meaning becomes attached to the high, suspended violin figuration through its unfolding relation to Kafka's words. The dreamy hanging of the flower on its high stem is reflected through the lofty position of the G♭, perched as it is more than an octave above the F, the note used in the voice for the first syllable of "Träu-mend" (dream-ing) as well as for the verb "hing" (hung). The span of more than an octave reflects the stem as bearer of the flower, as is conveyed musically by the stirring shift in the vocal part from F to F♯ first at "Blu-[me]" (flow-[er]) and then more decisively at "hohen Sten-[gel]" (high stem).[22] Only here does one begin to perceive the significance of the static, suspended alternation of the minor ninth G♭–F from the outset, which is associated poetically with the image of the tall flower. As the words "am hohen Stengel" resonate in the voice, the violin elaborates its figuration, harmonically and contrapuntally. Yet the peak of the vocal line is reserved for the end of Kafka's concise text: "Abenddämmerung umzog sie" (dusk enveloped it). Here darkness embraces the splendid flower as the soprano sustains G, resolving this pitch at the end of the measure to the F♯ corresponding to the earlier setting of "Sten-[gel]" (stem). Though enveloped in darkness—that quintessential romantic image—the flower does not vanish in the music, since the violin ultimately returns, at the end of its long meditative postlude, to its point of origin on the pitches F and G♭.[23] This song has a circular form, refusing closure in favor of endless dreaming.

Text and Music in the *Kafka Fragments*

Aspects of the interaction and blending of Kafka's suggestive texts with Kurtág's remarkable music can be illustrated through some of the concise settings in the *Kafka Fragments*. The song following "Der begrenzte Kreis" is "Ziel, Weg, Zögern" (III/7), in which underlying existential issues are given forceful expression. The text asserts: "Es gibt ein Ziel, aber keinen Weg; was wir Weg nennen, ist Zögern" (There is a goal but no path; what we call a path is hesitation). Through his musical setting, Kurtág probes the paradoxical meaning lodged in Kafka's concentrated formulation. In contrast to the syllabic declamation of the rest of the song, the final word "Zögern" (hesitation) is enormously elongated. The syllable "Zö-" is protracted over a dozen beats. It therefore embodies in itself a static waiting, a hesitation. What is involved is not a path toward a goal but a more spontaneous shift in perspective, an enlarged temporal awareness and magnified sensibility.

The interplay between soprano and violin deepens the meaning of Kafka's aphorism while moving beyond the strictly verbal sphere, for the accented augmented-octave interval C♯–C in the violin in mm. 5–7 already anticipates the vocal setting of "Zögern" spanning the same minor-ninth interval heard a half step lower: C–B. This sonority too is protracted, and the lower pitch of the dyad, C, prepares the upper pitch of the soprano at the first syllable of "Zö-gern." This anticipation in the violin of the vocal setting of "Zögern" enhances the independent contrapuntal role of that instrument. The violin gesture acts in urgent counterpoint to the voice and points beyond anything that *could* be sung.

The positioning of the sharply accented, syncopated minor ninth sonority at the midpoint of the song is significant. The rejection of a *Weg*, or "path," in favor of an immediate *presence* is at issue here. Only in this context can we appreciate the closing gesture in the violin in the final measure, for the arpeggiated penultimate sonority combines two minor-ninth intervals: A♭–G and C–B. The pitches associated with hesitation are doubled here and then resolved downward to the final note, A, which represents the continuation from the vocal motive heard moments before.

In the ensuing setting of "So fest" (So tight) (III/8), the metaphor of a tightly held stone to be hurled into the distance defines the path as a remote goal. Crucial words here are "jene Weite" (that distance), to be sung "meditatively." As he did in the setting of "weit" in the unused song "Du bist die Aufgabe," Kurtág expands the range here to stretch from middle C at "je-[ne]" to high G at "Wei-[te]," an octave and a fifth higher. The emphasis lies on the distance and not on the path as such. On the other hand, a sudden manifestation of an astonishing uncanny presence occupies the penultimate position in this part of the cycle in "Staunend sahen wir das grosse Pferd" (Amazed we saw the great horse) (III/11). This song, marked *Largamente, alla breve*, begins with lofty, widely spaced chords in half notes in the violin, played *forte*, with the highest voice descending by step from C to G. That

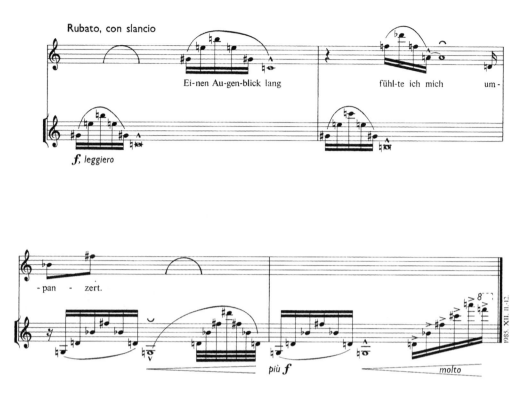

Ex. 6.4. Kurtág, *Kafka Fragments*, "Umpanzert." Editio Musica Budapest.
Printed with permission.

the opening sonority, which sounds C in three octaves, conveys the presence of the great horse is confirmed by the later setting of "Pferd" as octave unisons with the soprano on G in m. 8. The harmonic approach at "das gros-se" leading up to "Pferd" would imply G♭/F♯, but Kurtág instead supplies the octave G here, ending the phrase with impressive effect. The stirring poetic idea of the great white horse with flowing mane breaking through the ceiling invites comparison with the contrasting dark image of leopards breaking into the temple in "Leoparden" (IV/5). Ironically, the breaking in of the marauders occurs again and again and becomes a predictable part of the ceremony. Consequently, Kurtág's setting, which begins with the direction "wild and fast," ends gently, più lento and dolcissimo.

The concentrated chemistry of Kurtág's Kafka is evident in "Umpanzert" (Fortified) (I/14), which is but four measures in length (Ex. 6.4).[24] This setting is characterized by a paradoxical wit that finds unsuspected potential in a mere bundle of words. "Einen Augenblick lang" means literally "for a moment" or "a moment long." Kurtág recognizes a latent meaning here, recalling the sense of immediate presence of "Ziel, Weg, Zögern." Regarded dualistically, "Einen Augenblick" (A moment) and "lang" (long) are contraries; the word "long" contests the import of "moment." The verb *umpanzert* (armored or fortified) lends a character of sturdiness and solidity that is reflected in the musical setting. The initial musical motive set to "Einen Augenblick" might seem stable and solid: a rising sixth from G♯ to E is followed by a rising perfect fifth to high B. A descent through the same pitches of E and G♯ provides a strong sense of symmetry, with all five pitches grouped rhythmically into a pattern of sixteenth notes.

Nevertheless, the landing on a prolonged accented C confirms the harmonic underpinning as an augmented triad. The upwardly arching gesture to the high B set to the syllable "Au-" is poised above the whole note C almost two octaves below. Rhythmically, the setting of "lang" is *long*: the accented whole note on C stands in sustained opposition to the two words preceding it. The sense of negation of the preceding words is paradoxical, since the sustained character amounts to an affirmation, a sonorous *presence*. From this insight Kurtág builds his setting. The dualistic motive is heard first in the violin, then in the soprano. In the second measure, the existential reference of "lang" to the self is affirmed through the assignment of the long, accented A to "mich" (me). With the setting of "um-pan-zert" through the rising intervals D–B♭–F♯, Kurtág again employs the augmented triad, stressing the last two syllables through the broadening of rhythmic values, while the violin duplicates the B♭–F♯ step in its rapid figuration to coincide with the last syllable of the vocal part.

An ecstatic character emerges in the violin postlude. A new variant of the "Augenblick" motive arises at the end of the penultimate measure. The motivic intensification is written here in thirty-second notes instead of sixteenths, and it peaks by extending upward the F♯ heard in the soprano at "-zert," thereby reaching a high D♯. This is the highest pitch yet reached in the piece, but it is transcended in the final measure. Beginning on the downbeat, Kurtág now recapitulates the "Moment" motive in an emphatic form. Grounded on G, the lowest note of the violin, the motive sweeps up through fifths and sixths for nearly two octaves before collapsing symmetrically once more to the G.

We become aware here of tensional aspects lodged in Kurtág's dualistic idea. How long can this alternation of arpeggiated gestures and long-held notes continue? Is there an end in sight? Can the energy of the energetic, upward-thrusting rhythmic figure overcome its antithesis? Despite its extreme brevity, "Umpanzert" both raises and answers such questions. In its closing gesture, the violin breaks free from constraints, passes into the stratosphere, and disappears into silence.

A very different kind of dualism is embodied in the following song, "Zwei Spazierstöcke" (Two walking sticks). Like "Ruhelos" (I/4) and a number of other songs, this piece assumes a vivid dramatic character yet collapses at its conclusion into distanced introspective irony. The comparison pivots on the sung inscriptions of the two walking sticks, each of which is introduced by spoken words. The French novelist's cane, which is set with jewels, is contrasted here with the simple stick of the wanderer protagonist. Balzac's walking stick bears the self-confident claim of overcoming: "I break all barriers." Kurtág supports these words with pure triads in the violin, while the vocal part reaches its peak at "Hin-der-nis-se" (barriers). As Kurtág notes at the head of the song, the setting is "authentisch-plagal," employing with metaphorical effect the two basic kinds of cadential progressions. The strong "authentic" form affirms the dominant harmony; the weaker "plagal" form utilizes the subdominant. Displaying mirror symmetry, the setting of "Ich breche alle" (I break all) passes through the G and C major triads to reach a D major chord, whereas "Mich brechen alle" (I am broken by all) is expressed by the identical harmonies moving in the weaker subdominant direction, passing through the D and C major triads to a G major sonority.

The "authentic" Balzac sequence of triads on G major, C major, and D major leads to a further upward shift by semitone in all voices, peaking at "Hin-[der-nis-se]." This harmonic shift resembles a deceptive cadence; one is reminded distantly perhaps of the protracted moment on a high, sustained E♭ chord in Beethoven's Ninth Symphony choral finale at "Über Sternen muß er wohnen" (Above the stars he must dwell). In the second phrase of "Zwei Spazierstöcke," on the other hand, the violin chords and vocal line descend rather than ascend, as they do at the proclamation of Balzac's proud dictum. In this reversal of the harmonic progression, a telling moment is reached at the setting of "Hindernisse." Here, the upward semitone shift is shadowy, moving in the vocal part from G to G♯. The voice fails, recalling the exhausted delivery of "Ru-he-los" at the end of I/4 or the collapse of the singer near the end of "Nichts dergleichen" (I/19). The whispered "Hindernisse" conveys brokenness; the same word that had been mastered by Balzac can now scarcely be uttered at all. The two opposing perspectives have little in common besides the modifier "alle" (all), which is spoken to conclude the song.

This extraction of a nugget of meaning out of persistent repetitions is the subject of I/7, "Wenn er mich immer frägt" (But he just won't stop asking me). This song is one of the wittiest of all (Ex. 6.5). The text stems from the beginning of Kafka's diary from 1910, where it forms the second entry: "'Wenn er mich immer frägt.' Das ä, losgelöst vom Satz, flog dahin wie ein Ball auf der Wiese" ("But he just won't stop asking me." The *a*, detached from the sentence, flew away like a ball across the meadow). Kurtág's response fastens on the word "immer," meaning "again and again." This is a pretext for nagging repetition, and he directs that the singer deliver the line in a "squeaking" fashion.[25] The first half of the song is built almost exclusively from the interval of a fourth, underscoring the repetitiousness. Furthermore, Kurtág alters the text from Kafka's diary to repeat the word "immer" (always). He brings that word to life by allowing it to manifest its essential nature, its influence and omnipresence within the verbal confines of its domain. The squeaking "immer" motive initially dominates the setting, and the ensuing quality of obsessiveness is conveyed as well through two imitations of the opening vocal phrase in the violin, first *mezzo piano* to *mezzo forte* and then *forte*.

3 Ein wenig quäkend
  A bit squeaking
4 Sich wichtig machend
  Putting on airs
5 (den Bogen nierderlegen)
  (put down the bow)

Ex. 6.5. Kurtág, *Kafka Fragments*, "Wenn er mich immer frägt."
Editio Musica Budapest. Printed with permission.

The first nodal point in this song comes at the word "frägt" (asks). Kurtág concentrates his structure of fourths on this word. The soprano is given upward and lower grace notes on G♯ and A with the main note, D♯, falling on a downbeat; concurrently, the violin begins its first statement imitating the opening vocal phrase. The dogged insistence of "immer, immer" reaches a threshold here, and the grace notes in the voice at the distance of an upper fourth and lower tritone suggest a virtual fourth chord without yet actually realizing it in sound. Moments later, at "Das ä" (the *a*), Kurtág returns to this virtual chord, which now receives more embodiment, since the A has become an eighth note set to "Das" and the upper G♯ a longer ornament preceding the D♯. The expression at this juncture assumes a theatrical aura: "putting on airs."

The following words, "losgelöst vom Satz" (detached from the sentence), represent a surprising trigger point: the overused, questioning "ah" breaks off from the sentence. At "losgelöst vom Satz" Kurtág continues to hammer away at the strict structure of fourths and tritones; the descending sequence E–B♭–F–C is the inversion of the opening notes in the vocal part, whereas the violin gesture emphasizing D♯ echoes the vocal setting of "ä."

How does Kurtág convey the *separation* of the vowel from its consonants? At "Satz" (sentence), the soprano leaps through a seventh to a B, a qualitatively new gesture, though one still closely related to the opening phrase of the voice part.[26] At this moment, we hear a sonority in the violin that includes A, D♯, and G♯, the pitches identified with the "ä." By escaping to the violin part—from the sphere of language into the sphere of instrumental sound—this sound indeed emancipates itself from the straitjacket of repetition! No longer imprisoned by the four guardian consonants of "frägt," the "ä" is set free, *losgelöst*. The refugee can now celebrate. Like a ball on the meadow, it shall fly away, in waltz tempo! The deliciously subtle, leggierissimo execution of the concluding dancelike phrases changes the tone, setting the final measures at a vast distance from the nagging repetition of the opening of the song.

The following song, "Es zupfte mich jemand am Kleid" (I/8), displays a similar expressive logic as does "Wenn er mich immer frägt." The rhythm of Kafka's lines as set by Kurtág reinforces the meaning: the insistent tugging is reflected by triplet eighth note groups in the voice, with accents and emphatic violin chords occupying the strong beats. At the word "Kleid" (clothes), the sense of physical contact is conveyed through more rapid and intense *forte* chords in the violin. This phrase then sets the scene for an action: the shrugging off of the unwelcome tugging. Here, as in the preceding piece, annoying persistent interference is overcome through a liberating deed. Notable too is the linear continuity between the accented C♯ at "Kleid" and the nimble chromatic sixteenth notes rising from D♯ to F♯ that belong to the setting of "Aber ich schüttelte ihn ab" (but I shrugged him off). The moment of *disjuncture* at "shrugged" is conveyed above all through the gesture of the rapid, downwardly unfolding, broken chord, with a contrary-motion arpeggio on the downbeat in the violin. The final triple fortissimo gesture in the violin confirms and also celebrates the act of liberation.

It is fascinating to observe how Kurtág's musical miniatures in the *Kafka Fragments* were triggered by Kafka's aphorisms in his diaries and excerpts from letters to his closest confidante, Milena Jesenská.[27] One is reminded of other documented instances in which chance occurrences yielded potentially rich artistic material. One of the most provocative is recorded by Bálint András Varga in his collection of interviews with Kurtág. Varga describes Kurtág's encounters with the influential American composer John Cage, mentioning how Kurtág met Cage at the International Bartók Seminar and Festival in Szombathely, Hungary, in 1986. Varga relates further: "Kurtág also told me that a year later [in 1987], he bumped into Cage in Zurich. 'He was standing in the lobby of the Opera House. I went up to him and told him my name: Kurtág. Whereupon Cage: guten Tag! Me: I'm Kurtág. He: guten Tag! (as a stage instruction: Kurtág giving up): Bye-bye! It was something like a composition; I jotted it down on a piece of paper.'"[28] On the basis of the *Kafka Fragments*, we can well understand why Kurtág bothered to write down his curiously amusing nonencounter with Cage at Zurich, regarding it as "something like a composition," and we may hope he will sometime yet write the music. As a tensional encounter that suddenly breaks off, "Kurtág—guten Tag!" shows a structure comparable to some of the tersely paradoxical songs we have discussed, such as "Wenn er mich immer frägt."

Vulnerability and the "True Path"

Human vulnerability is a prominent theme in part IV of the cycle, the part of the *Kafka Fragments* most concerned with love. This section opens with "Zu spät" (Too late), composed at Szombathely in August 1985. The springboard is Kafka's diary entry of 22 October 1913, in which he reflects on his fleeting love relationship with Gerti Wasner, an eighteen-year-old Swiss woman whom he met during his stay in a sanatorium in Riva, on the Lago di Garda in northern Italy:

> 22. Oktober. Zu spät. Die Süßigkeit der Trauer und der Liebe. Vor ihr angelächelt werden im Boot. Das war das Allerschönste. Immer nur das Verlangen, zu sterben und das Sich-noch-Halten, das allein ist Liebe.

> [22 October. Too late. The sweetness of grief and love. To be smiled at by her in the boat. That was the most beautiful of all. Again and again that yearning to die and yet the holding back, that alone is love.]

In Kurtág's setting, the arresting import of the words "Too late" is conveyed through a rising half step F♯–G in the soprano; the chromaticism implied through this pair of notes is taken up at once by the violin. A semitone juxtaposition of F♯

and G is heard in the first full measure, since the violin sustains an F♯ whole note against the G in the voice, whereas in the second measure the violin itself shifts its sustained whole note up to G, thereby composing out the opening half step motive of the soprano. The second voice in the violin creeps around these sustained pitches chromatically. Every note is strictly derived from the opening vocal gesture set to "Too late."

"Zu spät" is the most chromatic of all the songs in the *Kafka Fragments*, the most suffused with a yearning for love and death, that archetypal cultural theme. The associations raised by Kafka's concise entry based on his experience at Riva are far-reaching, blending a masochistic "sweetness of grief" with the urge to preserve in memory that "most beautiful of all," the smile in the boat. The watery setting as well as the endless longing for a love shadowed by death suggest a parallel to Wagner's *Tristan und Isolde*, and this background doubtless left an impact on Kurtág's music. As we have seen, a pervasive rising chromaticism punctuated by wide, falling intervals is characteristic of the music of erotic yearning in works like *Tristan* and the Adagietto of Mahler's Fifth Symphony. Comparable elements surface in Kurtág's "Zu spät" (Ex. 6.6). His setting of "Liebe" (love) is set apart through its melodic span of a falling minor ninth, whereas smaller intervals are otherwise prominent.

In the violin part following "Liebe," for instance, the lower voice in whole notes rises from C♯ through D and then through a whole step to E, while the upper voice traces a chromatic trajectory a fifth higher, reaching C at the end of m. 10. In the following measures, the violin lines separate to the distance of an octave and then stress the expressive dissonance of a minor ninth over and over: D above C♯, E♭ above D, and then D above C♯. Kurtág marks this passage *doloroso, lontano* (lamenting, distant). From whence does it derive its sonorous content? This is a distillation of the sustained setting of "Liebe" in the soprano, where the same falling minor ninth, D to C♯, resonated across two full measures. The violin sustains and compresses this musical content even as we move to the next line of text, which is delivered "softly and fleetingly, as if from a distance."

"To be smiled at by her in the boat": this gentle, soft musical utterance is held in rigorous relation to all that precedes and follows it. The vocal part suggests a siciliano rhythm; the words are delivered gently, as if from a distance. Whereas the highest previous pitch in the song had been reached at the sustained D at "Lie-[be]," the inward reflection of the loving smile motivates the further ascent to E at "Boot" (boat), which shifts down chromatically in sustained notes to recapture the earlier pitch level of D and then lift it up to D♯. The way the high sustained E is then delicately reaffirmed at "Das" (that) deserves comment. "Das" might seem to be a colorless word, but this impression is superficial. Kurtág's "Zu spät" is a superbly organic conception that embodies the rich content latent in Kafka's choice words. In this musical setting, the word "Das" acts as a kind of magnet,

Ex. 6.6. Kurtág, *Kafka Fragments*, "Zu spät," beginning.
Editio Musica Budapest. Printed with permission.

a point of compression, absorbing the experience of the smile in the boat. The intimate glance on the water and gentle setting of "Das war das Allerschönste" is the inward climax, since it breaks the "closed circle," the isolation of the self. The affinity here to the "glance" motive in Wagner and Mahler is not accidental; the proverbial image of eyes as windows to the soul reaches back to antiquity.

In the remainder of Kurtág's setting, the parallel setting of "Verlangen" (yearning) and "sterben" (to die) is striking. From the lower E—an octave below the climax bridging "Boot" and "Das"—the sliding chromatic steps are opened to the space of the augmented second G♭–A at "Verlangen" and the major third G–B at "sterben." The still wider falling intervals at "Sich-noch-Hal-ten" recall the earlier melodic shape at "Al-ler-schön-ste." Kurtág then takes the cue from Kafka's text for a recapitulation of the stirring vocal gesture at "Liebe," spanning the descending minor ninth D–C♯. Echoes of the minor ninth permeate the violin postlude, which now is dominated by descending chromatics, inverting the linear direction from the beginning of the song.

Yet another dimension of "Zu spät" lies in its connection to Samuel Beckett's 1958 play *Krapp's Last Tape*. The affinity lies not only in the backward-looking mood of melancholy reminiscence of Beckett's play but in specific layers of floating erotic imagery, as in the following passage, which is punctuated by silences as Krapp stops and rewinds the tape:

> —my face in her breast and my hand on her. We lay there without moving.
> But under us all moved, and moved us, gently, up and down, and from side to side.
> [*Pause*]
> Past midnight. Never knew such silence. The earth might be uninhabited.
> [*Pause*]
> Here I end—
> [*Krapp switches off, winds tape back, switches on again*]
> —upper lake with the punt, bathed off the bank, then pushed out into the stream and drifted.[29]

In "Zu spät" pregnant silences occur near the beginning and end of the song after "Die Süßigkeit der Trauer und der Liebe" and preceding the final words:, "das allein ist Liebe."

Kurtág returns in an entirely different way to the idea of the erotic glance at the outset of the next song, "Eine lange Geschichte" (A long story) (IV/2), which begins with a halting setting of "Ich sehe einem Mädchen in die Augen" (I look a girl in the eye) and then unfolds as a huge crescendo, peaking ecstatically at "Donner und Küsse und Blitz" (thunder and kisses and lightning). The following two songs explore the theme of vulnerability in contrasting fashion. "In Memoriam Robert Klein" (IV/3) is dominated by the disturbing image of hunting dogs destined to vanquish their prey, whereas in "Aus einem alten Notizbuch" (From an old notebook) (IV/4), the writer observes how his left hand compassionately grips the exhausted fingers of his right hand. The expressive weight of this music falls on the last three phrases, with tender stress on motives falling from E and set to "Mitleid" (compassion), "Fingern" (fingers), and "umfasst hielt" (gripping).

If a moment of telling, or *erzählen*, enables the inward climax in "Zu spät," the setting "Im Memoriam Joannis Pilinszky" (IV/6), whose title alludes to the Hungarian poet, questions the very possibility of narrative communication. As such, it belongs to the critical framework of Kurtág's aesthetics, in which dream states are pitted against hard realism, undue pretensions punctured or mocked. The beginning of the text "Ich kann nicht eigentlich erzählen, ja fast nicht einmal reden" (I can't actually tell a story, in fact, I am almost unable even to speak) lies at the threshold of noncommunication, of stuttering yielding to silence. The long violin prelude is punctuated by pauses. It begins timidly on a single note. The textures are sparse throughout, with restricted treatment of register and an avoidance of any double-stops in the violin. In the vocal part, the gaps between words are long; the delivery of words unfolds in a stammering fashion. Even the word "erzählen" is slightly interrupted between its first two syllables.

The would-be narrator communicates something important: the feeling that the act of telling is like the experience of little children taking their first steps. In the halting setting of these last words, "die die er-sten Geh-ver-su-che ma-chen," the violin serves as close partner to the voice, shadowing it in a state of virtual identity. Although the violin often echoes the voice, sometimes it anticipates, as with the second syllable of the last word, "[ma]-chen" (make), which steadies the toddler. A remarkable feature of this setting is its depiction of precarious balance, or imbalance, of strained efforts and setbacks, which convey an emotional quality close to anguish or despair. Bipedal locomotion is not taken for granted here.

In an interview with Varga, Kurtág makes reference to this *Hommage à Pilinszky* as *ars poetica* and states: "I cannot speak, and basically, I cannot tell a story. Like a child who tries to learn to walk. That is a state that I actually seek. As if I did not want to know my material."[30] The movement is from stuttering toward communication. Here as elsewhere, the goal of a creative process can be to capture tensional uncertainty, avoiding predictable paths while safeguarding vitality.

While working at the Archivio Luigi Nono in Venice, Friedemann Sallis came across a manuscript by Kurtág, a fair copy of "In Memoriam Joannis Pilinszky." Kurtág scrawled "Für Gigi, he[r]zlichst, gyuri" near the top of the first page; he had sent the manuscript to Nono as both a greeting and a message. Since this Kafka fragment concerns an inability to communicate and a need to relearn this capability, it complements and corresponds to a phrase that Nono repeated incessantly in personal notes, memos, titles, and program notes during the last decade of his life: "No hay caminos, hay que caminar" (There are no pathways, there is only traveling itself). For Nono, this motto meant that forms and formulas from the past are not reliable. Reinventing his style and technique late in his career, Kurtág's fellow traveler created a series of innovative chamber works as well as his monumental *Prometeo, tragedia dell'ascolto* (1985). Kurtág's greeting acknowledges this achievement as well as their shared perspective. During the 1980s, Nono often claimed that he had seen the phrase "No hay caminos, hay que caminar" written on a wall in Toledo and that both the wall and the inscription dated from the late Middle Ages. At the same time, the motto paraphrases a poem by Antonio Machado, a poet whom Nono knew well because he had been setting his texts since the early 1960s.[31]

That brings us to the last and longest of the songs we shall examine in detail here: "Der wahre Weg," which forms the whole of part II. Like "Abschied" in the *Hommage à R. Sch.*, this is an extended slow movement, an antipode to the agitated, driven pieces in the *Kafka Fragments* like "Ruhelos" (I/4), "Nichts dergleichen" (I/19), and "Wiederum, wiederum" (IV/7). Kurtág entitles this highly unified piece an "Hommage-message à Pierre Boulez." The precarious balancing act between voice and violin heard in the "Im Memoriam Joannis Pilinszky" is reflected in this Adagio through the contrapuntal balance between the two lines of the violin, which begin an octave apart in the lowest available register, on G. "Der wahre Weg" is almost unbearably demanding for the performers. The violinist never reaches the E string; a sense of struggle is fundamental to adequate interpretation. The violinist must play like two musicians at once, achieving a tensional balance of the paired voices, whereas the soprano must successfully sustain those long, low notes that convey the central message of the song: "Der wahre Weg geht über ein Seil . . . knapp über den Boden" (The true path goes by way of a rope . . . just above the ground).

The "doubled" violinist balanced "just above the ground" thus contributes to the poetic image of the musical setting. This carries implications for the voice leading, register, and harmonic structure. The pitches for the soprano as well are low and fall between the two lines of the violin. The very first syllable of the voice, the C♯ set to "Der" in m. 4, lies between two A♭s in the violin. Even if C♯ is not enharmonically equivalent to D♭ in this instance, a strongly tonal framework is felt, and this tonal foundation is more broadly characteristic of the song, which ends with a varied recapitulation of the opening violin passage leading to a consonant tenth—G–B—as the final sonority.

The tonal balance unfolds here on a vast timescale relative to the many fleeting miniatures heard in part I of the *Kafka Fragments*. In connection with the notion of a path over a suspended rope, it is natural for Kurtág to employ quarter tones in the violin, since these convey subtle nuances, corrections, and adjustments, and they register the constant instability that confronts the wanderer protagonist in navigating the "true path." The notion of the "true path" is of course regarded ironically by Kafka/Kurtág; the purpose of the rope "scheint mehr bestimmt, stolpern zu machen als begangen zu werden" (seems to be more to make one stumble than to be walked on). This part of the text is delivered parenthetically in two segments, in a compressed, quasi-speaking manner, which makes the protracted slowness of the rest of the song stand out even more in relief. Its first phrase is rendered as a "quasi cadenza" with allusion to siciliano rhythm ("Es scheint mehr bestimmt, stolpern zu machen"), whereas the second is conveyed in a more distanced manner, in the character of a chorale ("als begangen zu werden").

The song begins with three measures for the violin alone. The opening octave G emerges from silence and is played triple pianissimo, yet the atmosphere is immediately infused with tension because of inward shifts of the two voices, which cannot retain their octave positions. Were it not for the use of quarter tones, there would be a clear implication here of augmented sixths emerging out of the octaves and resolving back into them. The smaller intervallic span achieves an analogous effect with more subtlety: balance on the suspended rope demands vigilance and tiny adjustments. After both voices shift to the A♭ octave beginning m. 2—a half step higher than their starting point on G—the lower voice drops back to G, and the upper part falls in turn to this octave. After another inward shift at the outset of m. 3, the two voices pass over the G octave to reach the A♭ octave that sounds as the soprano is first heard.

The voice traces a similar vacillating path through its sustained notes, shifting from C♯ to D, reaching E♭ at "geht" (goes) in m. 8, yet sinking back through D to C♯ at "Seil" (rope) in m. 10 (Ex. 6.7). Though the voice returns here to its opening pitch, change has occurred in the music, as reflected in the gradually rising pitch levels of the violin. A trigger is the word "geht" (goes) in m. 8, which motivates groupings of eighth notes in slow triplet configurations, first in the lower and then in the upper part. Thus at "Seil" the voice rests on the same C♯ as the lower voice of the violin, with its upper voice reaching more than an octave higher.

After so much slow, sustained motion by semitone, the detached accented notes in the violin in the middle of m. 12, with the upper part spanning the descending augmented third from A♯ to F, are conspicuous, even surprising. The following words of the soprano act as a commentary on all of the music we have heard so far: "das nicht in der Höhe gespannt ist" (that is suspended not high up). The word "Hö-[he]" (high) is set here not to a high note but to one of the lowest notes in the vocal part. The sense of a suspended line is conveyed with vivid, almost overwhelming immediacy in the music, which embodies the position of the rope as "not high up."

Yet the meaning of the whole is clarified only with the last line in the vocal part: "Es scheint mehr bestimmt, stolpern zu machen als begangen zu werden" (Its purpose seems to be more to make one stumble than to be walked on"). The "true path" as stumbling block, not as something lifted up high but as something low down, immediate, and close to the ground: this is Kafka's vision as realized in Kurtág's song, which seems gigantic in context, following the many genuine "fragments" in part I.

This "nonfragment" has a circular aspect, yet paradoxically, it also attains a sense of closure. The open cyclical dimension is conveyed through Kurtág's handling of the last word, "wer-den" (to be), which spans the rising tritone F♯–C and sets into motion the recapitulation of the violin passage heard at the outset. "Werden" is a future tense and points toward what is to come; the return of the earlier music in this context implies the continuing undiminished presence of all that has yet been heard. That Kurtág does not change the recapitulated music is striking and

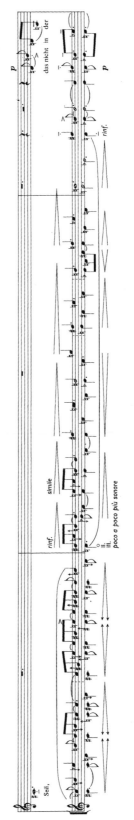

Ex. 6.7. Kurtág, *Kafka Fragments*, "Der wahre Weg," beginning. Editio Musica Budapest. Printed with permission.

unusual; only the final measure, with its ultimate settling onto the consonant major tenth, G–B, is altered. One can well imagine, therefore, that the return of the violin postlude overlaps or blends with the prelude, implying an endless succession of repetitions as we continue to experience "Der wahre Weg" in our mind's ear. For this "true path" is long and indeed endless. The static slowness and hypnotic repetitions of the song, together with its motive of stumbling, may remind us at least distantly of another culminating *Wanderlied*, Schubert's "Der Leiermann" (The hurdy-gurdy man) at the end of *Winterreise*.

Kurtág's extensive use of quarter tones in "Der wahre Weg" might be regarded in relation to the treatment of quarter tones in the lowest register of the violin in the last movement of the last work Bartók completed, his Sonata for Violin Solo.[32] This lowest violin pitch on G returns prominently at the end of the concluding song of the entire cycle, "Es blendete uns die Mondnacht" (The moonlit night dazzled us). Here too the low sound is associated with deep, earthly ground: "Wir krochen durch den Staub, ein Schlangenpaar" (We crawled through the dust, a pair of snakes). A series of descending chromatic figures in the violin reach their endpoint on G; the matching sound in the penultimate vocal phrase is spoken: "Staub" (dust).

The earlier coloratura passages for both soprano and violin in this impressive final song carry the artistic expression beyond the limits of language. The entire second section, marked *Lento, rubato*, is framed by a double statement of the last line of text with its image of the two serpents. At the end of the first statement, the final word, "paar" (pair), serves as a springboard, triggering astonishing melismatic passages for the voice and violin. With extraordinary freedom, the vocal line unfolds as intricate embellishment, vibrations, and seemingly endless melody; the violin suggests a kind of fantastic sitar improvisation, hovering in the uncanny landscape inhabited by the "Schlangenpaar" (pair of snakes). The three-note rhythmic figure heard at the outset of the Lento, rubato section (as C–B–C or C–G–C in the violin and slightly later as C–G–C at "wir" in the soprano) is inverted as the music rises to the climax in the lofty high register, reaching an unforgettable peak at the vocal motive G–B–G. The spectacular cadenza caps the song, whose textures now descend to the original low register for the close, which is strangely transfigured through the animalistic imagery yet firmly grounded by the final low G in the voice at "paar." The pair of protagonists have dispensed with human form, and the imaginative setting opens a final paradoxical level of meaning: the symbolic identification of György and Márta Kurtág as metamorphosed creatures creeping through the dust. The following ascent in the violin, pianissimo and dolcissimo, conveys an open ending, for the journey remains ever incomplete.

We recall Kurtág's comment about his original encounter with Kafka—that it was "through *The Metamorphosis* that I found access."[33] The text of the second song of the *Fragments* already alludes to constant transformation of the path: "Wie ein

Weg im Herbst: Kaum ist er reingekehrt, bedeckt er sich wieder mit den trockenen Blättern" (Like a pathway in autumn: hardly has it been swept clean, it is covered again with dry leaves). In Kafka the transformation of the protagonist is conveyed in the initial sentence of the tale;[34] in Kurtág's work the parallel event is withheld until the end. The notion of metamorphosis involves a rich ambiguity that can only be accommodated in the imagination; one recalls Kafka's horror in recoiling from the notion that the insect might be drawn to furnish a frontispiece for the publication of *Die Verwandlung*: "Please, not that—anything but that! . . . The insect itself cannot be drawn. It cannot even be shown in the distance."[35] The premature resolution of ambiguity can diminish meaning. This is a point that demands empathy and respect for aesthetic autonomy even as we confront an unusually detailed and suggestive array of contextual evidence.

In diverse ways, the notion of transformation has remained central to all our investigations. Mozart's inspired afterthought of resolving the opening of his Fantasia as a culminating gesture ending his C Minor Sonata, the *creatio ex nihilo* of Beethoven's plan for his incomplete F Minor Trio, Schumann's metamorphosis of Beethoven, Mahler's of Bach and Wagner, Bartók's assimilation of folkloric elements into his chain of interconnected dances: each of these creative endeavors exposes a fresh path, clearing away impatient habitual solutions.

In 1987, soon after completing the *Kafka Fragments*, Kurtág declared at the Bremer Podium composition workshop that "my mother tongue is Bartók, and Bartók's mother tongue was Beethoven."[36] Studies of the creative process have reminded us time and again of the importance of such productive continuities, as successive generations of composers invent new forms and new means of expression while building on the legacy of the past. Their pieces can be explored concretely and vividly through the approach of genetic criticism, whereby the artwork is regarded not as a closed entity but as a cultural deed, some of whose traces of "lived experience" can still be retrieved. In this context, the illusion of a singular "true path" yields to the recognition of a long path often obscured by historical debris, a path sustained not by traditionalism but by a productive living heritage of vast dimensions. For as Beethoven himself put it, quoting the ancient maxim attributed to Hippocrates, "ars longa, vita brevis"—art is long, life is short.

Notes

Introduction

1. The source was the Engelmann Sketchbook from 1823, which is now held in the collection of the Beethoven-Haus at Bonn. Brahms wrote to Wilhelm Engelmann about the manuscript on 23 February 1897. In 1913 it became the first Beethoven sketchbook to be published in facsimile.

2. Recent contributions to genetic criticism include Jed Deppman, Daniel Ferrer, and Michael Groden, eds., *Genetic Criticism: Texts and Avant-Textes* (Philadelphia: University of Pennsylvania Press, 2004), and William Kinderman and Joseph E. Jones, eds., *Genetic Criticism and the Creative Process: Essays from Music, Literature, and Theater* (Rochester: University of Rochester Press, 2009). An interdisciplinary forum for genetic studies is the French journal *Genesis: Revue internationale de critique génétique*. The term "genetic criticism" does not yet have such wide currency outside of France but is used in the present study in broad reference to studies of the creative process. An important monograph series for genetic studies of musical works has been Studies in Musical Genesis, Structure, and Interpretation, published by Oxford University Press and edited by Lewis Lockwood from 1985 until 1997 and Malcolm Gillies since 1997. A number of analytical studies of twentieth-century music have made productive use of manuscript sources, especially those held in the Paul Sacher Stiftung in Basel, Switzerland. One such recent study is Gretchen G. Horlacher, *Building Blocks: Repetition and Continuity in the Music of Stravinsky* (New York: Oxford University Press, 2011). Much remains to be done, and the Sacher Archive, for instance, holds many extensive collections, including more than twenty thousand pages of sketches by György Kurtág and more than one hundred thousand pages of documents from Elliott Carter.

3. In the "musicology" entry of the 2001 edition of *The New Grove Dictionary of Music and Musicians*, for instance, at least eleven largely autonomous divisions are described. On the increasing lack of integration of the discipline, see, among other sources, Lütteken's foreword to *Musikwissenschaft: Eine Positionsbestimmung*, ed. Laurenz Lütteken (Kassel: Bärenreiter, 2007), 10.

4. See Douglas Johnson, "Beethoven Scholars and Beethoven's Sketches," *19th-Century Music* 2 (1978): 3–17, and my discussion of the issue in the introduction to Kinderman and Jones, *Genetic Criticism*, 6–7.

5. Kevin Korsyn, *Decentering Music: A Critique of Contemporary Musical Research* (New York: Oxford University Press, 2003), 99–100. Korsyn observes that even when Schenker's analytical graphs reveal structural relations between movements, he cannot acknowledge them, which "constitutes a remarkable blind spot in his work but one with its own logic" (99). In practice, the "intertextuality of the *déjà entendu*" need not be regarded as infinite, as Robert Hatten observes in "The Place of Intertextuality in Music Studies," *American Journal of Semiotics* 3 (1985): 69–82.

6. Joseph Kerman, *Contemplating Music: Challenges to Musicology* (Cambridge, MA: Harvard University Press, 1985), 126. Kerman cites in this connection his earlier article "On William Byrd's *Emendemus in melius*," *Musical Quarterly* 44 (1963): 431–49, in which he already sought to draw in the results of "musicological" disciplines in order to explore "the aesthetic quality of the music itself" (*Contemplating Music*, 125).

7. Lawrence Kramer, *Classical Music and Postmodern Knowledge* (Berkeley: University of California Press, 1995), 25; Susan McClary, *Conventional Wisdom: The Content of Musical Form* (Berkeley: University of California Press, 2000), 169.

8. Robert Hatten, *Interpreting Musical Gestures, Topics, and Tropes: Mozart, Beethoven, Schubert* (Bloomington: Indiana University Press, 2004), 6.

9. McClary, *Conventional Wisdom*, 5.

10. See Lydia Goehr, *The Imaginary Museum of Musical Works: An Essay in the Philosophy of Music* (Oxford: Clarendon, 1992), and the critique of her position by Reinhard Strohm, "Looking Back at Ourselves: The Problem with the Musical Work-Concept," in *The Musical Work: Reality or Invention?*, ed. Michael Talbot (Liverpool: Liverpool University Press, 2000), 128–52.

11. See my essay "Improvisation in Beethoven's Creative Process," in *Musical Improvisation: Art, Education, and Society*, ed. Gabriel Solis and Bruno Nettl (Urbana: University of Illinois Press, 2009), 298–312, esp. 308; and Hatten's chapter in the same volume, "Opening the Museum Window: Improvisation and Its Inscribed Values in Canonic Works by Chopin and Schumann" (281–95).

12. Hoffmann elevates the expressive role of music as a medium conveying "unaussprechliche Sehnsucht" (unspeakable yearning). Nor should Hoffmann be regarded solely as a proponent of a canon of musical works as autonomous entities. As Abigail Chandler observes in her book *E. T. A. Hoffmann's Musical Aesthetics* (Burlington: Ashgate, 2006), Hoffmann also "fomented a critical methodology for the deconstruction of the musical 'canon'" (180).

13. See in this regard especially Carl Dahlhaus, *The Idea of Absolute Music*, trans. Roger Lustig (Chicago: University of Chicago Press, 1989), 19–20. In his writings from 1849

and 1851, Wagner polemically describes as "absolute" all "partial arts" severed from the *Gesamtkunstwerk* (total work of art). Although Dahlhaus's study is cited by Goehr, she does not acknowledge that this point contradicts her argument.

14. A probing study of allusion in music of this period is offered by Christopher Reynolds in *Motives for Allusion: Context and Content in Nineteenth Century Music* (Cambridge, MA: Harvard University Press, 2003).

15. See Karl Geiringer, *On Brahms and His Circle*, rev. and enl. George S. Bozarth (Sterling Heights, MI: Harmonie Park Press, 2006), 86.

16. If any kind of cultural orientation or activity is regarded as "ideological," the term is rendered virtually meaningless. Lawrence Kramer writes of "musical immediacy" in "mystified or idealized form" becoming "a powerful means of ideological seduction or coercion," but he does not explain how and why aesthetic effects become ideological (*Classical Music and Postmodern Knowledge*, 17).

17. The Beethoven sketchbook is cataloged as Vienna A 45, now held at the Gesellschaft der Musikfreunde in Vienna, and is discussed in Douglas Johnson, Alan Tyson, and Robert Winter, *The Beethoven Sketchbooks: History, Reconstruction, Inventory* (Berkeley: University of California Press, 1985), 351–54.

18. For detailed discussion of the role of descending chains of thirds in the "Hammerklavier" Sonata, see especially Charles Rosen, *The Classical Style: Haydn, Mozart, Beethoven* (New York: Norton, 1997), 404–34.

19. See Marie Rivers Rule, "The Allure of Beethoven's *Terzen-Ketten*: Third-Chains in Studies by Nottebohm and Music by Brahms," PhD dissertation, University of Illinois at Urbana-Champaign, 2011.

20. Malcolm McDonald suggested the possibility that the symphony may represent "a symbolic memorial to the great musicologist" in his book *Brahms* (London: Dent, 1990), 312n6.

21. For more detailed discussion, see my essay "Sieben Fantasien für Klavier op. 116," in *Brahms: Interpretationen seiner Werke*, ed. Klaus Bockmaier and Siegfried Mauser (Laaber: Laaber, forthcoming).

22. Styra Avins, ed., and Josef Eisinger and Styra Avins, trans., *Johannes Brahms: Life and Letters* (Oxford: Oxford University Press, 1997), 706.

23. Walter Frisch, *Brahms and the Principle of Developing Variation* (Berkeley: University of California Press, 1984), 152.

24. For a study of similar attitudes concerning the staging of earlier opera, see Rachel Cowgill, "Mozart Productions and the Emergence of *Werktreue* at London's Italian Opera House, 1780–1830," in *Operatic Migrations: Transforming Works and Crossing Boundaries*, ed. Roberta Montemorra Marvin and Downing A. Thomas (Burlington, VT: Ashgate, 2006), 145–86.

25. Leopold von Schröder, *Die Vollendung des arischen Mysteriums in Bayreuth* (Munich, 1911), cited in Stephan Mösch, *Weihe, Werkstatt, Wirklichkeit: Wagners "Parsifal" in Bayreuth 1882–1933* (Kassel: Bärenreiter and Metzler, 2009), 366.

26. Alfred Lorenz, *Der musikalische Aufbau von Richard Wagners "Parsifal"* (Berlin: Max Hesses Verlag, 1933).

27. "Wagner hat seine prophetischen Gedanken über Führertum und Wiederaufstieg

in diesem Werke ausgesprochen und ihm damit eine h o h e S e n d u n g anvertraut" (Lorenz, *Der musikalische Aufbau*, n.p. [preceding the table of contents], emphasis in original).

28. For detailed discussion of this point, see my introduction to William Kinderman and Katherine Syer, eds., *A Companion to Wagner's "Parsifal"* (Rochester: Camden House, 2005), 20–23.

29. Katherine Syer, "'It left me no peace': From Carlo Gozzi's *La donna serpente* to Wagner's *Parsifal*," *Musical Quarterly* 94 (2011): 325–80.

30. "W i r s o l l e n d e n V e r f a l l ü b e r w i n d e n u n d a l s r a s s i s c h h o c h g e z ü c h t e t e s V o l k z u m S i e g e s c h r e i t e n , will Wagner" (Lorenz, *Der musikalische Aufbau*, 153, emphasis in original). Lorenz footnotes at this point his essay "Die Religion des Parsifal," which appeared in *Die Musik*, February 1933, 342–47.

31. See Alfred Rosenberg, *Selected Writings*, ed. with an introduction by Robert Pois (London: Jonathan Cape, 1970), 139. This quotation comes from Rosenberg's widely circulated book *Der Mythus des 20. Jahrhunderts* (1930; Munich: Hoheneichen Verlag, 1939), 434.

32. For a more detailed discussion, see my book *Wagner's "Parsifal"* (New York: Oxford University Press, 2013).

33. Reinthaler prepared the first complete performance of the work in Bremen on Good Friday of 1868. Since he was disturbed by the absence of any strict doctrinal statement, Reinthaler urged Brahms to write another movement of incontrovertibly Christian content, a suggestion rejected by the composer. The term "German" in Brahms's title refers not specifically to nationality but to the language of the text.

34. Lorenz, "Die Religion des Parsifal," 344, 347.

35. Thomas Mann, *Briefe*, vol. 2, *1937–1947*, ed. Erika Mann (Frankfurt: Fischer, 1961), 444.

36. Susanne Langer, *Philosophy in a New Key: A Study in the Symbolism of Reason, Rite, and Art* (1942; New York: Mentor, 1961), 204.

37. Kramer's requirement that "what we call musical experience needs to be systematically rethought" through "modes of hermeneutic and historical writing" betrays an overestimation of his own role and can be safely dismissed (*Classical Music and Postmodern Knowledge*, 17).

38. This prophetic inscription was entered into the young composer's album by Count Ferdinand Waldstein.

39. The Csengery-Keller recording was issued on Hungaroton (B000027C4K); the Banse-Keller version appeared with ECM Records (ECM New Series 1965, 476 3099). A 2009 recording on DVD with soprano Tony Arnold and violinist Movses Pogossian includes excerpts of a rehearsal with the composer (Bridge 7867358).

40. Hans Ulrich Gumbrecht, *The Powers of Philology: Dynamics of Textual Scholarship* (Urbana: University of Illinois Press, 2003), 84. (A German version appeared as *Die Macht der Philologie* [Frankfurt: Suhrkamp Verlag, 2003].) Gumbrecht cites in this regard the work of Wilhelm Dilthey and Hans-Georg Gadamer, particularly Gadamer's subchapter "Der Begriff des Erlebnisses," in *Wahrheit und Methode: Grundzüge einer philosophischen Hermeneutik*, 2nd ed. (Tübingen: Mohr, 1965), 60–66. See also in this

context Thomas Christensen, "Music Theory and Its Histories," in *Music Theory and the Exploration of the Past*, ed. Christopher Hatch and David Bernstein (Chicago: University of Chicago Press, 1993), 9–40.

41. On this point, see also Nicholas Cook, "Analysing Performance and Performing Analysis," in *Rethinking Music*, ed. Nicholas Cook and Mark Everist (Oxford: Clarendon, 1999), 239–61.

42. Alex Ross, "Hold the Mozart: New Works by John Adams and György Kurtág in Vienna," *New Yorker*, 4 December 2006, 103.

1. Mozart's Second Thoughts

1. A comprehensive study of Mozart's sketches is offered in Ulrich Konrad, *Mozarts Schaffensweise* (Göttingen: Vandenhoeck und Ruprecht, 1992). This book is supplemented by Konrad's article "Neuentdecktes und wiedergefundenes Werkstattmaterial Wolfgang Amadeus Mozarts: Erster Nachtrag zum Katalog der Skizzen und Entwürfe," in *Mozart-Jahrbuch 1995*, 1–28.

2. Franz Niemetschek, *W. A. Mozarts Leben*, facsimile reprint of the first edition (Prague: Herrlischen Buchhandlung, 1798), including the revisions and additions of the second edition from 1808, ed. Ernst Rychnovsky (Prague: T. Taussig, 1905), 45.

3. Georg Nikolaus Nissen, *Biographie W. A. Mozarts* (Leipzig: Breitkopf und Härtel, 1828), 649. The original quotation is as follows: "Man glaube überhaupt dem Geschwätz nicht, als habe er seine bedeutenden Werke nur flüchtig und schnell hingeworfen. Er trug sich sehr lange mit den Hauptideen herum, zeichnete sie sich oft kurz auf, arbeitete im Kopfe die Hauptsachen ganz fertig: dann erst schrieb er das Ganze schnell nieder—und auch nicht so schnell, als man sich einbildet: er besserte sorgfältig nach, nur war er in solchen Compositionen, auf die er selbst Werth legte, äußerst streng gegen sich."

4. See Alan Tyson, "Mozart's Piano Concerto Fragments," in *Mozart's Piano Concertos: Text, Context, Interpretation*, ed. Neal Zaslaw (Ann Arbor: University of Michigan Press, 1996), 67–69.

5. A facsimile of this manuscript is reproduced in the volume *Fragmente*, ed. Ulrich Konrad, Neue Mozart Ausgabe, Serie X, Supplement 30/4, 121–22.

6. This catalog has been published in facsimile as *Mozart—eigenhändiges Werkverzeichnis Faksimile*, ed. Albi Rosenthal and Alan Tyson, British Library, Stefan Zweig MS 63 (Kassel: Bärenreiter, 1991).

7. The manuscript has been published in facsimile as *Wolfgang Amadeus Mozart: Fantasie und Sonate c-Moll für Klavier, KV 475 + 457. Faksimile nach dem Autograph in der Bibliotheca Mozartiana Salzburg*, introduction by Wolfgang Plath and Wolfgang Rehm (Salzburg: Internationale Stiftung Mozarteum, 1991). Also see Eugene K. Wolf, "The Rediscovered Autograph of Mozart's Fantasy and Sonata in C minor, K. 475/457," *Journal of Musicology* 10 (1992): 3–47; and John Irving, *Mozart's Piano Sonatas: Contexts, Sources, Style* (Cambridge: Cambridge University Press, 1997), 73–82.

8. See the discussion of the passage in Jürgen Uhde and Renate Wieland, *Denken und Spielen: Studien zu einer Theorie der musikalischen Darstellung* (Kassel: Bärenreiter, 1988), 372.

9. One is reminded here of the extreme contrasts in register in the first movement of Beethoven's C Minor Sonata, op. 111 (mm. 48–49, 114–15).

10. Siegbert Rampe, *Mozarts Claviermusik: Klangwelt und Aufführungspraxis* (Kassel: Bärenreiter, 1995), 270–71.

11. Robert Hatten, *Interpreting Musical Gestures, Topics, and Tropes: Mozart, Beethoven, Schubert* (Bloomington: Indiana University Press, 2004), 164.

12. László Somfai, "Mozart's First Thoughts: The Two Versions of the Sonata in D Major, K. 284," in *Early Music* 19 (1991): 601–13, quotations from 602, 605. Somfai provides a transcription of the draft, which I have reproduced with emendations in Ex. 1.3. For instance, the bass note in the opening sonority of the draft is D, not C♯, as is printed in his Ex. 3 (p. 606).

13. In this instance, the phrases overlap, so that each six-measure unit includes the cadence that forms the beginning of the next phrase.

14. One can also regard the beginning of the revised version as corresponding to m. 6 of the draft, which already contains the full tonic harmony. Seen from this perspective, Mozart's first critical decision was to discard the first five measures of the draft version.

15. Charles Rosen, *The Classical Style: Haydn, Mozart, Beethoven* (New York: Norton, 1971; reprint, expanded ed., 1997), 228–33, quotation from 228.

16. The measures replaced include the last seven of the draft as well as m. 43, whereas mm. 44–45 are retained in their original form.

17. Such figures have of course a conventional aspect, and similar motivic configurations can be found in other works, such as in the transition to the second group in the opening Allegro of the preceding Sonata in G Major, K. 283. Nevertheless, the specific network of motivic relations within a movement or work often assumes much significance in Mozart's music.

18. Somfai, "Mozart's First Thoughts," 603.

19. Alfred Einstein, *Mozart, His Character, His Work* (New York: Oxford, 1945), 242.

20. Walter Gerstenberg, "Zum Autograph des Klavierkonzertes KV. 503 (C-Dur): Anmerkung zu Mozarts Schaffensweise," in *Mozart-Jahrbuch 1953*, 38–46.

21. Alan Tyson, *Mozart: Studies of the Autograph Scores* (Cambridge, MA: Harvard University Press, 1987), 125.

22. Konrad, *Fragmente*.

23. For perspectives on Mozart's fragmentary notation and the role of improvisation in the concertos, see among other studies Robert Levin's essays "Improvisation and Musical Structure in Mozart's Piano Concertos," in *L'interpretation de la musique classique de Haydn à Schubert: Colloque international, Evry, 13–15 octobre 1977* (Paris: Minkoff, 1980), 45–50, and "Improvised Embellishments in Mozart's Keyboard Music," *Early Music* 20 (1992): 221–33, esp. 226–32; and Friedrich Neumann, *Ornamentation and Improvisation in Mozart* (Princeton: Princeton University Press, 1986), esp. 240–56. Also see Levin, "Improvising Mozart," in *Musical Improvisation: Art, Education, and Society*, ed. Gabriel Solis and Bruno Nettl (Urbana: University of Illinois Press, 2009), 143–49.

2. Beethoven's Unfinished Piano Trio in F Minor from 1816

1. The manuscript of this letter in English is held by the Ira Brilliant Center for Beethoven Studies, San Jose, California; it appears in *Beethoven Briefe*, ed. Sieghard Brandenburg (Munich: Henle, 1996), vol. 3, Letter 982. This letter is in the hand of Johann von Härings and signed by Beethoven.

2. A facsimile edition of this autograph score has been published as *Ludwig van Beethoven: Klaviersonate A-Dur Opus 101* (Munich: Henle, 1998). This edition includes a commentary by Sieghard Brandenburg. The manuscript is inscribed and dated by the composer as follows: "Neue Sonate / für Piano / von L. v. Beethowen / 1816 / im Monath / November."

3. Willy Hess, comp., *Verzeichnis der nicht in der Gesamtausgabe veröffentlichte Werke Ludwig van Beethovens* (Wiesbaden: Breitkopf und Härtel, 1957).

4. Nicholas Marston, "In the 'Twilight Zone': Beethoven's Unfinished Piano Trio in F Minor," *Journal of the Royal Musical Association* 131 (2006): 227–86. The additional sketch leaf is folio 20 of the miscellany Add. MS 29997 held at the British Library in London. Not all pages listed by Marston as containing work on the unfinished piano trio actually hold material for the trio. On page 236 of his article, he lists pages 86–107 of the Scheide Sketchbook as related to the trio, but no such material is found on pages 92–93, 99, or 106.

5. Gustav Nottebohm, "Ein Skizzenbuch aus den Jahren 1815 und 1816," in *Zweite Beethoveniana: Nachgelassene Aufsätze von Gustav Nottebohm* (Leipzig: Peters, 1887), 321–48. Nottebohm's comments on the F Minor Trio are found on pages 345 and 348.

6. Douglas Johnson, Alan Tyson, and Robert Winter, *The Beethoven Sketchbooks: History, Reconstruction, Inventory* (Berkeley: University of California Press, 1985). The article on the Scheide Sketchbook is found on pages 241–46. Brief mention is given to the F Minor Trio by Lewis Lockwood in "The Beethoven Sketchbook in the Scheide Library," *Princeton University Library Chronicle* 37 (1976): 141, 145; by Joseph Kerman in the published summary of a panel discussion, "Future Directions in Sketch Research," in *Beethoven, Performers, and Critics: The International Beethoven Congress, Detroit, 1977*, ed. Robert Winter and Bruce Carr (Detroit: Wayne State University Press, 1980), 145, and *The New Grove Beethoven*, by Kerman and Alan Tyson (New York: Norton, 1980), 69; and in Barry Cooper, *Beethoven* (New York: Oxford University Press, 2000), 250–51, 253.

7. Karl Dorfmüller, "Beethovens Kompositionen für Klaviertrio: Eine chronologische Übersicht," in *Beethovens Klaviertrios: Symposion München 1990*, ed. Rudolf Bockholdt and Petra Weber-Bockholdt (Munich: Henle, 1992), 19. The sketches for the trio on the two leaves removed from Scheide are listed as well by Tyson in Johnson, Tyson, and Winter, *The Beethoven Sketchbooks*, 246. Brief entries on the "Partitur-Skizzen" in the Grasnick 29 MS are found in Eveline Bartlitz, ed., *Die Beethoven-Sammlung in der Musikabteilung der deutschen Staatsbibliothek: Verzeichnis* (Berlin: Deutsche Staatsbibliothek, 1970), 110; and in Hans Schmidt, "Verzeichnis der Skizzen Beethovens," *Beethoven-Jahrbuch* 6 (1969): 37.

8. Georg Kinsky and Hans Halm, eds., *Das Werk Beethovens: Thematisch-Bibliographisches Verzeichnis seiner sämtlichen vollendetem Kompositionen* (Munich: Henle, 1955), 276.

9. This is twelve-stave paper of type 57 in the list compiled by Joseph Schmidt-Görg in "Die Wasserzeichen in Beethovens Notenpapieren," in *Beiträge zur Beethoven Bibliographie: Studien und Materialien zum Werkverzeichnis von Kinsky-Halm*, ed. Kurt Dorfmüller (Munich: Henle, 1978), 167–95.

10. For more detailed discussion of this work, see Bernd Edelmann, "Wenzel Müllers Lied vom 'Schneider Wetz' und Beethovens Trio-Variationen Op. 121a," in Bockholdt and Weber-Bockholdt, *Beethovens Klaviertrios*, 76–102.

11. Kinsky and Halm, *Das Werk Beethovens*, 462.

12. Brandenburg, *Beethoven Briefe*, vol. 3, Letter 939.

13. See Lewis Lockwood, "Beethoven's Unfinished Piano Concerto of 1815: Sources and Problems," *Musical Quarterly* 56 (1970): 624–46; Nicholas Cook, "Beethoven's Unfinished Piano Concerto: A Case of Double Vision?," *Journal of the American Musicological Society* 42 (1989): 338–74; and the exchange between Lockwood and Cook in *JAMS* 43 (1990): 376–82, 382–85.

14. For a study of the genesis of this work and a complete transcription of the sketches and draft from 1819, see William Kinderman, *Beethoven's Diabelli Variations* (Oxford: Clarendon, 1987; reprinted 2008); also see the facsimile edition of the Diabelli Variations autograph score, including my commentary (*Ludwig van Beethoven: Facsimile-Ausgabe der Diabelli-Variationen op. 120* [Bonn: Verlag Beethoven-Haus (Carus), 2010]). My CD recording of the Diabelli Variations (studio recording and lecture recital) is available through Arietta Records (ART-001).

15. In 2003 I completed the transcription of the Grasnick 29 draft and recorded the torso of the first movement of the trio for a paper presented at the annual meeting of the American Musicological Society in Houston on 16 November 2003. The audio recording (http://www.press.uillinois.edu/FMinorTrio) of an edited version of the unfinished first movement is performed by William Kinderman, piano; Christina Lixandru, violin; and Diana Flesner, cello. Willem Holsbergen independently attempted to reconstruct a version of the movement. He describes the movement as Biamonti 637, according to a little-known thematic catalog compiled by Giovanni Biamonti by 1968; see the website http://www.unheardbeethoven.org.

16. Gustav Nottebohm, "Ein Skizzenbuch aus den Jahren 1815 und 1816," *Musikalisches Wochenblatt* 7 (1876): 609–11, 625–27, 637–39, 653–55, 669–70; reprinted with minor changes in Nottebohm, *Zweite Beethoveniana* (Leipzig: Peters, 1887), 321–48; cited in Johnson, Tyson, and Winter, *The Beethoven Sketchbooks*, 246.

17. Nottebohm, "Ein Skizzenbuch," in *Zweite Beethoveniana*, 345, 348. When Nottebohm studied this sketchbook, it was owned by Eugen von Miller in Vienna.

18. These leaves fit into the sketchbook before page 93, as shown in Johnson, Tyson, and Winter, *The Beethoven Sketchbooks*, 243.

19. Tyson, following Nottebohm, places a question mark next to the attribution of this sketch in Johnson, Tyson, and Winter, *The Beethoven Sketchbooks*, 245.

20. See Wolfgang Osthoff, "Die langsamen Einleitungen in Beethovens Klaviertrios

(Op. 1 Nr. 2; Op. 121a; Op. 70 Nr. 2)," in Bockholdt and Weber-Bockholdt, *Beethovens Klaviertrios*, 119–29; and Bernd Edelmann, "Wenzel Müllers Lied," 99.

21. As notated in the Grasnick 29 draft, the slow introduction and exposition would not allow for much change in the basic tempo, and the length of a quarter note would remain similar in both sections. Nevertheless, these tempo indications are significant as indications of musical character.

22. This watermark is illustrated as paper type 33 in Johnson, Tyson, and Winter, *The Beethoven Sketchbooks*, 555, and also shown in Brandenburg, *Ludwig van Beethoven: Klaviersonate A-Dur Opus 101*, vii. It is type 57 in the list compiled by Joseph Schmidt-Görg in "Die Wasserzeichen in Beethovens Notenpapieren," in Dorfmüller, *Beiträge zur Beethoven Bibliographie*, 182–83.

23. Johnson, Tyson, and Winter, *The Beethoven Sketchbooks*, 555.

24. Johnson, Tyson, and Winter, *The Beethoven Sketchbooks*, 241, 244. An end date of May 1816 was taken over by Sieghard Brandenburg in his essay "Die Skizzen zur Neunten Symphonie," in *Zu Beethoven: Aufsätze und Dokumente*, ed. Harry Goldschmidt (Berlin: Verlag Neue Musik, 1984), 94. In his recent study of sources for the trio, Marston also suggests that "Tyson's dating of Scheide . . . may be too restrictive" and that work on the trio may have extended until September 1816 ("In the 'Twilight Zone,'" 240).

25. For a recent discussion of Beethoven's use of this term, see William Kinderman, *Artaria 195: Beethoven's Sketchbook for the "Missa solemnis" and the Piano Sonata in E Major, Opus 109* (Urbana: University of Illinois Press), 1:109–10.

26. Marston writes concerning the second subject of the sonata design that "what does seem fairly certain is that Beethoven did not envisage a 'textbook' lyrical *Seitensatz*: the only passage that might fulfil this particular formal role is the one beginning at bar 90, and repeated in a varied and expanded form from bar 103 onward" ("In the 'Twilight Zone,'" 241). He overlooks thereby the lyrical second subject in mm. 71–83, which is so clearly set apart from the first subject by its key of D♭ major and its pervasive ascending linear motion.

27. Marston, "In the 'Twilight Zone,'" 241.

28. Another example of Beethoven's emphasis on D♭ major in the context of F minor is offered by the recapitulation of the *Egmont* Overture. James Hepokoski has recently drawn attention to this feature of the overture in his essay "Back and Forth from *Egmont*: Beethoven, Mozart, and the Nonresolving Recapitulation," *19th-Century Music* 25 (2001–2): 127–54. Of course, Beethoven's avoidance of tonic resolution in the second subject area of the overture's recapitulation is surely bound up with the ensuing *Siegessymphonie* in F major, following the silence in m. 178, which stands for the death of Count Egmont. To avoid undercutting the closing apotheosis in the tonic major, Beethoven avoided the tonic major in the recapitulation.

29. For a discussion of Beethoven's expansion of sections through the insertion of extra phrases of paragraphs into the overall form and tonal plan, see Barry Cooper, *Beethoven and the Creative Process* (Oxford: Clarendon, 1990), 128–29.

30. Consequently, I have included in the accompanying sound recording of the movement just the slow introduction and the exposition of the sonata form up to the second subject in D♭ major. In order to supply a cadence, I have supplied editorially a D♭ at the end of the recorded excerpt, at m. 84.

31. Marston, "In the 'Twilight Zone,'" 233n18, 241.

32. Charles Rosen, *The Classical Style: Haydn, Mozart, Beethoven*, expanded ed. (New York: Norton, 1997), 434.

33. Rosen, *The Classical Style*, 424, 427.

34. For a discussion of the evolution of this theme, see Kinderman, *Artaria 195*, 1:65–72.

35. Maynard Solomon, "Beethoven's Tagebuch," in *Beethoven Essays* (Cambridge, MA: Harvard University Press, 1988), 275, entry no. 91. Also see Solomon, "Beethoven's Tagebuch of 1812–1818," in *Beethoven Studies 3*, ed. Alan Tyson (Cambridge: Cambridge University Press, 1982), 255, entry no. 91; and the German edition published as *Beethovens Tagebuch* (Mainz: Hase und Koehler Verlag, 1990), 89, 158.

36. Beethoven's folksong arrangements for Thomson from this period are discussed by Barry Cooper in *Beethoven's Folksong Settings: Chronology, Sources, Style* (Oxford: Clarendon, 1994), 25–29.

37. Barry Cooper, *Beethoven* (Oxford: Oxford University Press, 2000), 250. It is also evident that Beethoven envisioned the F Minor Trio as a challenging large-scale composition, quite unlike the easy piano trio movement in B♭ major, WoO 39, that he wrote for the ten-year-old Maximiliane Brentano in 1812.

38. Theodore Albrecht, trans. and ed., *Letters to Beethoven and Other Correspondence* (Lincoln: University of Nebraska Press, 1996), vol. 2, Letter 235; Brandenburg, *Beethoven Briefe*, vol. 3, Letter 996.

39. See in this regard Alan Tyson, *The Authentic English Editions of Beethoven* (London: Faber and Faber, 1963), 19–21.

40. There was confusion for several months concerning £5 that Birchall sent to Beethoven for expenses, while the publisher waited in vain for the composer's receipt of a larger sum. The matter was only clarified with Beethoven's letter to Birchall of 14 December 1816 (Brandenburg, *Beethoven Briefe*, vol. 3, Letter 1013).

41. The autograph score of the quartet is dated "1810 im Monath October," and the score of the "Archduke" Trio is dated "3ten März 1811" (Kinsky and Halm, *Das Werk Beethovens*, 267, 272). The delay in publication of these works has encouraged speculation that the scores might have been backdated. In a recent source study, however, Seow-Chin Ong has confirmed the 1811 date of completion of the "Archduke" autograph, observing that Beethoven had offered the work for publication to Breitkopf und Härtel soon after it was finished, in April of that year, but then withheld it from publication because his fee was not met. See Ong, "The Autograph of Beethoven's 'Archduke' Trio," *Beethoven Forum* 11 (2004): 181–208.

42. Elliot Forbes, ed., *Thayer's Life of Beethoven* (Princeton: Princeton University Press, 1964), 2:646.

43. Solomon, "Beethoven's Tagebuch," 274, entry no. 88.

44. This pocket sketchbook is tentatively described as "Paris MS 78 and MS 103" in Johnson, Tyson, and Winter, *The Beethoven Sketchbooks*, sources that need to be augmented by several additional leaves contained in the miscellany Mendelssohn 2 at the Biblioteka Jagiellońska, Cracow, as Sieghard Brandenburg has observed. See Johnson, Tyson, and Winter, *The Beethoven Sketchbooks*, 344–45n3, 346.

45. See Kinsky and Halm, *Das Werk Beethovens*, 618–19. Beethoven enjoyed his friendship with these two young women. Fanny Giannattasio del Rio, who was twenty-six at the time, recorded her affection for the composer in her diary. Anna (Nani) was two years younger. Two years later, in January 1819, Beethoven wrote his "Hochzeitslied," WoO 105, for the occasion of Anna's wedding to Joseph Schmerling.

46. Kinsky and Halm, *Das Werk Beethovens*, 618–19. This autograph score of the song has been in the possession of Dr. Matthew Malerich of Bakersfield, California, who kindly allowed me access to the manuscript.

47. The entire letter is printed in *Ludwig van Beethovens Leben von Alexander Wheelock Thayer*, ed. Hermann Deiters and Hugo Riemann (Leipzig: Breitkopf und Härtel, 1923), 4:516–18; also see Kinsky and Halm, *Das Werk Beethovens*, 617.

48. This single leaf was formerly in the archive of the music publishing firm Schott in Mainz. The high price level of this sale was sustained at the more recent auction at Sotheby's in London in 2003, when the corrected copy of Beethoven's Ninth Symphony fetched £2.1 million.

49. Nottebohm was aware of the sketch in Scheide and its chronology but regarded it as a stray entry that did not yet belong to the genesis of the symphony when it was made. The recognition of closely related contemporaneous sketches for the symphony such as the Weimar sketch leaf weakens Nottebohm's argument, however. See Nottebohm, "Ein Skizzenbuch," in *Zweite Beethoveniana*, 157. A facsimile of page 51 of the Scheide Sketchbook is provided in Brandenburg, "Die Skizzen zur Neunten Symphonie," as plate 5 after page 206.

50. This sketch leaf is held in the Nationale Forschungs- und Gedenkstätten der klassischen deutschen Literatur, Liszt-Nachlaß, Weimar; it is no. 389 in the "Verzeichnis der Skizzen Beethovens" compiled by Hans Schmidt, who does not mention the presence of sketches for the Ninth Symphony. For a detailed survey of sketches for the Ninth Symphony from this period, see Brandenburg, "Die Skizzen zur Neunten Symphonie," 88–129, esp. 90–103. Brandenburg provides transcriptions of the sketches for the Ninth on the Mainz and Weimar leaves on pages 96–97.

51. For a discussion of the complexities of Beethoven's relationship with the society, see "Beethoven and the Philharmonic Society," in *Beethoven and England: An Account of Sources in the British Museum*, ed. Pamela J. Willetts (London: British Museum, 1970), 43–48.

52. Beethoven in 1817 entertained the idea of composing two symphonies, including a choral symphony involving a "celebration of Bacchus," recalling his rudimentary sketches for a pastoral opera on Bacchus in the Scheide Sketchbook, pages 52–53. For a more detailed discussion, see William Kinderman, *Beethoven* (Oxford: Oxford University Press, 2009), 292.

53. Solomon, "Beethoven's Tagebuch," 119, entry no. 119.

54. Martin Cooper, *Beethoven: The Last Decade, 1817–1827* (Oxford: Oxford University Press, 1970), 14; Maynard Solomon, *Beethoven* (New York: Schirmer, 1998), 322.

3. Schumann, Beethoven, and the "Distant Beloved"

1. In his second edition of the *Davidsbündlertänze*, Schumann changed the title, eliminated the references to Florestan and Eusebius, and made other changes. The Symphonic Études also exist in two different editions, and several remarkable Eusebian pieces composed for that work but excluded from both versions by Schumann have been reinstated by pianists such as Alfred Cortot and Alfred Brendel. See in this regard Brendel's essay "Theme and Variations: Schumann and Beethoven" in his book *Alfred Brendel on Music: Collected Essays* (Chicago: A Capella, 2001), 229–31, and his fine recording in the collection *The Art of Alfred Brendel* (Philips CD 446 948–2), which includes these extra pieces. Other works by Schumann, such as the *Novelletten*, op. 21, and the piano sonatas, also underwent a complex genesis that is reflected in part in the surviving sources. For a recent study of Schumann's creative process in general, see Bernhard Appel, *Vom Einfall zum Werk—Robert Schumanns Schaffensweise*, Schumann-Forschungen, Band 13 (Mainz: Verlag Schott, 2010). As Appel observes, the Symphonic Études received no fewer than seven different titles during the course of their genesis and publication (169).

2. This title page is held at the Beethoven-Haus Bonn as manuscript BH 270 accessible as "Robert Schumann, Fantasie für Klavier op. 17, Titelblatt, Autograph, Konzept" through their digital archives.

3. In his letter of 19 March 1838 Schumann informs Clara Wieck that he had completed the three movements in the form of a detailed draft by June 1836: "Außerdem habe ich eine Phantasie in drei Sätzen vollendet, die ich im Juni 36 bis auf das Detail entworfen hatte" (*Clara und Robert Schumann: Briefwechsel. Kritische Gesamtausgabe*, ed. Eva Weissweiler [Frankfurt, 1984], 1:126). Despite this letter, Nicholas Marston has speculated that Schumann had composed only the first movement by that time (*Schumann: Fantasie, Op. 17* [Cambridge: Cambridge University Press, 1992], 8, 23); that opinion is echoed in John Daverio, *Robert Schumann: Herald of a "New Poetic Age"* (New York: Oxford University Press, 1997), 133, 151.

4. Bodo Bischoff, *Monument für Beethoven: Die Entwicklung der Beethoven-Rezeption Robert Schumanns* (Cologne-Rheinkassel: Chr. Dohr, 1994), 194, 205–6, and the studies cited in note 3.

5. This source is discussed and reproduced in Alan Walker, "Schumann, Liszt and the C Major *Fantasie*, Op. 17: A Declining Relationship," *Music & Letters* 60 (1979): 156–65. An updated version of Walker's essay appeared in his book *Reflections on Liszt* (Ithaca, NY: Cornell University Press, 2005), 40–50. See also Margit L. McCorkle, ed., *Robert Schumann: Bibliographisches Werkverzeichnis* (Mainz: Schott, 2003), 74–78.

6. This original ending is printed in the score edited by Wolfgang Boetticher (Robert Schumann, *Fantasie C-dur Opus 17* [Munich: Henle, 1987], 39), who comments that "we consider it interesting enough to reproduce" (iii).

7. Hermann Abert, *Robert Schumann*, 2nd ed. (Berlin: Harmonie Verlagsgesellschaft für Literatur und Kunst, 1910), 64.

8. Charles Rosen, *The Classical Style: Haydn, Mozart, Beethoven*, expanded ed. (New York: Norton, 1997), 513. Also see in this regard Janet Schmalfeldt's keynote address "Coming Home," *Music Theory Online* (*MTO*) 10 (2004).

9. Marston, *Schumann: Fantasie, Op. 17*, 23, 32.

10. Bischoff, *Monument für Beethoven*, 186, 417, 419. Bischoff notes that Schumann heard the trio "Gut Söhnchen, gut" from the opera in January 1829 (418).

11. In an apt formulation, Richard Taruskin writes that Schumann's Florestan, "named after Beethoven's imprisoned freedom-fighter, represented his embattled '*innerliches Ich*,' his 'inmost I,' a concept we have associated with German romanticism from its Beethovenian beginning" (*The Oxford History of Western Music*, vol. 3, *The Nineteenth Century* [New York: Oxford University Press, 2005], 293).

12. Yet another parallel is Klärchen's longing to don male clothes in order to follow her beloved Egmont into battle, as expressed in her first song, "Die Trommel gerühret"; Leonore is of course disguised as a man until the climax of the dungeon scene.

13. In a portion of a letter to Schumann dated 17 November [1837], Clara explained that on account of her father she needed to write hastily with her door open and that he should address his next letter to her to "Julius Kraus" while including the name and address of "D. Reuter" and taking other precautions to avoid discovery (Weissweiler, *Clara und Robert Schumann: Briefwechsel*, 1:43).

14. Weissweiler, *Clara und Robert Schumann: Briefwechsel*, 1:66. The spelling "Lenore" appears in the original source.

15. Weissweiler, *Clara und Robert Schumann: Briefwechsel*, 1:312. This poem was presumably included with Schumann's letter to Clara Wieck from 1 December 1838.

16. Weissweiler, *Clara und Robert Schumann: Briefwechsel*, 1:542–43.

17. Joseph Kerman, "An die ferne Geliebte," in *Beethoven Studies 1*, ed. Alan Tyson (Cambridge: Cambridge University Press, 1966), 126–27, 129.

18. Elliot Forbes, ed., *Thayer's Life of Beethoven* (Princeton: Princeton University Press, 1967), 647.

19. Solomon devotes a chapter of his biography to this issue (*Beethoven* [New York: Schirmer, 1998], 207–46), but debate continues concerning the identity of Beethoven's beloved.

20. Kerman, "An die ferne Geliebte," 131.

21. "Der 'Ton' im Motto bist Du wohl? Beinahe glaub ich's" (Weissweiler, *Clara und Robert Schumann: Briefwechsel*, 2:562).

22. This motto stems from Schlegel's poem "Die Gebüsche" in the collection *Abendröthe*, which Schumann consulted in one of three available editions and then copied into his extensive collection of mottos (*Mottosammlung*), at the latest by early 1838, before placing a slightly modified version at the head of the fantasie. See Leander Hotaki, *Robert Schumanns Mottosammlung: Übertragung—Kommentar—Einführung* (Freiburg im Breisgau: Rombach, 1998), 164, 206–8.

23. Weissweiler, *Clara und Robert Schumann: Briefwechsel*, 2:577.

24. Berthold Hoeckner, *Programming the Absolute: Nineteenth-Century German Music and the Hermeneutics of the Moment* (Princeton: Princeton University Press, 2002), 98–202.

25. Marston, *Schumann: Fantasie, Op. 17*, 8.

26. Robert Schumann, *Gesammelte Schriften über Musik und Musiker*, ed. Martin Kreisig (Leipzig, 1914), 1:133, cited in Bischoff, *Monument für Beethoven*, 209n.

27. "Nun will ich einmal recht mit Ihnen reden, plaudern, lachen—könnte man wie man wollte, so reichten kaum Ballen von Briefen, hin, die Sie von mir zu erhalten hätten—so aber wenn ich recht, recht an Sie denke, sitze ich flugs am Clavier und schreibe lieber mit [Nonenaccorden] z.B. dem bekannten Terzdecimenaccord." Schumann includes the music example in his letter, which appears in Weissweiler, *Clara und Robert Schumann: Briefwechsel*, 1:13–14.

28. Charles Rosen, *The Romantic Generation* (Cambridge, MA: Harvard University Press, 1995), 112.

29. Anthony Newcomb, "Schumann and the Marketplace," in *Nineteenth-Century Piano Music*, ed. R. Larry Todd (New York: Schirmer, 1990), 295.

30. Marston, *Schumann: Fantasie, Op. 17*, 40–42. Marston is highly ambivalent concerning the issue of a Beethoven allusion. He states that "there is no certainty that Schumann *was* alluding to the Beethoven work" while maintaining that "it is precisely the music set to the words 'Take them then, these songs' ('Nim[m] sie hin denn diese Lieder') which is alluded to in bars 295–7 of the *Fantasie*. Given its autobiographical suitability, it is difficult to believe that the allusion was not consciously intended" (36–37).

31. R. Larry Todd, "On Quotation in Schumann's Music," in *Schumann and His World*, ed. R. Larry Todd (Princeton: Princeton University Press, 1994), 95.

32. Weissweiler, *Clara und Robert Schumann: Briefwechsel*, 2:368.

33. Rosen, *The Romantic Generation*, 111.

34. Rosen, *The Romantic Generation*, 111.

35. Brendel, "Theme and Variations," 229, 230.

36. Rosen, *The Romantic Generation*, 663. One thinks in this regard of Schumann's own statement, which he attributed to Meister Raro, the judicious intermediary character between Florestan and Eusebius: "Die erste Konzeption ist immer die natürliche und beste. Der Verstand irrt, das Gefühl nicht" (The first conception is always the most natural and best. The intellect errs, feeling doesn't) (Robert Schumann, *Gesammelte Schriften über Musik und Musiker*, ed. Heinrich Simon [Leipzig: Philipp Reclam, 1888], 38).

37. Appel, in his study *Vom Einfall zum Werk*, 95, draws attention to Schumann's reluctance about and even dread of probing the artistic creative process, as expressed in comments like the following: "Wir würden schreckliche Dinge erfahren, wenn wir bei allen Werken bis auf den Grund ihrer Entstehung sehen könnten" (We would experience terrible things, if we could examine all works to the core of their genesis) and "Der Phantasie des Musikers auf den Grund sehen zu wollen, ist gefährlich" (It is dangerous to want to explore the source of the fantasy of the musician).

38. Christopher Reynolds, *Motives for Allusion: Context and Content in Nineteenth-Century Music* (Cambridge, MA: Harvard University Press, 2003), 127.

39. Commentators differ in their views concerning Schumann's reference to an allusion to Beethoven's Seventh Symphony in the finale of the fantasie. Hermann Erler believed that Schumann removed his intended allusion from the finished work (*Robert Schumann's Leben, aus seinen Briefen geschildert* [Berlin, 1887], 1:102); Gustav Jansen thought that the allusion consisted merely of Schumann's use of a long-short-short rhythm beginning in m. 30 (*Die Davidsbündler: Aus Robert Schumanns Sturm- und Drangperiode* [Leipzig, 1883], 537). Charles Rosen regards the "Etwas bewegter" pas-

sage as "more cryptically a quotation from Beethoven" (*The Romantic Generation*, 102). Also see in this regard Bischoff, *Monument für Beethoven*, 198.

40. For a vivid description of these events, see Alan Walker, *Franz Liszt*, vol. 1, *The Virtuoso Years 1811–1847* (New York: Alfred A. Knopf, 1983), 417–25.

41. Erik Michael Horak-Hult, "The 'Distant Beloved' Archetype in Works of Ludwig van Beethoven and Robert Schumann," master's thesis in musicology, University of Illinois at Urbana-Champaign, 2003, 92.

42. Alan Walker, "Schumann, Liszt and the C Major Fantasie, Op. 17: A Declining Relationship," *Music & Letters* 60 (1979): 165.

4. Aesthetics of Integration in Mahler's Fifth Symphony

1. This is not the only relationship to a song in the Fifth Symphony. Donald Mitchell has drawn attention to the affinity between the opening Funeral March and the last *Wunderhorn* song, "Der Tamboursg'sell," composed in July 1901. See "Eternity or Nothingness? Mahler's Fifth Symphony," in *The Mahler Companion*, ed. Donald Mitchell and Andrew Nicholson (Oxford: Oxford University Press, 1999), 236–43. Another allusion, to the *Wunderhorn* song "Lob des hohen Verstandes" in the finale, will be discussed below.

2. Record companies have been eager to market the Adagietto as love music. While the performance of the Adagietto by itself ties into a tradition that antedates Visconti's film, recent recordings have emphasized its detachment from the rest of the symphony. Philips has offered a CD packaged in gold-leaf book format entitled *The Music of Love* and containing slow movements from Symphonies 2, 3, 4, and 6 as well as the Adagietto, accompanied by facsimiles of love letters from Gustav to Alma and portraits of the two on the CD cover presented as miniature love lockets. The Adagietto is conducted by Bernard Haitink with the Royal Concertgebouw Orchestra (ASIN B000025FNN). Less lavishly produced but cheaper in price as a gift option is a Naxos disk entitled *Adagio Mahler* that features the Adagietto with other Mahler slow movements conducted by Antoni Wit with the Polish National Radio Symphony—this CD has a large red rose on its cover (Naxos 8.552243). A recording of the Adagietto with the London Symphony Orchestra conducted by Gilbert Kaplan features the rose image and the title *Adagietto/From Mahler with Love* (IMP Classic ASIN B000000TRM). Other recordings have excerpted the Adagietto from the Fifth Symphony to join it with the five Rückert songs, as in the CD with the Prague Chamber Philharmonic Orchestra conducted by Jírí Bělohlávek with Dagmar Pecková as soloist on Supraphon (SU 3030-2231). Against the general background of musical reception, Bernd Sponheuer explores the movement's relation to kitsch in "Zu schön? Mahler, Čajkovskij und der musikalische Kitsch," in *Gustav Mahler und die Symphonik des 19. Jahrhunderts: Referate des Bonner Symposions 2000*, ed. Bernd Sponheuer and Wolfram Steinbeck (Frankfurt: Peter Lang, 2001), 169–81.

3. Theodor W. Adorno, *Mahler: Eine musikalische Physiognomik* (Frankfurt: Suhrkamp, 1960).

4. Theodor W. Adorno, *Mahler: A Musical Physiognomy*, trans. Edmund Jephcott (Chicago: University of Chicago Press, 1992), 136.

5. Adorno, *Mahler: A Musical Physiognomy*, 137–38.

6. Adorno, *Mahler: A Musical Physiognomy*, 32.

7. Alma Mahler, *Gustav Mahler: Memories and Letters*, trans. Basil Creighton (New York: Viking, 1946), 45.

8. Contributions to the debate include Bernd Sponheuer's book *Logik des Zerfalls: Untersuchungen zum Finalproblem in den Symphonien Gustav Mahlers* (Tutzing: Hans Schneider, 1978), 219–79, and the very different view advanced by John Williamson in "Liszt, Mahler, and the Chorale," *Proceedings of the Royal Musical Association* 108 (1981–82): 115–25.

9. Mitchell, "Eternity or Nothingness?," 319.

10. This full score is cataloged as Cary 509 in the Mary Flagler Cary Collection at the Pierpont Morgan Library.

11. See the facsimile edition of the Adagietto published as Gilbert E. Kaplan, ed., *Gustav Mahler: Adagietto: Facsimile, Documentation, Recording* (New York: Kaplan Foundation, 1992). A color facsimile of the first page of this score of the Adagietto, including the text and Mengelberg's comments, also appears in Truus de Leur, "Gustav Mahler in the Netherlands," in *Gustav Mahler: The World Listens*, ed. Donald Mitchell (Haarlem: Tema Uitgevers, 1995), 1:25. Also see Rudolf Stephan, *Mahler, Werk und Interpretation: Autographe, Partituren, Dokumente* (Cologne: A. Volk, 1979), plates 38 and 39. Mengelberg's conducting score is held at the Willem Mengelberg Foundation in Amsterdam.

12. Natalie Bauer-Lechner, *Recollections of Gustav Mahler*, trans. Dika Newlin, ed. Peter Franklin (Cambridge: Cambridge University Press, 1980), 174 (first published in German in 1923).

13. Stephen E. Hefling, "The Rückert Lieder," in Mitchell and Nicholson, *The Mahler Companion*, 359.

14. For critical discussion of Visconti's film in relation to Mahler, see especially Philip Reed, "Aschenbach Becomes Mahler: Thomas Mann as Film," in *Benjamin Britten: Death in Venice*, ed. Donald Mitchell (Cambridge: Cambridge University Press, 1987), 178–83; and Kurt von Fischer, "Gustav Mahlers Adagietto und Luchino Viscontis Film *Morte a Venezia*," in *Verlust und Ursprung: Festschrift für Werner Weber* (Zurich: Ammann, 1989), 44–52, repr. in Kurt von Fischer, *Aufsätze zur Musik* (Zurich: Hug, 1993), 125–30. Also see Hans Rudolf Vaget, "Film and Literature: The Case of *Death in Venice*: Luchino Visconti and Thomas Mann," *German Quarterly* 53 (1980): 159–75. Of special interest is *Visconti e la musica* (Lucca: Libreria Musicale Italiana, 1994) by Franco Mannino, who conducted the music for *Death in Venice* and other films by Visconti.

15. See Mann's letter of 18 March 1921 to the Munich painter Wolfgang Born, cited in Reed, "Aschenbach Becomes Mahler," 180. Mann had met Mahler in Munich in 1910. Also see Jürgen Kolbe, *Heller Zauber: Thomas Mann in München 1894–1933* (Munich: Siedler Verlag, 1987), 222–23.

16. Thomas Mann, *Stories of Three Decades*, trans. H. T. Lowe-Porter (New York: Knopf, 1936), 384. Mann's *Death in Venice* also resonates in ways quite divorced from Mahler, and Venice was of course the city in which Richard Wagner died in 1883. For a discussion of the aesthetic context of the novella, see the chapter "Music and Repression:

Death in Venice," in *Undertones of Insurrection: Music, Politics, and the Social Sphere in the Modern German Narrative*, by Marc A. Weiner (Lincoln: University of Nebraska Press, 1993), 75–99.

17. According to a well-publicized report, Tadzio was Wladyslaw Moes, whom Thomas Mann observed at Venice in 1911. See "I Was Thomas Mann's Tadzio," in Mitchell, *Benjamin Britten*, 184–85.

18. Henry-Louis de La Grange, *Vienna: The Years of Challenge, 1897–1904*, vol. 2 of *Gustav Mahler* (New York: Oxford University Press, 1995), 817.

19. De La Grange, *Vienna: The Years of Challenge*, 817.

20. De La Grange, *Vienna: The Years of Challenge*, 818. Also see in this regard Mitchell, "Eternity or Nothingness?," 313. Bernard Haitink's second recording from 1988 lasts thirteen minutes and fifty-five seconds. It is this recording by Haitink that is used in the aforementioned Phillips CD *The Music of Love*. Antoni Wit's recording on the *Adagio Mahler* disk lasts twelve minutes and seven seconds. Gilbert Kaplan's aforementioned recording was offered in the spirit of countering "slow motion" performances of the Adagietto and restoring the basic tempo employed by Mengelberg.

21. See Stephen E. Hefling, "The Composition of 'Ich bin der Welt abhanden gekommen,'" in *Gustav Mahler: Wege der Forschung*, ed. Hermann Danuser (Darmstadt: Wissenschaftliche Buchgesellschaft, 1992), 96–158.

22. Adorno, *Mahler: A Musical Physiognomy*, 22.

23. Donald Mitchell, "Mahler: Symphony No. 5," in Mitchell, *Gustav Mahler: The World Listens*, 2:67.

24. Maynard Solomon has discussed these Mozartian movements as an adagio/andante archetype in the chapter entitled "Trouble in Paradise" in his *Mozart: A Life* (New York: HarperCollins, 1995), 187–209. For a discussion of this phenomenon in Schubert, see William Kinderman, "Wandering Archetypes in Schubert's Instrumental Music," *19th-Century Music* 21 (1997): 208–22.

25. Henry-Louis de La Grange, Günther Weiss, and Knud Martner, eds., *Ein Glück ohne Ruh': Die Briefe Gustav Mahlers an Alma* (Berlin: Siedler, 1995), letter 107, cited in Henry-Louis de La Grange, *Vienna: Triumph and Disillusion, 1904–1907*, vol. 3 of *Gustav Mahler* (Oxford: Oxford University Press, 1999), 27. Vladimir Kurbusicky has traced these images in Jean Paul in *Gustav Mahler und seine Umwelt* (Darmstadt: Wissenschaftliche Buchgesellschaft, 1978), 93.

26. An analogy could be made to the slow movement of the Fourth Symphony, in which the serene opening section yields to a plaintive oboe melody at m. 62. The ensuing lyrical string passage, whose striving character culminates in crisis at mm. 88–91, bears comparison with the middle section of the Adagietto of the Fifth Symphony.

27. The use of this term stems from Paul Bekker in his book *Gustav Mahlers Sinfonien* (Berlin: Schuster and Loeffler, 1921). A recent discussion of the notion of *Durchbruch* in Mahler is contained in James Buhler, "'Breakthrough' as Critique of Form: The Finale of Mahler's First Symphony," *19th-Century Music* 20 (1996): 125–43. See also Bernd Sponheuer, "Der Durchbruch als primäre Formkategorie Gustav Mahlers," in *Form & Idee in Gustav Mahlers Instrumentalmusik*, ed. Klaus Hinrich Stahmer (Wilhelmshaven: Heinrichshofens Verlag, 1980), 117–64.

28. Sponheuer, *Logik des Zerfalls*, 237–79; Carolyn Baxendale, "The Finale of Mahler's Fifth Symphony: Long-Range Musical Thought," *Journal of the Royal Musical Association* 112 (1987): 257–89.

29. Allen Forte, "Middleground Motives in the Adagietto of the Fifth Symphony," *19th-Century Music* 8 (1984): 153–63.

30. Constantin Floros, *Gustav Mahler: The Symphonies*, trans. Vernon Wicker (Portland, OR: Amadeus, 1985), 155; published in German as *Gustav Mahler: Die Symphonien*, vol. 3 (Wiesbaden: Breitkopf und Härtel, 1985), 149.

31. In his essay "Eternity or Nothingness?," Mitchell writes: "A conscious, knowing—if covert—'quote' from *Tristan*? I don't hear it" (316n104). In a different context, James Buhler also takes aim at Floros's emphasis on Mahler's apparent allusions to or quotations of other composers, stating that "compositional originality is the steep price Floros's hermeneutics exact for allowing Mahler's music to become meaningful" ("'Breakthrough' as Critique," 142n55).

32. Alma Mahler, *Gustav Mahler: Erinnerungen und Briefe* (Amsterdam: Allert de Lange, 1949), 262; Alma Mahler, *Gustav Mahler: Memories and Letters*, trans. Basil Creighton (New York: Viking, 1946), 209; cited and commented on in Hefling, "The Rückert Lieder," 360. Hefling corrects some inaccuracies in Alma's account by comparing it to her personal diary, observing that the Wagner score in question was *Siegfried*, which she received on 10 August 1902. According to Alma's report, she failed to open the score as soon as Mahler expected, and he grew impatient, opening it himself, whereupon the song fell out.

33. An extraordinary feature of this passage is the clear tonal articulation of A minor moments later, at Isolde's words "das Schwert—ich liess es fallen!" (the sword—I let it drop!). For it is A minor that is often implied from the very beginning of the prelude yet without the confirmation of its actual triad. More detailed discussion of this point is offered in William Kinderman, "Dramatic Recapitulation and Tonal Pairing in Wagner's *Tristan und Isolde* and *Parsifal*," in *The Second Practice of Nineteenth-Century Tonality*, ed. William Kinderman and Harald Krebs (Lincoln: University of Nebraska Press, 1996), 180–81.

34. This blending of D minor and F major triads and Mahler's practice of juxtaposing third-related keys elsewhere in the Adagietto illustrates a practice that has become known as tonal pairing. More detailed discussion of this issue is offered in Kinderman and Krebs, *The Second Practice*.

35. Sponheuer, *Logik des Zerfalls*, 251.

36. Floros, *Gustav Mahler: The Symphonies*, 156–57.

37. In the formal shaping of sections of the finale, the theme drawn from the Adagietto functions as a kind of middle unit, following the opening thematic complex and the first contrapuntal sections while leading into the triumphant brass chorale. In a recent dissertation, Songtaik Kwon emphasizes the polarity of the two main thematic complexes, distinguished as A and C, with the latter referring to the Adagietto theme. Kwon discerns an overall design of A–B–A–B–C–B–C–B–A–B–A–C coda, in which the B sections represent areas of heightened contrapuntal activity and the coda is regarded as beginning with the chorale. See Kwon, "Mahler and Bach: Counterpoint and Polari-

ties in Form," PhD diss., University of North Carolina at Chapel Hill, 2002, 153–55. Another commentator, Edward Murphy, finds that the movement "is not a traditional classical rondo by any means" and describes its form as a "long, unusual and asymmetrical pattern." See his "Unusual Forms in Mahler's Fifth Symphony," *Music Review* 47 (1986–87): 109.

38. It should be noted that although all three appearances of the theme from the Adagietto are marked *grazioso* (in mm. 191, 373, and following 606), the first grazioso section starting in m. 100 does not yet contain this thematic material.

39. Warren Darcy, "Rotational Form, Teleological Genesis, and Fantasy-Projection in the Slow Movement of Mahler's Sixth Symphony," *19th-Century Music* 25 (2001): 52.

40. Darcy, "Rotational Form," 52.

41. Mahler's annotations in his Bach edition are discussed in detail by Kwon in "Mahler and Bach," 26–49, 58–73. As Kwon reports, the present owner of Mahler's Bach edition is Dr. Ralph Kohn in London. This source also contains Mahler's markings in the Orchestral Suites in B Minor, BWV 1067, and D Major, BWV 1068, from which he excerpted several dances, fusing them into an arrangement given for the New York Philharmonic Society in 1909.

42. Bauer-Lechner, *Recollections of Gustav Mahler*, 116.

43. Hans Redlich, *Bruckner and Mahler*, ed. Jack Westrup (London: J. M. Dent, 1963), 158.

44. Mahler's cuts and other changes in Bruckner's symphony drew criticism from Vienna's Bruckner's supporters, and de La Grange comments that Mahler's treatment of the symphony revealed "the profound ambiguity of his feelings about Bruckner's music" (*Vienna: The Years of Challenge*, 331).

45. Bauer-Lechner, *Recollections of Gustav Mahler*, 137.

46. De La Grange, Weiss, and Martner, *Ein Glück ohne Ruh'*, 72.

47. These and other related documents are cited in de La Grange, *Vienna: The Years of Challenge*, 436–37.

48. Sachs is so detached from events around him that his apprentice David has great difficulty getting his attention. For a discussion of these aspects of the character of Sachs, see William Kinderman, "Hans Sachs's 'Cobbler's Song,' *Tristan*, and the 'Bitter Cry of the Resigned Man,'" *Journal of Musicological Research* 13 (1993): 161–84.

49. The expression "summons to the 'real world'" stems from James Zychowicz and is cited by de La Grange, *Vienna: The Years of Challenge*, 821n95.

50. Donald Mitchell, *Gustav Mahler: The Wunderhorn Years: Chronicles and Commentaries* (Berkeley: University of California Press, 1975), 261n36.

51. The full name of the author is Jean Paul Richter. Herta Blaukopf has discussed Mahler's deep interest in Richter against the background of the "Jean Paul–Renaissance" in Vienna around 1880 and concludes that he must have obtained an edition of Jean Paul's works, a desire mentioned in a letter to his friend Albert Spiegler in the summer of that year. See Blaukopf, "Jean Paul, die erste Symphonie und Dostojewski," in *Gustav Mahler: Werk und Wirken: Neue Mahler-Forschung aus Anlaß des vierzigjärhigen Bestehens der Internationalen Gustav Mahler Gesellschaft*, ed. Erich Wolfgang Partsch (Vienna: Pasqualatihaus, 1996), 35–42. For a discussion of the relevance of Jean Paul to

Mahler's *Wunderhorn* symphonies, see Mirjam Schadendorf, *Humor als Formkonzept in der Musik Gustav Mahlers* (Stuttgart: Metzler, 1995).

52. Bruno Walter, *Gustav Mahler: Ein Portrait* (Wilhelmshaven: Heinrichshofen, 1981), 102.

53. Jean Paul, *Vorschule der Ästhetik*, vol. 9 of *Jean Paul Werke*, ed. Norbert Miller (Munich: Hanser, 1975), 129.

54. Paul, *Vorschule der Ästhetik*, 132.

55. See in this regard Theodor Veidl, *Der musikalische Humor bei Beethoven* (Leipzig: Breitkopf und Härtel, 1929), 15n2: "Jean Paul vergleicht den Witz sehr witzig mit einem verkleideten Priester, der jedes ungleiche Paar kopuliert" (Jean Paul slyly compares wit to a person disguised as a priest who marries the most unfitting of partners).

56. See Leon Botstein's recent discussion of ways that Mahler "suggests the contradictory, incomplete, and multifaceted faces of realism" in "Whose Gustav Mahler? Reception, Interpretation, and History," in *Mahler and His World*, ed. Karen Painter (Princeton, NJ: Princeton University Press, 2002), 41.

57. Botstein, "Whose Gustav Mahler?," 40.

58. One model for this type of narrative musical design is the finale of Beethoven's penultimate piano sonata, op. 110, with its alternation of lament ("Klagender Gesang") and aspiring fugue. Only at its second appearance and development does the fugue lead to a positive resolution. If Adorno's description of the second movement passage in the symphony as a *Durchbruch* might be questioned in view of its subsequent negation, the corresponding passage in the finale still sounds like a "breakthrough" while arising from a stronger sense of context and showing more staying power.

59. Adorno, *Mahler: A Musical Physiognomy*, 32, 51. As Mitchell observes, Adorno's German in the second instance is "more powerfully dismissive," since the phrase "kulinarische Sentimentalität" might be rendered as "dished-up sentimentality." See "Eternity or Nothingness?," 308n81.

60. Yet another dimension of the overall design is its parallel to Beethoven's C♯ Minor Quartet, op. 131, which was for Mahler the "greatest and most difficult" of the quartets, demanding presentation in a string orchestra. See de La Grange, *Vienna: The Years of Challenge*, 136–37. Like Mahler's symphony, Beethoven's op. 131 begins with a slow movement in C♯ minor, and it places much emphasis on the Neapolitan D major, which becomes the tonic key of the second movement. It is a measure of the more radiant and optimistic trajectory of Mahler's work that the symphony closes in D, moving beyond the C♯ minor of the Funeral March.

61. In a sketch for the movement in the Landsberg 8 Sketchbook, Beethoven refers to it as "too tender," presumably too remote from action; a dissonant intrusion from without in the so-called terror fanfare (*Schreckensfanfare*) leads into the choral finale. In *Die Meistersinger*, the ethereal high string writing in the prelude to act 3 is associated with the "angel" who holds Sachs in an artistic paradise with the "world at his feet," as we learn from the last stanza of his "Cobbler's Song" in act 2. Although Sachs, unlike Mahler, avoids a marriage commitment to his Evchen, he still remains firmly rooted in the social world of his beloved Nuremberg.

5. Folklore Transformed in Bartók's *Dance Suite*

1. Stefan Zweig, *Die Welt von Gestern* (Frankfurt am Main: Fischer, 1953), 14. Despite Zweig's emphasis on the "world of security," a powerful current of German nationalism and racial anti-Semitism had arisen by the 1890s. For discussions of this development, see, among other studies, Brigitte Hamann, *Hitler's Vienna: A Dictator's Apprenticeship*, trans. Thomas Thornton (New York: Oxford University Press, 1999; first published as *Hitlers Wien: Lehrjahre eines Diktators* [Munich: Piper, 1996]). Also see in this context the epilogue "The Twilight of Liberalism" in Margaret Notley, *Lateness and Brahms: Music and Culture in the Twilight of Viennese Liberalism* (New York: Oxford University Press, 2007), 204–20.

2. Zweig was born in Vienna; Bartók came from the town of Nagyzentmiklós (now Sànnicolau Mare, Romania) in the Banat region, where György Kurtág was born at Logoj in 1926.

3. Theodor Adorno, "Béla Bartóks Tanzsuite," in *Musik-Konzepte 22 Béla Bartók*, ed. Heinz-Klaus Metzger and Rainer Riehn (Munich: Vollendorf, 1981), 123. This review originally appeared in *Pult und Taktstock 2/6*, ed. Erwin Stein (Vienna, 1925).

4. Ofen is an alternative name for Buda, which remained a separate city from Pest until 1873, when these two cities were merged and joined as well with a third distinct, Óbuda (Ancient Buda). The *Dance Suite* was originally conceived as an orchestral work, but Bartók also completed a version for piano by 1925.

5. Vera Lampert's book *Folk Music in Bartók's Compositions: A Source Catalog: Arab, Hungarian, Romanian, Ruthenian, Serbian, and Slovak Melodies* (Budapest: Hungarian Heritage House, 2008) provides a geographical map of Bartók's sources on pages 40–41.

6. Béla Bartók, "Die Volksmusik der Völker Ungarns," in *Documenta Bartókiana*, vol. 4, 112, cited in Tibor Tallián, *Béla Bartók: Sein Leben und Werk*, German trans. by Susanne Rauer Farkas (Gyoma: Kner, 1988; first published Budapest, 1981), 140. This essay was not published during Bartók's lifetime.

7. This long letter is found in János Deménysch, ed., *Bartók Béla levelei* (Letters of Béla Bartók) (Budapest, 1955), 3:189–95; the part quoted here is excerpted in Bence Szabolcsi, ed., *Béla Bartók: Weg und Werk* (Kassel: Bärenreiter, 1972; first published Budapest: Corvina, 1957), 261–62. Beu was preparing a lecture about Bartók for the Romanian radio, presumably in connection with the composer's fiftieth birthday. The shifting of boundaries according to the Treaty of Trianon, which had placed Bartók's birthplace in Romania, surely helps explain Beu's use of the term *compositorul român*.

8. See the discussion of Lorenz in the introduction to this volume.

9. See in this regard also Harald Kaufmann's essay "Nachbarn im Donauraum" in his *Fingerübungen: Musikgesellschaft und Werttungsforschung* (Vienna: Verlag Elisabeth Lafite, 1970), 44.

10. Deménysch, *Bartók Béla levelei*, 1:147.

11. The letter is cited in György Kroō, *Bartók Hand-Buch*, trans. Erzsébet Székács (Vienna: Universal, 1974; first published Budapest: Franklin, 1974), 112–13.

12. Judit Frigyesi, *Béla Bartók and Turn-of-the-Century Budapest* (Berkeley: University

of California Press, 1998), 6. Frigyesi refers to the cultural situation already preceding World War I, but the issue became much more problematic by the early 1920s.

13. See László Somfai, "Dating Béla Bartók's Sketches," in *A Handbook to Twentieth-Century Musical Sketches*, ed. Patricia Hall and Friedemann Sallis (Cambridge: Cambridge University Press, 2004), 125.

14. This sequence of events is outlined in László Somfai, *Béla Bartók: Composition, Concepts, and Autograph Sources* (Berkeley: University of California Press, 1996), 56–57. The sheet containing Bartók's sketch for the ritornello is held at the Sacher Foundation in Basel. A facsimile of Bartók's autograph full score fair copy of the *Dance Suite* has been published as *Béla Bartók. Dance Suite for Orchestra. Reprint of the Original Manuscript (Budapest Historical Museum)*, with a commentary by Ferenc Bónis (Budapest, 1998).

15. The song with text and translation is drawn from Lampert, *Folk Music in Bartók's Compositions*, 135–36.

16. Nevertheless, Bartók makes subtle reference to the ritornello in the scherzando phrases in mm. 125–26 and in the longer quiet passage in mm. 135–47 preceding the robust close of the third movement.

17. Aesthetic aspects of this work have been discussed recently by Julia Brown in her book *Bartók and the Grotesque: Studies in Modernity, the Body and Contradiction in Music* (Burlington, VT: Ashgate, 2007), 86–131.

18. Kroó, *Bartók Hand-Buch*, 116.

19. In his Harvard lectures from 1943, Bartók described this theme as his first "chromatic" melody and compared it to an Arab melody ("Harvard Lectures," in *Béla Bartók Essays*, ed. Benjamin Suchoff [Lincoln: University of Nebraska Press, 1992; first published London: St. Martin's Press, 1976], 379). In describing it as "chromatic" he was evidently referring to the use of small intervals. The melodies Bartók heard in Algeria often made use of intervals smaller than the semitone. An outstanding resource for the study of Bartók's folk song collection at Biskra, Algeria, is the 2006 CD-ROM *Bartók and Arab Folk Music* created by László Vikárius with János Kárpái and István Pávai, which includes Bartók's phonograph recordings and autograph transcriptions. This CD-ROM has been issued through the UNESCO European Folklore Institute, Institute for Musicology of the Hungarian Academy of Sciences.

20. Benjamin Suchoff, "Bartók's Fusion of National Styles," in *Béla Bartók: A Celebration* (Lanham, MD: Scarecrow, 2004), 62.

21. This is a compositional strategy with a history. A comparable example is Wagner's procedure in the *Tristan* prelude of employing the so-called Tristan chord (a minor triad with added sixth) in three emphatic sonorities at the climax of the developmental section before returning to the original quiet version of that sonority in the ensuing varied reprise of the beginning of the piece.

22. One early British critic expressed his distaste of this trombone slide as follows: "We shall slip away before it, next time it occurs. It is time that some protest was registered against glissandos on the trombones, even if every other atrocity is admitted to the concert room" (cited in Malcolm Gillies, "Dance Suite," in *The Bartók Companion*, ed. Malcolm Gillies [Portland, OR: Amadeus Press, 1994; first published London: Faber and Faber, 1993], 490).

23. For instance, the motivic idea of the descending glissando third on the same pitch level played *pianissimo* in the trombones occurs at the end of *The Miraculous Mandarin*, when the mandarin's yearning is stilled and his wounds bleed, causing his death. A different version of the slide through a minor third in the cellos using quarter tones is heard when the mandarin's longing protects him from death by suffocation at the hands of the tramps.

24. This source is cited and translated from Hungarian into German in Tibor Tallián, "Quellenschichten der Tanz-Suite Bartóks," *Studia Musicologica Academiae Scientiarum Hungaricae* 25 (1983): 215–26. Tallián gives the source as Bartók Archive Budapest, BA-N: 4066. See also Somfai, *Béla Bartók: Composition*, 17–18.

25. Szabolcsi, *Béla Bartók: Weg und Werk*, 262; also see note 7 above.

26. Beethoven made 179 arrangements of songs for the Edinburgh publisher George Thomson between 1809 and 1820 in addition to variations on sixteen folk songs, which were published as his opp. 105 and 107.

27. One of Beethoven's richest contributions in this vein is his set of thirty-three transformations ("Veränderungen") of Anton Diabelli's commonplace waltz in his longest work for piano: the "Diabelli" Variations, op. 120.

28. This diagram is based on the outline in Ernő Lendvai's essay "Einführung in die Formen- und Harmonienwelt Bartóks," in Szabolcsi, *Béla Bartók: Weg und Werk*, 126.

29. Lendvai's analytical approach is developed in his book *Béla Bartók: An Analysis of His Music* (London: Kahn and Averill, 1971); also see Lendvai's study *Bartók stilusa* (Budapest: Zeneműkiadó, 1955), in English as *Bartók's Style*, trans. Paul Merrick and Judit Pokoly (Budapest: Akkord Music Publisher, 1999). For a critique of his approach, see Paul Wilson, *The Music of Béla Bartók* (New Haven, CT: Yale University Press, 1992); and Malcolm Gillies, "Bartók and His Music in the 1990s," in Gillies, *The Bartók Companion*, who writes that "Bartók studies suffered their greatest normalizing threat in the theories of the Hungarian Ernő Lendvai" (13). Also see Ivan F. Waldbauer, "Analytical Responses to Bartók's Music: Pitch Organization," in *The Cambridge Companion to Bartók*, ed. Amanda Bayley (Cambridge: Cambridge University Press, 2001), 218–20; and Roy Howat, "Bartók, Lendvai and the Principles of Proportional Analysis," *Music Analysis* 2 (1983): 69–95.

30. Halsey Stevens, *The Life and Music of Béla Bartók*, ed. Malcolm Gillies (1953; New York: Oxford University Press, 1993), 271.

31. Somfai comments on the excision of the Slovakian dance that "Bartók removed it . . . for purely musical reasons, rendering the original plan incomplete but improving the composition as a whole" (*Béla Bartók: Composition*, 190).

32. Cf. Lendvai, "Einführung," 126.

33. This translation of the passage is offered in János Kárpáti, "Bartók in North Africa: A Unique Fieldwork and Its Impact on His Music," in *Bartók Perspectives: Man, Composer, and Ethnomusicologist*, ed. Elliott Antokoletz, Victoria Fischer, and Benjamin Suchoff (New York: Oxford University Press, 2000), 179.

34. Malcolm Gillies writes about the close of the work that, "given the mass of excitement that he has generated in this movement, its ending sounds too abrupt and suggests that same weakness in resolution of momentum which caused him twenty years later to

revise the ending of his composition's spiritual successor, the Concerto for Orchestra" ("Dance Suite," 495).

35. See Balázs Mikusi, "Bartók and Scarlatti: A Study of Motives and Influence," *Studia Musicologica* 50 (2009): 3–27, who discusses conflicting views about synthesis in Bartók's music on pages 5–8. An expanded version of his article appeared as "Bartók és Scarlatti: Oknyomozás és hatástanulmány," *Magyar Zene*, February 2008, 7–29.

36. Bence Szaboleci, *Bartók Béla élete* (The life of Béla Bartók) (Budapest: Zeneműkiadó, 1956), 20.

37. János Kárpáti, *Bartók's Chamber Music*, trans. Fred Macnicol and Mária Steiner (Stuyvesant, NY: Pendragon Press, 1994), 235; in Hungarian as *Bartók kamarazenéje* (Budapest: Zeneműkiadó, 1976), 171.

38. Arnold Whittall, *Musical Composition in the 20th Century* (Oxford: Oxford University Press, 1999), 114.

39. Mikusi, "Bartók and Scarlatti," 7.

40. David E. Schneider, *Bartók, Hungary, and the Renewal of Tradition: Case Studies in the Intersection of Modernity and Nationality* (Berkeley: University of California Press, 2006), 187.

41. Noteworthy in this regard are the "international aspects of creating a national music scene or a national music," which made "Bartók's music and outlook . . . so controversial in early twentieth-century Hungary, yet . . . are often downplayed in conventional music historiography," in the formulation of Lynn Hooker ("Modernism on the Periphery: Béla Bartók and the New Hungarian Music Society of 1911–1912," *Musical Quarterly* 88 [2005]: 274–319, quotation from 298), who discusses the "cosmopolitan Bartók in action" during the years preceding the First World War. On the negative response in Hungary to Bartók's cosmopolitan stance, see David E. Schneider, "Hungarian Nationalism and the Reception of Bartók's Music, 1904–1940," in Bayley, *Cambridge Companion*, 180–81.

42. Schneider, *Bartók, Hungary*, 188.

43. Szabolcsi, *Béla Bartók: Weg und Werk*, 262–63.

6. Kurtág's *Kafka Fragments* and *Hommage à R. Sch.*

1. Kurtág draws especially on Kafka's diaries from the period beginning in 1910, which have been published as *Franz Kafka Tagebücher 1910–1923*, ed. Max Brod (1937; Frankfurt: Fischer, 1950).

2. The *Kafka Fragments* represents Kurtág's longest work to date, although it is bound to be surpassed in this regard by his current project, an opera based on Samuel Beckett's *Endgame* that is scheduled to premiere at the Salzburg Festival in 2013. Kurtág has entertained the idea of writing an opera based on Beckett for many years. Two performances at Paris in 2008 of Beckett's *Rockaby* directed by Peter Brook stimulated this interest; by 2011 Kurtág had accomplished much work on his opera. See in this connection Bálint András Varga, comp. and ed., *György Kurtág: Three Interviews and Ligeti Homages* (Rochester, NY: University of Rochester Press, 2009), 43, 153.

3. A study exploring this dimension of Kurtág's art is Ulrich Mosch's essay "What Presence of the Past? Artistic Autobiography in György Kurtág's Music," in *Centre and*

Periphery, Roots and Exile: Interpreting the Music of István Anhalt, György Kurtág, and Sándor Veress, ed. Friedemann Sallis, Robin Elliott, and Kenneth DeLong (Waterloo, ON: Wilfrid Laurier University Press, 2011), 347–71. Mosch observes that "to date, Kurtág has written some one hundred . . . 'Hommages'" (355); as Mosch puts it, Kurtág seeks to "find the path to himself through productive reformulation" (361).

4. Discussion of this vocal setting is offered by Alvaro Oviedo in "Arracher la figure au figurative: La musique vocale de György Kurtág," in Sallis, Elliott, and DeLong, *Centre and Periphery, Roots and Exile*, 267–70.

5. György Kurtág, *Werkeinführung: Kafka-Fragmente op. 24*, in *Ligeti und Kurtág in Salzburg: Programmbuch der Salzburger Festspiele 1993*, ed. Ulrich Dibelius (Salzburg, 1993), 80, cited in Claudia Stahl, *Botschaften in Fragmenten: Die großen Vokalzyklen von György Kurtág* (Saarbrücken: Pfau, 1998), 22.

A core experience of isolation and unfulfilled expectation had been associated with Kurtág's first compositional effort in his youth. Around 1942, at the age of about sixteen, he wrote a movement for piano in response to a vocal setting of his composition teacher Max Eisikovits; the text was a poem by Endre Andy, *Mintha valaki jönne* (as if someone were coming). As Kurtág recalled, "its basic experience—I am waiting and they are not coming—was painfully familiar" (Varga, *Three Questions for Sixth-Five Composers* (Rochester: University of Rochester Press, 2011), 139, and *Three Interviews*, 6). Many years later, at Paris in 1956, Kurtág suffered a psychological crisis that made it impossible for him to compose. The Hungarian psychologist who helped him find his way back to composition, Marianne Stein, received the dedication of the *Kafka Fragments* when the work was completed two decades later.

6. The sketch material for the unfinished piano concerto, *Kafka Fragments*, *Hommage à R. Sch.*, and other works by Kurtág is held in the collection of the Paul Sacher Stiftung in Basel, Switzerland.

7. Kurtág, *Werkeinführung*, 81.

8. The International Bartók Seminar began in 1967. By 1985 it had expanded with a festival and adopted the "Bartók New Music" motto. The Twenty-Seventh International Bartók Seminar and Festival (Nemzetközi Bartók Szeminárium és Fesztivál) took place at Szombathely in July 2011 and was coordinated with an International Musicological Colloquium on Scholarly Research and Performance Practice in Bartók Studies, an event celebrating the fiftieth anniversary of the foundation of the Budapest Bartók Archives.

9. Varga, *György Kurtág: Three Interviews*, 58.

10. Dibelius, *Ligeti und Kurtág in Salzburg*, 94. In my interview with Kurtág, he acknowledged the input of Wilheim as reflected in the ordering in Figs. 6.2–6.4.

11. A basic inventory compiled by Friedemann Sallis is available at the Sacher Archive in Basel. Sallis identifies five sketchbooks containing sixty-three pages of work on the *Kafka Fragments* in addition to even more material in the form of loose sketch pages, drafts, and scores, which also contain revisions. Also see Sallis, "Skizzen zu den Kafka-Fragmenten op. 24: Ein Blick in György Kurtágs Werkstatt," *Neue berlinische Musikzeitung* 11/2 (1996): 13–23.

12. Kurtág concurred with this suggestion in my interview with him on 20 June 2010.

13. The music used in the last movement of the *Hommage à R. Sch.* first appeared in 1976 as sketches for a piece for piano and trombone, one of which is entitled *Nagy Sirató* (Great lament), referring to the ancient oral tradition of conveying bereavement through song. The same music was adapted in 1979 to become the final movement of an unpublished version of *Grabstein für Stephan*. See Friedemann Sallis, "Coming to Terms with the Composer's Working Manuscripts," in *A Handbook to Twentieth-Century Musical Sketches*, ed. Patricia Hall and Friedemann Sallis (Cambridge: Cambridge University Press, 2004), 56–57. Sallis observes further that "rather than discovering teleological source chains, the study of Kurtág's sketch material reveals a complex web of hermeneutic and structural relationships, which may or may not impinge on our apprehension of the completed work" (57).

14. For more details about the genesis of this work, see the following studies by Sallis: "The Genealogy of György Kurtág's *Hommage à R. Sch.* op. 15d," *Studia Musicalogica Academiae Scientiarum Hungaricae* 43/3–4 (2002): 311–22; and "La musica da camera di György Kurtág (1950–2005): Dall'estetica del frammento ai 'programmi da concerto,'" *RATM—Rivista di Analisi e Teoria Musicale* 16 (2010): 18–21.

15. Schumann alluded to Hoffmann's Kreisler in various ways, such as in the title of his cycle of fantasies, op. 16: *Kreisleriana*.

16. Brod, *Franz Kafka Tagebücher*, 229, entry for 30 August 1913.

17. Thomas Bösche, "György Kurtág," in the program book of the Musiktage Mondsee Festival 1998, ed. Otto Biba, 9.

18. One also senses an aesthetic affinity of this song to Schumann's Eichendorff setting "Mondnacht."

19. In my interview with Kurtág, he acknowledged his long-standing fascination with Beethoven's treatment of such suspended musical textures.

20. Schumann altered the second note of the vocal part in the opening song of *Dichterliebe* in his autograph manuscript from B to C♯ so that the setting of the second word, "wunderschönen" (beautiful), would begin with the dissonance of C♯ against D in the piano. See the facsimile edition *Robert Schumann Dichterliebe Opus 48 Liederkreis aus Heinrich Heines "Buch der Lieder," Faksimile nach dem Autograph in der Staatsbibliothek zu Berlin Preußischer Kulturbesitz*, ed. Elisabeth Schmierer (Laaber: Laaber, 2006).

21. *György Kurtág: Kafka-Fragmente op. 24*, Juliane Banse, soprano, András Keller, violin (ECM Records, 2006).

22. In an entry in his Sketchbook 62 held at the Sacher Foundation (320-1006), Kurtág tried a setting of "ho-hen" ascending from the lower G♭ to the high F, leading to a semitone ascent at "Sten-[gel]." In the finished version, the use of the grace note in the lower octave in the voice enhances the immediacy of this poetic image.

23. One is reminded here of the moving piano postlude at the end of *Dichterliebe*, which recalls the postlude of the earlier song "Am leuchtenden Sommermorgen" (no. 12) suffused with the image of speaking flowers. The fifth piece of Kurtág's *Hommage à R. Sch.* is also associated with night: "In der Nacht" (At night).

24. In Kafka's diary for 21 February 1911, the entry for "Umpanzert" precedes "Wie fern sind mir zum Beispiel die Armmuskeln," a setting that Kurtág sketched but did not

include in the finished work. See Brod, *Franz Kafka Tagebücher*, 31. A discussion of "Umpanzert" in the context of Kurtág's settings of Kafka's texts is offered by Stephen Blum, "L'articulation des rythmes de Kafka selon Kurtág (Fragments de Kafka op. 24)," in *Ligatures: La pensée musicale de György Kurtág*, ed. Pierre Maréchaux and Grégoire Tosser (Rennes: Presses universitaires de Rennes, 2009), 177-91, esp. 185-86.

25. In describing such tightly woven settings, Gyula Csapó writes that "Kurtág lets the text structure the music, he speaks the text with utter intensity through the music, attached utterly to every word, to every aspect of every word, be it phonetic or semantic" ("Singing as an Altered State of Speech: Questions of Contemporary Prosody and Text Handling through the Prism of French Post-Modern Thought [a Continuation of a Conversation with György Kurtág]," paper given at the Sixth Annual Hawaii International Conference on the Arts and Humanities at Honolulu, 2008).

26. The B at "Satz" corresponds to the same note at "mich" in the opening phrase.

27. Milena Jesenská was a Czech writer and translator, twelve years younger than Kafka, with whom he had a passionate relationship that is documented in his numerous surviving letters to her. Kafka confessed to her: "To you I can tell the truth, for your sake as well as mine, as to nobody else." Because of her activities in resistance to the Nazi regime, Jesenská was apprehended by the Gestapo in 1939. She died in the concentration camp at Ravensbrück on 17 May 1944. See among other sources Idris Parry, "A Path in Autumn," in *The World of Franz Kafka*, ed. J. P. Stern (New York: Holt, Rinehart and Winston, 1980), 229-37.

28. Varga, *György Kurtág: Three Interviews*, 118.

29. *The Collected Shorter Plays of Samuel Beckett* (New York: Grove Weidenfeld, 1984), 60-61.

30. Varga, *György Kurtág: Three Interviews*, 65.

31. See Friedemann Sallis, "Le paradoxe postmoderne et l'oeuvre tardive de Luigi Nono," *Circuit: Musiques contemporaines* 11, no. 1 (2000): 68-84, esp. 73. As Sallis has observed, this manuscript of "In Memoriam Joannis Pilinszky" is one of many manuscripts Kurtág sent to Nono.

32. Cf. Friedrich Spangemacher, "*Der wahre Weg geht über ein Seil*: Zu György Kurtágs Kafka-Fragmenten," in *MusikTexte* 27 (1989): 33; and Stahl, *Botschaften in Fragmenten*, 223. The version of the last movement with quarter tones was not included in the 1947 publication of this work edited by Yehudi Menuhin.

33. In Kafka's fantastic tale *Die Verwandlung* (*The Metamorphosis*) from 1912, the main character, Gregor Samsa, finds himself transformed into a huge verminous insect, which is swept away and thrown out.

34. "Als Gregor Samsa eines Morgens aus unruhigen Träumen erwachte, fand er sich in seinem Bett zu einem ungeheueren Ungeziefer verwandelt" (When Gregor Samsa awoke one morning from disturbing dreams, he found himself in his bed transformed into a monstrous insect). For a recent discussion of Kafka's tale in a broad cultural context, see David Gallagher, "*Metamorphosis*: Transformations of the Body and the Influence of Ovid's Metamorphoses on Germanic Literature of the Nineteenth and Twentieth Centuries" (Amsterdam and New York: Rodopi, 2009), 117-58.

35. Alan Blunden, "A Chronology of Kafka's Life," in Stern, *The World of Franz Kafka*, 22. For a probing discussion of the genesis of Kafka's tale, see Hartmut Binder, *Kafka: Der Schaffensprozeß* (Frankfurt: Suhrkamp, 1983), 136–90.

36. See Hartmut Lück, "Kurtág, György," in *Metzler Komponisten Lexikon*, ed. Horst Weber (Stuttgart: J. B. Metzlersche Verlagsbuchhandlung and Carl Ernst Poeschel Verlag, 1992), 406.

Index

74–75; creative process interpretation, 2–4; folk song experience, 152–53, 219n26, 219n27; harmonic practice comparison with Schumann, 91–92; influence on Bartók, 161; Kurtág foreshadowing, 183; Mahler foreshadowing, 134; on Mozart and Haydn influences, 10; polyphony, 129; primary sources, 1. *See also* Piano Trio in F Minor (unfinished) (Beethoven)

Beethoven Monument, 77, 79, 100, 101

Beethoven's diary (*Tagebuch*), 72

The Beethoven Sketchbooks (Nottebohm chapter), 43

Berlin Staatsbibliothek, 46

Berlioz, Hector, 91

Beu, Octavian, 140–41, 157

Biblioteka Jagiellońska, 21

biographical context: Beethoven, 71–75, 87–88, 92; Kurtág, 164; Mahler, 103, 104, 118, 130–31, 132; Schumann, 85–88, 90, 91, 93, 94, 99–101

Biographie W. A. Mozarts (Nissen), 17

Birchall, Robert, 42–43, 46, 72

Botstein, Leon, 133

Brahms, Johannes, 1, 5–7, 7, 199n16

Brandenburg, Sieghard, 46

Brendel, Alfred, 98

Brentano, Antonia, 87, 92

Brentano, Maximiliana, 92

British Library (London), 48

Brod, Max, 166

Bruckner, Anton, 129, 215n44

Carnaval (Schumann), 80, 88, 89, 90

central European tradition, 10

Chamberlain, Houston Stewart, 7–8

compositional strategies context, 4–7

Concerto in A Major, K.464a (Mozart), 32

Concerto in C Major, K. 467 (Mozart), 32

Concerto in C Minor, K. 503: First Movement (Mozart), *34–39*; draft version, 32–33; final version of piano entrance, 40; first performance, 41; ink colors as clue, 32–33, 38, 41; missing cadenzas, 41; opening piano passage, 33–36; overview, 20; paper type clues, 31–32; piano passage turning point, 36–38

Concerto in D Minor, K. 466 (Mozart), 29–30, 32

Concerto in F Major, K. 459 (Mozart), 32

Cook, Nicholas, 46

Cooper, Barry, 72

Cooper, David, 161

Cooper, Martin, 75

creative contexts. *See* biographical context; compositional strategies context; cultural context; performance context; political context; reception context

creative process studies, 2

creativity myth, 17

Csengery, Adrienne, 10, 166–67, 200n39

cultural context, 132, 152, 161, 164, 166

Dance Suite (Bartók): Allegro Molto, 148–49, 218n22; Allegro vivace, 153–54, 156; Arabic influences, 161; Bach influence, 161; Beethoven influence, 161; Comodo, 157–58, 160; components, 146; current location, 154; fifth dance, 157–60; finale, 157–60; folk idiom assimilation, 152–57, 161–62; fourth dance Arabian association, 156–57; Liszt influence, 161; Meno vivo, 160; *The Miraculous Mandarin* relationships, 146–52, 160, 219n23; missing/discarded Slovakian dance, 154–56, 162; Moderato movement, 147–48; Molto tranquillo section, 160; nationalism combined with multicultural perspective, 162, 220n42; opening Moderato, 153; opening theme, 147, 218n21; overview, 13–14; political context, 139–40, 161, 217n1; Presto section, 160; *Rite of Spring* (Stravinsky) comparison, 147, 149; ritornello, 142, 144–46, 149, 218n16; Strauss influence, 161; stylistic synthesis, 160–61; third movement theme, 153–54; *verbunkos* style, 142; Vivo passage, 147

Fragments), 172–75; Webern influence, 10; working method, 172–73

Kurtág, Márta, 10, 164

Kwon, Songtaik, 216–17n37

Langer, Suzanne, 10

Lendvai, Ernö, 153–54, 161, 219n29

Leonore, 84

Leonore (*Beethoven*), 91

Leonore Prohaska, WoO 96 (Duncker), 46

Letter to Robert Birchall (Beethoven), *44–45*, 203n1

Ligeti, György, 10

Liszt, Franz, 79, 100, 101, 161

"lived experience" concept of creativity, 11–14. *See also* biographical context

Lixandru, Christine, 61, 204n15

Lockwood, Lewis, 46

London Philharmonic Society, 75

Longfellow, Henry Wadsworth, 8

Lonsdale, Christopher, 72

Lorenz, Alfred, 8–9, 141

Machaut, Guillaume de, 176–77

Mahler: Eine musikalische Physiognomik (Adorno), 103

Mahler, Gustav: Bach influence, 131–32; biographical context, 103, 104, 118, 130–31, 132; Bruckner relationship, 129, 215n44; comic opera influence, 131; on "Ich bin der Welt abhanden gekommen," (Rückert), 104; imaginative writers influence, 132; polyphony, 129; reception context, 132; Richter influence, 132; on Scherzo, Fifth Symphony, Adagietto, mm. 56–103 (Mahler), 115–16; Verdi influence, 131; Wagner influence, 10, 13, 118, 119, 129–30, 132, 214n31; *Wunderhorn* years, 102, 132

Mann, Thomas, 9, 10, 104–5

Marston, Nicholas, 42, 67–68, 70, 90, 94, 203n4, 205n26

McClary, Susan, 3, 4

Mengelberg, William, 102, 104

The Metamorphosis (Kafka), 166, 194–95, 223n34

Mikusi, Balász, 161

Military March, WoO24 (Beethoven), 65

The Miraculous Mandarin, 142–52

Missa solemnis (Beethoven), 5, 6–7, 71, 87

Mitchell, Donald, 103, 106–7, 211n1

Montez, Lola, 100

Mozart, Constanze, 32

Mozart, Wolfgang Amadeus, 11. *See also* Sonata in D Major, K. 284/205b ("Dürnitz") First Movement (Mozart)

MS Grasnick 20a, 48

MS Grasnick 29, 1–6, 44–45, 48–61, 65–71; transcriptions, pages 1–6, *55–60*

Müller, Wenzel, 43

Müller, Wilhelm, 167

musicology, 1–3, 198n3

Musikalisches Opfer (Bach), 18

Mussorgsky, Modest, 146

myth of creativity, 17

National Socialist ideology, 8–9

National Széchényi Library (Budapest), 79

Neate, Charles, 74–75

Neue Mozart Ausgabe (Konrad, ed.), 32

Neue Zeitschrift für Musik (Schumann), 79, 100

Newcomb, Anthony, 94

new musicology, 2–3

Niemetschek, Franz, 17

Ninth Symphony (Beethoven), 7, 74, 75, 134, 153, 183

Nissen, Georg Nikolaus, 17

Nottebohm, Gustav, 4, 5–6, 43, 47–51, 74

Nuttall, Geoff, 10

"Obulus" op.12 (Schumann), 78

Osthoff, Wolfgang, 61

paper type as composition clue, 43, 64, 204n9

Paul Sacher Stiftung (Basel), 154

performance context, 10, 80, 114, 167. *See also* reception context

Pessiak-Schmerling, Anna, 74

WILLIAM KINDERMAN is a professor of music at the University of Illinois at Urbana-Champaign and the author or editor of ten books, including *The String Quartets of Beethoven* and the three-volume study *Artaria 195: Beethoven's Sketchbook for the* Missa solemnis *and the Piano Sonata in E Major, Opus 109.*

The University of Illinois Press
is a founding member of the
Association of American University Presses.

Designed by Jim Proefrock
Composed in 11.2/14 Bulmer
at the University of Illinois Press
Manufactured by Sheridan Books, Inc.

University of Illinois Press
1325 South Oak Street
Champaign, IL 61820-6903
www.press.uillinois.edu